FIERCE GODS

Fierce Gods

INEQUALITY, RITUAL, AND THE POLITICS OF DIGNITY IN A SOUTH INDIAN VILLAGE

DIANE P. MINES

Indiana University Press
Bloomington and Indianapolis

This book is a publication of

Indiana University Press
601 North Morton Street
Bloomington, IN 47404-3797 USA

http://iupress.indiana.edu

Telephone orders 800-842-6796
Fax orders 812-855-7931
Orders by e-mail iuporder@indiana.edu

The paper used in this publication meets the minimum requirements of American National Standard for Information Sciences—Permanence of Paper for Printed Library Materials, ANSI Z39.48-1984.

Manufactured in the United States of America

Library of Congress Cataloging-in-Publication Data

Mines, Diane P., date-
Fierce gods : inequality, ritual, and the politics of dignity in a South Indian village / Diane P. Mines.
p. cm.
Includes bibliographical references and index.
ISBN 0-253-34576-6 (cloth : alk. paper) — ISBN 0-253-21765-2 (pbk. : alk. paper)
1. Rites and ceremonies—India—Tirunelveli (District) 2. Caste—India—Tirunelveli (District) 3. Religion and politics—Indian—Tirunelveli (District) 4. Tirunelveli (India : District)—Religious life and customs. 5. Tirunelveli (India : District)—Politics and government. 6. Tirunelveli (India : District)—Social conditions. I. Title.
GN635.I4M553 2005
306.4'0954'82—dc22

2004025823

1 2 3 4 5 10 09 08 07 06 05

Raman, Norman, K. P.

CONTENTS

ACKNOWLEDGMENTS

George Herbert Mead argued that the self is not fundamentally "individual" but is foremost a product of social relations, and so it must be of any book. While I am this book's author and any errors or omissions are my own, the book has also taken shape only by virtue of its being in relationship to others who have influenced me in a variety of ways, whether through material, intellectual, or emotional support.

My fieldwork in India was funded by the Fulbright-Hays Program, the American Institute of Indian Studies, the National Science Foundation, and the Office of Graduate Research at Appalachian State University. I received additional support for periods of writing from the Charlotte Newcombe Foundation, the Committee on Southern Asian Studies at the University of Chicago, and an Andrew W. Mellon Foundation post-doctoral fellowship at Washington University in St. Louis. In India, the Fulbright Foundation and American Institute of Indian Studies provided not only financial support but other forms of assistance and personal support as well, and here I wish to thank Geeta Nayar from the Fulbright Foundation and Dr. Venugopala Rao from AIIS in Chennai. Tanjavur University in Tamilnadu provided my research affiliation, and my advisor there, Dr. S. S. Thekkamalai, offered unfailing support and aid, especially in the initial phases of my project. It was he who introduced me to the faculty at the Folklore Research Center at St. Xavier's College in Palayamkottai, especially Dr. S. D. Lourdu, who headed the program while I was there. Dr. Lourdu is a wonderful teacher and researcher, and I learned a great deal by watching him conduct interviews. He and his colleagues offered me intellectual support and encouragement, as they also fed me countless cups of coffee in the college canteen and gave me both friendship and generous research assistance whenever I needed it. I cannot thank them enough for their kindness and their intellectual input into my research.

This book has been a long time in the making, and over the years I have had the chance to rethink the material in many ways thanks to the diverse comments and criticisms I have received from many individuals. To begin with, my teachers at the University of Chicago and elsewhere had a deep influence on how I developed many of my ideas. While this book is quite different from my dissertation, it has grown out of that dissertation in significant ways. McKim Marriott read deeply the drafts I gave him and provided many hours of his time discussing, challenging, and pushing my interpretations. A. K. Ramanujan, K. Paramasivam, and Norman Cutler sustained my love for Tamil language. Ramanujan especially bolstered my confidence even as I slogged through drafts of my unruly chapters. Nancy Munn, Terry Turner, and Bernard Cohn each helped me see different aspects of my work and pointed me to wider spheres of interpretation and theory. Val Daniel first introduced me to the semeiotic perspective that underlies much of my thinking, and he continues to influence my work through his words and writings.

Many other colleagues and friends have, through reading, criticism, and discussion, and sometimes simply through their encouraging support, helped me move forward in my work, offered details of interpretation that have made a big difference, helped me think about my work in terms broader than I might have otherwise, and helped me persevere. They include A. Chellaperumal, Jeff Boyer, Steve Coleman, Dick Fox, Elvin Hatch, Sue Keefe, Laurie Lewis, Mattison Mines, Muthukumaraswamy, Indira Peterson, Greg Reck, Kathy Schroeder, Martha Selby, Robyn Stout, Sam Sudhananda, Gayle Turner, Brad Weiss, and Cynthia Wood. I wish especially to thank Sara Dickey for her close critical reading of the manuscript, which markedly improved the book's overall quality and helped me see better what is was about; Bernard Bate and Cathy Fisher for many hours of discussion, for friendship, and for a haven away from the sometimes infuriating intimacy of village life; and Sarah Lamb, who has read many drafts of these chapters and been a most encouraging friend and interlocutor from the very beginning.

I have had some important technical assistance with this manuscript. Line drawings, while designed by me, were first drafted by Sarah Nurmela. Richard Rapfogel amended the line drawings, helped prepare the tables and maps, converted and processed my own photography, and, as noted in the captions, contributed many of his own photographs. I am grateful to Rebecca Tolen, my editor at Indiana University Press, for her support and critical insights on this work, for her patience as I scrambled to finish it in bits and pieces, and, in an earlier guise, for her "letters from the field."

More than anyone, it is the people of Yanaimangalam (a pseudonym) who made my research possible. Their knowledge, generosity, humor, interest, and willingness to engage with me, initially a stranger and eventually a "sister" and "aunt" and "daughter," not only impacted my concepts but have impacted how I act and understand myself in the world more generally. It is impossible to name all of the people in Yanaimangalam who helped me. It was the whole village, the most inclusive whole. Among those for whose support I am most grateful include the following: Cudalaiyandi Pillai provided me a house to stay in, many delicious meals, and a most excellent outhouse. Ramayya Thevar and his family I thank for spending so many hours telling me how wrong and weird I was about almost everything and carefully explaining why. Arunacalampillai often sat down to tell me stories about the beginnings of things. Arumukampillai gave me the kindness of family, peace, fine meals, and textual knowledge. Pichaiya fed me some wonderful fish curry and a couple of very powerful stories that changed how I saw the reality of the place. Without B. S. Parvathi, my neighbor and friend with whom I shared hours in each day, my research would be empty. She looked after my well-being, made sure I had good help for doing my research, found out for me who was the local expert in which topic, and told me many good stories about the past. M. Aruna, more than any one person, made this research possible. She is my steadfast colleague, my brilliant friend who understood my intentions even when my Tamil was terrible, my feelings even when I tried to hide them, my questions when I could not quite form them myself.

I wish also to thank my family. My parents, Michael and Phyllis Mines, gave me freedom. They encouraged me to pursue such an unlucrative career as anthropology simply because I liked it. My Grandma Mildred Eastham always looked at me with love and helped all of her grandchildren love books. Richard Rapfogel, my husband, spent hours of his own time working on the artwork, talking through ideas, and traveling with me eagerly to Yanaimangalam and by so doing showing me new things about the place. He became part of my project, as of my life. He helped me to put aside the hurtful part of criticism (mostly self-inflicted) and embrace the useful part. Most of all, he loved me all through the hours. And I thank my daughter Lucy who, while now only two, has given me her time, too, and made me think a great deal about what matters most.

NOTE ON TRANSLITERATION

Tamil terms have been transliterated using the University of Madras Tamil Lexicon scheme. For the sake of readability, I have not transliterated proper names of individuals, deities, places, or most castes, using instead commonly recognized Anglicized forms of those terms. Indian terms are pluralized in the English manner, by adding an "s." Occasionally, terms are spelled according to the local spoken convention rather than literary convention. Most non-Tamil Indian terms are employed without diacritics, using commonly recognized Anglicized spellings.

FIERCE GODS

ONE
Introduction

"In this village, nothing changes," said Aruna in the summer of 2003 as we stood on her neighbor's flat roof and surveyed the terrain of Yanaimangalam, a village in Tamilnadu, South India. Aruna, 49 years old, had lived here most of her life, though she had grown up in a town about twenty miles away, the daughter of a textile-mill worker and union man. Wed to a poor farmer, living in a socially excluded "low caste" hamlet located out across the rice fields at some distance from the main village, Aruna had spent years trying to find a way to change her life, her family's financial situation, and her sense of being isolated from the middle-class town life that her sisters had achieved. When I first met her, in 1988, she was taking a correspondence course in typing and other secretarial skills. She later did a master's degree in social work through correspondence courses. She has worked as my research associate for all my fieldwork there, and she now works in the village preschool. She volunteers at the local polling place during elections. And all along—since 1984—she has been working for a World Bank–funded project as a nutritional consultant (Figure 1.1). This project aims at achieving population control through improved nutrition for babies and health education for young women and mothers. The theory is that if women feel confident that their babies will survive to adulthood, they will be more likely to limit the number of children they bear. For this work, which is practically a full-time job, Aruna earned (in 2003) about 20 dollars a month, enough to pay for two weeks of simple food for her small family. She says she doesn't do it for the money but out of a sense of public service (*cēvai*) to the village. If you speak to Aruna about her work with this development project, she glows. She knows that she has almost single-handedly halted the deaths of children. Her twenty years of careful data recording shows that in part through her own efforts, village population growth has slowed considerably. Yet despite her power

Figure 1.1. Aruna recording data with her colleague's daughters, 2003.
© Richard Rapfogel. Used by permission.

to implement positive social change, she still laments from the rooftop that in this village "nothing changes." When I asked her to explain, she described how caste inequities still dominate her life and the lives of others in painful ways. This she blames not on "caste" so much as on the "village."

A few days later, I was sitting and talking with Parvathi, an elderly Brahman woman who lives alone on the Agraharam, the Brahman street of the main village (Figure 1.2). Never married, she lives a simple existence supported by the monthly income she receives from a field she owns and occasional gifts from her cousin-brothers north in Allahabad and Benaras. "This village is ruined," she complained as she watched chickens scratch in the dirt in front of her house. "All these chickens and goats. . . ." For her, the village has changed irrevocably. All she remembers of her youth is gone. The Agraharam, an entire street with sixty houses of Brahmans in a tight-knit community, is gone. Her heyday as a young woman educated in Gandhian principles of self-sufficiency, which she brought to the women of her neighborhood in the form of sewing lessons and other crafts, is long gone. Now only ten or twelve houses on the street belong to (mostly poor) Brahmans, and the rest have been taken over by prosperous farmers from other powerful castes in the village. And their ways are different. Some keep and eat chickens and goats. They care little for the Krishna temple at

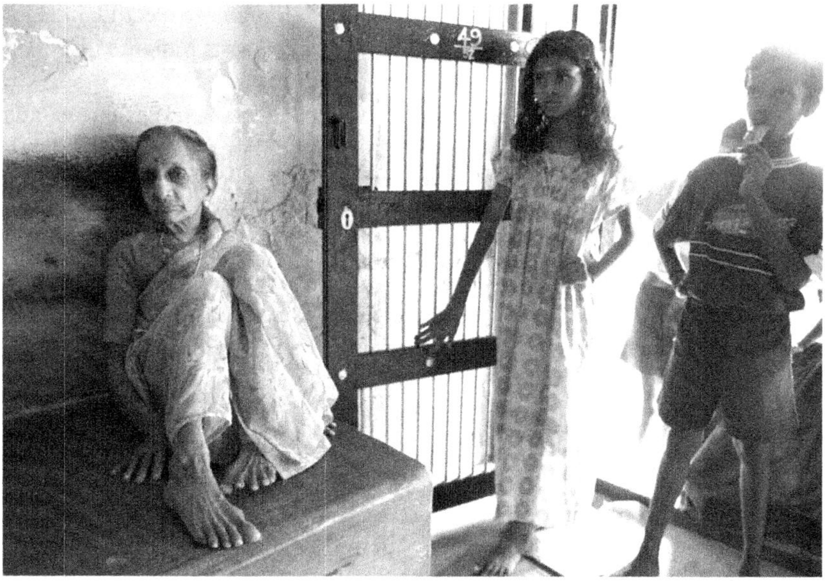

Figure 1.2. Parvathi with neighbor kids on her inner veranda, 2001.
© Richard Rapfogel. Used by permission.

the head of the street or the Siva temple at the other end, favoring rather the village goddess who oversees agriculture and the fierce gods who demand sacrifices of chickens and goats. Her days are steeped in remembrance of past days, which she talks about with great energy and enthusiasm, days when Brahmans were the center and power of her village.

Just down the street from Parvathi, I met with Vijayalaksmi and her husband Raja Pillai, a prosperous and high-caste agriculturalist. They had just moved out of their small house on Pillaimar Street (named for the caste group which populates it) and into a large abandoned house on the Brahman street. They prosper in this village and see as well as oversee its improvements. Active in politics and big supporters of a powerful state political party known as the All India Anna Dravida Munnetra Kazhagam (AIADMK), members of their family have served for years as members of the local panchayat, an elected town council representing both Yanaimangalam and a much larger village about two miles away. Her husband served on the panchayat board previously and both of them express their concern with serving the political-economic interests of the village through development projects funded by the state via the panchayat. In 2003, Vijayalaksmi was serving as the first female president of this council. Since 1994, in an attempt to legislate gender and caste equality in rural areas, the Tamilnadu state has mandated that panchayat boards in certain parts of the state elect women presidents. Others have mandates to elect Dalit (Untouchable) presidents, though in many areas these posts remained unfilled for fear of the violent backlash any such applicant may suffer at the hands of more dominant castes. I asked Vijayalaksmi if she experienced any difficulty in her position as a woman. She said no. For this family, which is dominant politically as well as economically, the village was a source of increasing power and prosperity.

What is this village that looks so different from different streets and different points of view, and even on different days to the same people? As we shall see, these three perspectives on the village (Aruna's that nothing has changed, Parvathi's that everything has changed, the panchayat members' that things are good and improving even more) illustrate several concepts crucial to the very purpose of this book. First, the village is a "sign," a concept as well as a material reality that has specific meanings to people. Second, the meaning of this sign is refracted through the lens of different social, political-economic, and even existential orientations, as the vignettes above illustrate. Finally, the village is a living sign. Its meaning and significance are still argued, still part of living discourse. The village—just what it is, was, or would be—matters very much to the living. For many academics working in South Asia today, the village appears as a dead sign, something not worth talking about much. But for the residents of Yanaimangalam the village is a vibrant and powerful trope in everyday life as well as in yearly political-ritual events that bring the sign, the village, to the forefront of life's concern.

This book is a village study and is based on research conducted continuously in Yanaimangalam between August 1988 and August 1990, with shorter return visits in 2000, 2001, and 2003. I explore some variety of the semeiotic resources—material, bodily, conceptual, and discursive—that village residents put to use as they constitute, alter, and contest the village as a place for their heterogeneous but intimately linked lives. The village cannot be understood without understanding power relations among village residents, so in speaking of the village, I am speaking too of the real relations of power that condition relations among village residents. While I study the production of both domination and subordination, I am particularly interested in exploring how the powerless make their voices heard in a village where the social power of some works to silence the discourses of others. What power do they have to "make" the village and their place in the world? As Ann Grodzins Gold and Ram Gujar have demonstrated beautifully in their ethnography of Rajasthani villagers' memories of domination under the kings of their region, the powers of the dominant are not necessarily hegemonic. Gold and Gujar find what Chatterjee (1993, 171) called "flashes of open rebellion" in everyday life, flashes which point to an "undominated region in peasant consciousness" (quoted in Gold and Gujar 2002, 18). They argue that "beyond these small defiances perhaps, are the still larger undominated regions of dignity and struggle" (ibid., 20).

For Yanaimangalam's powerless, their flashes of rebellion as well as their struggles to maintain dignity are aided in no small part by the gods who inhabit the world with them. That is, the powers of humans are not the only relevant powers at work in village politics, for the power of the gods who inhabit Yanaimangalam are part and parcel of villagers' makings and remakings of the village. This book is, therefore, also about the gods who inhabit Yanaimangalam. In particular, I argue that while the power of caste rank and political-economic dominance is produced in large part through relations to gods, it is the "fierce gods" of Yanaimangalam who, through their socially disordering powers, allow subordinate groups and persons to publicly turn the tables on domination and assert their own powerful alternatives of village relations. Below, I will outline more fully some of my perspectives on gods, villages, and social action. But let us begin by introducing the place of the humans and gods who populate this book.

ARRIVAL

Yanaimangalam is one in a loose strand of villages set along the banks of the Tambraparni River in Tirunelveli District, Tamilnadu (Figure 1.3). The river flows west to east and slips finally into the Bay of Bengal, but not before it floods and feeds the rice and banana fields that green Yanaimangalam for a good part of the year. Most village residents make a large part, if not all, of their living from farming small plots of rice and (increasingly) bananas, either as owners, tenants, or laborers (Table 1.1). The rich irrigated lands of the village support two crops of rice per year. Bananas take an entire year to mature and require crop rotation with rice as well, for they deplete the soil of nutrients. Farmers who can afford to build wells and install pumps depend less on river water and can therefore also grow summer crops of vegetables or pulses. During my research from 1988–1990, rice was by far the most common crop grown both for consumption and for sale. By 2003, farmers had planted bananas everywhere they could, for they proved a lucrative crop that helped residents increase their cash income and ensure against lean years. They grew rice to eat and bananas to sell. The move to bananas is not without other profound economic consequences.

The village has existed for some time. Inscriptions etched into the stone face of the riverside Visnu temple indicate that Yanaimangalam was certainly populated as early as 1400 C.E., almost certainly settled as a *brahmadeya*—that is, a village established by a king and granted to the support

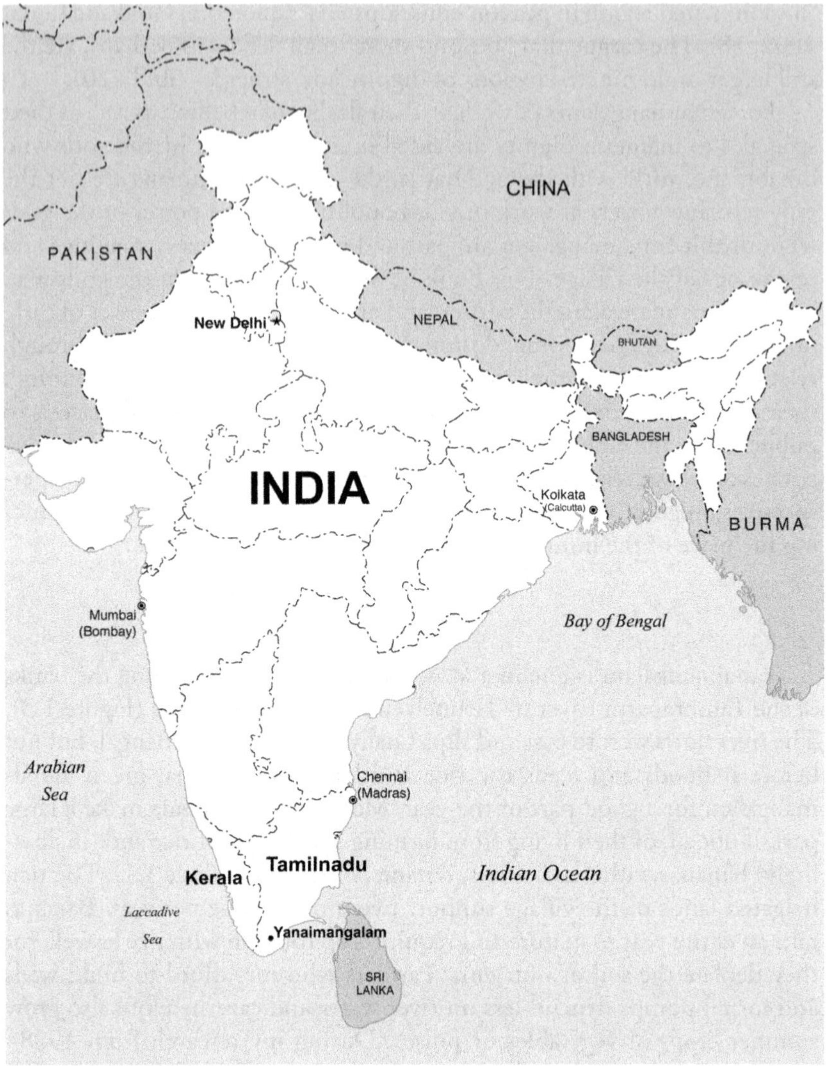

Figure 1.3. Map of India.

of a Brahman community.[1] By 1988, when I first arrived, Yanaimangalam's population belied this Brahmanical founding, a fact that led me to settle there by mistake. I had proposed my research to study a village that was explicitly not dominated by Brahmans. I was interested in alternative nonhierarchical models of social organization and exchange and thought that a non-Brahman village might present a clearer pattern of such alternatives.[2]

But, blinded by the current population statistics, I fell into the trap of mistaking present demography for the timeless eternity of the village, as if what it was in 1988 was the same as what it had been always. In 1988, and still in 2003, Brahmans in Yanaimangalam were a fairly impoverished small community that was far from dominant. As I was to learn, not forty years previously the number of Brahman households had been closer to sixty than ten and Brahmans had also owned a preponderance of the land and had been, indeed, the economically and politically dominant caste, or *jāti.*[3] Land reforms, beginning in the 1950s and culminating in the 1970s, had increasingly favored tenants over large nonlaboring landholders, leading to Brahman loss of dominance. Most Brahman residents had subsequently moved to white-collar jobs in towns and cities.

The sheepish grin and chagrined shrug I sometimes offer as an apology for my presumption—not so unusual in anthropological paradigms of the period—that the village was somehow immune to historical change resemble nothing so much as the grin and shrug I presented to the village residents when I made my clumsy—but no doubt entertaining—arrival in Yanaimangalam. It was my knees rather than my feet that first touched the earth of the village as I brought my bicycle to a prompt halt and then, just as promptly, fell off. My chaperone on this first visit was someone who knew how to dismount properly: a Tamil professor from St. Xavier's College in Palayamkottai, the colleague of a contact of a contact, whose cousin's cousin was a big man in the village. This big man was none other than the aforementioned Raja Pillai, who at that time was serving on the panchayat board.

The professor and I had taken the fast bus to the nearest roadside village, rented bicycles from a wary man at a roadside bicycle shop, and then cycled off up a side road that first wound through the dusty roadside village and then stretched out across cool, flooded paddy fields—the Western Ghats rising up blue in the near distance—toward Yanaimangalam. Once in the village, someone pointed out to us the big man's house, where we dismounted (or fell). We were ushered down a narrow lane that led into a bright whitewashed courtyard and then up a few steps onto the house veranda. We were invited to sit, and so we did—on cool concrete benches, polished and shined by many years of such sittings. Raja Pillai was not home, but his elderly and more prominent father was. He knew everything, we were informed. The professor established his kin connection, stated my purpose for coming to Yanaimangalam, and then turned the matter over to me. In what had become for me an unrelenting and nerve-racking quest for the perfect non-Brahman village in this part of Tamilnadu, I had become adept at stammering out in timid Tamil the first necessary question: "Which jātis live here?" The old man, Muttaiah Pillai—straight-backed with white hair, old, and very toothless and therefore difficult for me to understand—answered: "Pillaimar (his own), Muppanar, Thevarmar." Three jātis. Were there any Brahmans? I asked. Yes, but only about ten households. With effort, I elicited another few jāti names: Acari, Dhobi, Pallar, Palaiyar. After some time in the village, I learned that there were many jātis (Table 1.1). Clearly, Muttaiah Pillai was telling me not who *all* lived in this village, but rather to whom this village in some sense *belonged*: Pillaimar, Muppanar, Thevar.

I was thinking that demographically this village seemed promising for my research and that I might like to settle here in spite of the unsettling voice of Muttaiah Pillai's wife, who, the entire time I was discussing with her husband the possibility of moving into the village, was shouting out an accompaniment from inside the house: "Why would anyone want to live here? There is no bus, no shop, no convenience! What's the good in living here?" and so on. I later learned that she shouted out everything to everyone, as if their hearing was as blurred as her vision with its encroaching cataracts. At the time, I could barely understand a word anyway (the Tamil professor translated the gist for me later into English) and in the end it turned out there *were* a few small food shops and there *was* a bus from Tirunelveli Junction that came to the village five times a day (not counting the days of unpredictable breakdowns) after bumping for an hour or two through other villages up and down and across the river. The village had electricity, newspaper delivery, a post office, and, by the time I left in 1990, it even had treated water piped in from a nearby reservoir, though most people could not afford the fee for a private connection and relied on one of the four public pumps scattered throughout the settlement. Morning and evening, women and girls bunched up around these pumps to draw water, visit, and quarrel.

In the end, I settled in Yanaimangalam less for demographic reasons than for the generous and good-humored reception residents gave me, such as the group of women I met busily rolling incense sticks for pennies at another house on another street, at the aforementioned Parvathi's house. They seemed keen on my moving in, mostly in hopes of alleviating their boredom I think, for they warned me cheerfully and repeatedly that the village was not just boring, but *rompa pōrāka aṭikkum,* "reeeeaaally boring." There were several empty houses on Parvathi's street. The owner of the one right across the street from hers agreed not only to rent it to me but even to build a latrine, of sorts, out back. And so, after waiting one month for the latrine and then waiting another month—at the villagers' insistence—for an astrologically auspicious day for moving, I moved in. It turned out that my demographic blunder paid off. The recent history of the place, where Brahman dominance had given way to the dominance of other jātis, was often a topic of conversations that revealed quite clearly the

Table 1.1 Population of Yanaimangalam by Jāti, Number, and Occupation

Jāti	Households	Total Number	Attributed Occupations	Actual Occupations in Yanaimangalam[1]
Thevar	115	495	Cultivator, watchman	Owner-cultivator, watchman
Pallar	106	422	Agricultural laborer	Agricultural laborer
Pillaimar	66	295	Cultivator	Owner-cultivator
Muppanar	49	208	Cultivator	Owner-cultivator
Paraiyar	36	145	Agricultural laborer	Agricultural laborer
Illuttuppillai	22	82	Toddy tapper	Agricultural laborer
Brahmans[2]	11	47	Priest, scholar	Priest, salaried job, landowner
Acari[3]	4	32	Carpenter, smith	Carpenter, blacksmith, pot repair
Nacavan	4	22	Barber	Shopkeeper, tailor, salaried job
Saiva Pillai	4	13	Accountant	Landowner, salaried job
Vannan (Dhobi)	4	13	Washerman	Washerman
Naidu	3	4	Merchant	Retired
Muslim	1	4	Merchant	Bidi merchant
Kambar	1	1	Priest, musician	Retired
Totals	426	1,783		

1. Occupations listed are those common to most families. Many people also seek salaried employment both inside and outside the village instead of or in addition to the occupation listed here. "Owner-cultivator" refers to one who works the land he also owns. "Landowner" refers to one who owns land but who hires others to work it. "Agricultural laborer" refers to on who works on the land of others and owns little or none of his own.

2. All Brahmans here are Saivite Aiyars with the exception of one family of Vaisnavite Aiyangars who moved into the village to serve as priests in the Visnu and Krishna temples.

3. Three jātis of Acari are lumped together here. These are Carpenters, Blacksmith, and Pot-Makers.

processes, practices, and dimensions of dominance in the making, which is one of the major themes of this book.

VILLAGE TOUR

Had I been more familiar with South Indian villages, with rural house types, and with temple history and architecture, or had I been flexible enough to transpose my book knowledge about these subjects into my visual experience of the landscape, I would have discerned the village's Brahman history the first time I fell into the place. Architecture, temples, and residential patterns, plus the village's location on the banks of a large river with signs of an ancient irrigation system, fairly shouted out the village's past in a decisive narrative of bricks and stones, rice and water.

Yanaimangalam consists of five settlements: one central residential area usually referred to as the "big village" (*periya ūr*), or Big Yanaimangalam, and four smaller hamlets scattered around in the surrounding fields (Figure 1.4). Big Yanaimangalam consists of four parallel earthen streets linked by narrow pathways that run between packed rows of houses. Each of the four streets is named for the jāti who predominates among the street's residents. And their order, starting north and moving south, approximates the (contested) rank ordering of these jātis based on relative "purity" (*cuttam*).

The northernmost street is the Brahman street, which most villagers referred to as "*kirāmam,*" a word that means "village" yet here seems to be conflated with the Sanskrit term "*akkirakāram,*" or "Agraharam," which is the term I use in this text to connote this neighborhood's Brahmanical origins. Next comes Pillaimar Street, then Muppanar Street, and finally Thevarmar Street, with each street occupied not entirely but mostly by members of the jāti for which the street is named. These four streets languish in the heat of the day, especially during the hot summer season when temperatures ranged from 102F to 110F. People find shelter in the cooler dark interiors of their houses, where they nap or work quietly. But in the cooler early mornings and evenings, the streets and bylanes bustle.

During my stay, I would sit outside with my neighbors on house stoops and watch the traffic: men on cycles going to the bigger village down the road to hang out at the coffee shop with their cronies; children lingering on their way to or from the schoolhouse; women dressed in bright flowing saris sweeping the entrances to their houses and drawing decorations called *kōlam* on their thresholds. In the evenings, the house stoops would burst with gossip. Sometimes the streets offered entertaining distractions: the odd taxi bringing visitors or sometimes patients home from the hospital; jeeps blaring officious horns to announce the arrival of government officials or other VIPs, such as the district collector's wife, who came on tour one time; rented vans stuffed with wedding parties; one of the local tough guys

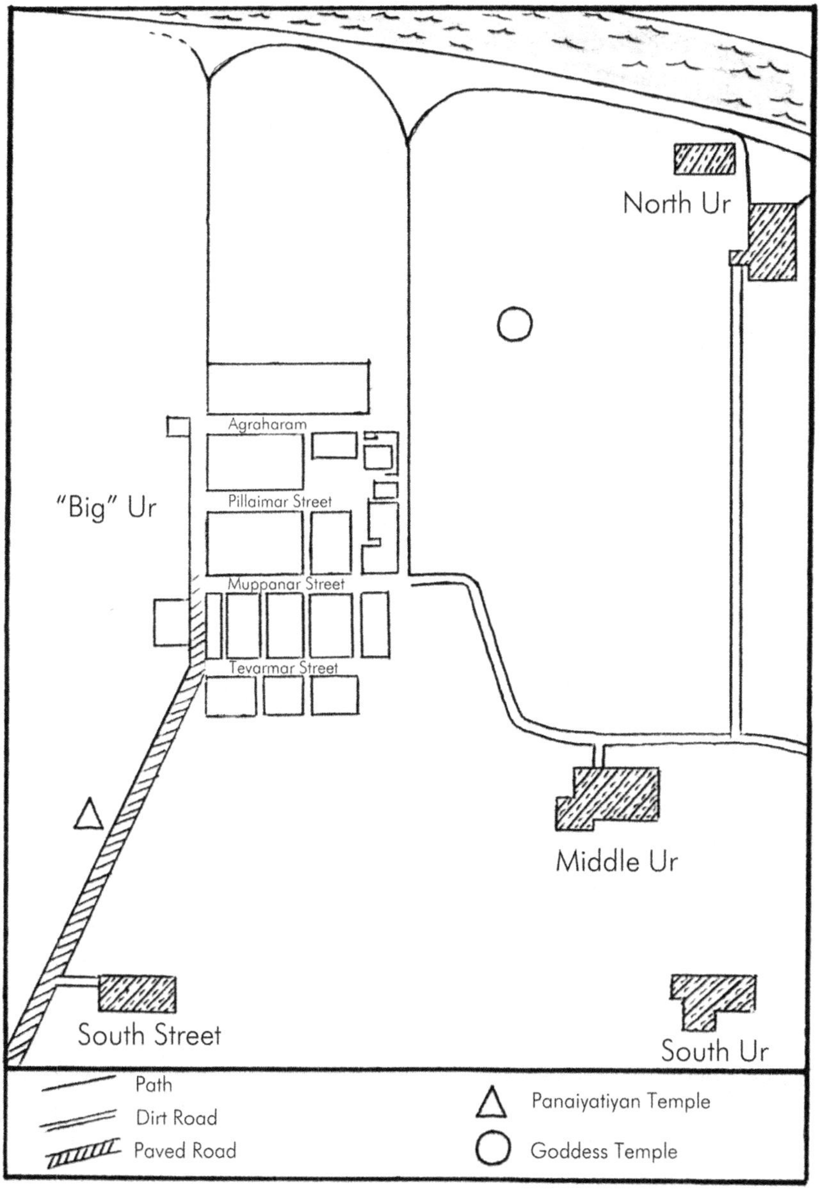

Figure 1.4. Sketch map of Yanaimangalam.

zooming back and forth on his maroon Yedzi (the Czech Harley), white *veṣṭi* billowing in his wake; a lorry delivering bulk goods to the ration shop; and even larger lorries accompanied by "agents" wearing gold chains who would come to haul banana crops away to Kerala from where they would be shipped off to Dubai and other destinations unknown; a temple elephant (with mahout) from some large temple in a nearby town collecting alms and giving blessings with his trunk; itinerant vendors hawking their goods with their long nasalized cries advertising plastic jugs or stainless steel or mangoes or onions or fortunes to be told. There were oxcarts rattling, an occasional motor scooter putting, and congeries of cattle and goats, whose hooves on the stone-hardened street sound like the rain starting to fall. By 2003, these sounds and scenes were accompanied and sometimes drowned out by numerous motorcycles, autorickshaw taxis, tractors, and even one car. These vehicles reflect a decade of prosperity brought about in part by increased banana cultivation and in part by the higher income commanded by young people who have found salaried jobs in town.

I lived on the Brahman street, the Agraharam. While most people were quite familiar with America and had a pretty good idea of my place in their lives, others sometimes thought I might be a Brahman, a mistake my research associate Aruna would often encourage among people she considered to be too nosey. Others thought maybe I was a North Indian Brahman ("Is America near Delhi?" I was asked on one occasion). Many people did wonder: What was my jāti? Aruna kept a village census as part of her nutrition-project job. Perusing that census one day, I found myself: name, address, age, gender, religion, and jāti all neatly recorded so that I could fit into the government census categories. My jāti Aruna had recorded as "Christian." I objected, saying that my jāti wasn't really "Christian." Eraser at the ready, she asked me what it was then. I said I didn't have one, a jāti that is. She laughed and then shouted out across the street to Parvathi, my neighbor, that I had no jāti. All the neighbors who overheard laughed out loud, and Parvathi slapped her hand on her knee in glee. To their ears such a statement meant something like "I don't exist as a kind of anything—living or dead—in this universe."

I settled on the Agraharam because this is where village residents I had contacted wanted me, where they thought I would be safest. And besides, this was where the empty houses were. The houses on this street are shotgun houses: long, narrow, and jammed together in two tight rows facing each other. At the western head of the street sits a small temple for Krishna, who, looking out from inside his abode, has an unobstructed view down the street in front of him toward the east, toward the rising sun. The houses, in their parallel rows, stand like temple devotees in line letting the god's eyesight flow past them. Behind the Krishna temple, the Western Ghats—now blue, now brown—rise straight up from the plains to over 5,000 feet, just twenty-five miles west. At the opposite, east end of the street, off to one side, sits a larger and old Siva temple. In 1990, it showed signs of age and neglect, but by 2003 it had been renovated, all expenses paid by a rich Brahman from Chennai (formerly Madras).

All Brahmans in Yanaimangalam live on this street. However, they are no longer the sole inhabitants of the street but rather a small and relatively impoverished minority of priests, teachers, civil servants (including the local postman), and old people. Most of those that could had long ago sold their property and left the village for more lucrative livings in cities and towns not only in Tamilnadu but as far away as Bombay, Delhi, and California. They sold their property not to other Brahmans but to those who gained from land reform, those who tilled the soil: Pillaimar, Muppanar, and Thevarmar jātis, the three jātis who are now the politically and economically dominant jātis of Yanaimangalam. The Agraharam has become the most jāti-integrated street in the village, while only forty years ago it was the least diverse and most exclusive.

The street just south of the Agraharam is Pillaimar Street, and most of its residents are of the high-ranking vegetarian Pillaimar jāti. As a group, Pillaimar are among the most prosperous landowners in the village, though included among their ranks are very poor families too, who eke out a living by working on the land and in the houses of their more well-to-do relatives. Several Pillaimar men both own land and commute to jobs in nearby towns, jobs ranging from bricklayer to office clerk to teacher. For example, in one well-to-do family with three sons, one stayed in the village to oversee the lands, one works as a naturalist for the forest service in the mountains of northern India, and one is a college history professor in another part of the state. Pillaimar houses—like the houses of most other village jātis—differ architecturally from the shotgun Brahman houses. They are often built around an interior courtyard. While the Brahman verandas face out onto the street (and into the auspicious gaze of Krishna), Pillaimar verandas face into their own inner courtyards. Sometimes several small houses are built around a central courtyard and larger houses are constructed with subdivisions in mind, as sons will marry and bring their wives to join the family and set up a separate hearth around the shared courtyard. Because of these architectural differences, in part, the street itself is less a center of social activity than was the Agraharam. Here the courtyards and rooftops are centers of social life, and social life mostly revolves around the extended family.

The third street, Muppanar Street, is the most commercial street in the village. Most of the vegetable and sundries shops are on this street, as are a couple of coffee stalls, a bicycle-repair shop, and, until recently, the post office. Pillaiyar (otherwise known as Vinayagar or Ganesh, the elephant-headed son of Siva and Parvathi) presides over this street in the same way that Krishna presides over the Agraharam, looking straight down the street from west to east. In this case, the temple doubles as a bus shelter, the large neem tree in the temple courtyard provides breezy shade, and the stone doorway shelter travelers from rain and sun alike. Like their Pillaimar neighbors, most Muppanars in the village own and/or work the land. Some work in nearby towns. Some run village shops. Some have sons working in factories as far away as Bombay or studying at college in towns not quite so far away, and many have daughters who have married into other towns, thus extending the reach of the kinship network regionally.

The fourth and last street of Big Yanaimangalam is Thevarmar Street. This narrowest and most crooked of streets, where tile roofs are sparser and thatched ones more common, is populated mostly by Thevarmar, or Thevars, whose local prominence as landowners and political powers is increasing not only in Yanaimangalam but throughout the region and the state. On the edges of this street, slightly behind and beyond the street itself, is the old compound of the Barbers, none of whom cut hair anymore (of the men, one is a tailor, one owns a shop in the village, and one works in the district engineer's office in a small town nearby as an assistant to the engineer). Behind them live the Dhobis, or Washermen, who do indeed wash clothes, though not just those of Yanaimangalam's residents, for one of them—who by 2003 was retired—was also attached to a laundry business in Tirunelveli town where he commuted daily by bus, one hour each way. His son works in Bombay and returns three times a year for a temple festival in which his father, and now he, play a significant role. On Thevarmar Street live also a family of Carpenters who build and repair plows, carts, doors, and shelves, and a family of Blacksmiths who forge plow tips, knives, and sickles over a fire in their courtyard, operating their bellows by foot. In 1988, there also lived a lone old Kambar woman (who by 2003 was deceased), who in her younger days had worked with her husband, the previous non-Brahman priest in the village goddess temple, until he died and she was forcibly removed from her priestly rights and replaced by Brahman priests. Her three sons left the village to find work and now live in various temple towns here and there in Tamilnadu, where they work as temple musicians. Her daughters were married and they live in other villages too.

Surrounding Big Yanaimangalam with its four main streets, its 1,000 residents, and its dozen or more temples, are fields. Rice fields and banana fields and a few small coconut and palmyra groves between. Hundreds of small fields are separated by narrow boundary paths—slippery balance beams in monsoon months. Across and amid these fields lie Yanaimangalam's four other settlements: North Ūr, Middle Ūr, South Street, and South Ūr.

Farthest south is South Ūr, inhabited almost entirely by members of the Palaiyar jāti, considered still by many to be "Untouchable." Middle Ūr and the southern half of North Ūr, which is located near the riverbank (Yanaimangalam's northern border), are populated by another "Untouchable" jāti called Pallar. (In the northern half of North Ūr live several Thevarmar families, a family of Washermen, and a Metalsmith who repairs pots.) Most Palaiyar and Pallar men and women work primarily as laborers in the fields and homes of more prosperous families in the Big Village. Some few own their land and are relatively prosperous. Many dream about migrating to larger towns and cities where they hope to find more lucrative, cash-paying jobs and where, as one man put it, hopefully, "jāti differences don't matter" (*jāti vityācam teriyātu,* lit. "jāti differences are not apparent"). These two Untouchable jātis, Palaiyar and Pallar, are sometimes still referred to by people from the Big Village as "Harijans." "Harijan" is a term coined by Gandhi to refer to those groups the British called "Untouchable"; it means "people or children of god." While the term "Harijan" is intended to be less derogatory than the actual jāti names (Pallar and Palaiyar in this case), many Untouchables in fact find that term to be patronizing. During the period of this research, Palaiyar and Pallar residents of Yanaimangalam preferred the designation "S. C.," for "Scheduled Caste," a government-reservation category (something akin to an affirmative action designation). Even by 2003, few used the more politically progressive term "Dalit," meaning "Oppressed" in Marathi. Throughout this book, when speaking of members of these jātis, I shift reference as village residents shifted it, according to context, because the term used—whether jāti name, Harijan, S. C., or Dalit—communicates pragmatically beyond simple reference, pointing to relative status, to attitudes, to ideology, to respect or the lack thereof.

Finally, a fourth hamlet, South Street, is situated near the road leading to and from Yanaimangalam. On South Street live two lineages of a jāti referred to as Illuttuppillai (the name they prefer) or Iluvar (the lower-status name others sometimes used to refer to them). These cultivators trace their descent to the neighboring state of Kerala and, more recently, to a textile-mill town about twenty miles east. Many own their own small plots of land where they eke out a minimal living. Two old women on that street liked to tell me about how they worked for white bosses in the textile mill (called Harvey Mill when it was still a British concern, but now owned by Madurai Coats) when they were young. They described how the white men shouted a lot and waved their guns about and how their wives wore "frocks." This was said with great expectancy as if I, myself, would don a frock or even wave a gun at any moment. (I learned several months into my stay, in fact, that my landlord had concocted a rumor that I was in possession of a gun given to me by my "husband"—also then a character in my landlord's fiction—who was in the military and that I had shown it to him once in my hotel room in town!) The Illuttuppillai of South Street are also considered to be quite low ranking. Their jāti is classified in the government category of "Most Backward Caste" (M. B. C.), just one step above the S. C. (The higher-ranking jātis in the big village were mostly ranked as F. C., Forward Castes, though many were trying for a lower category in hopes of having a better chance for government jobs and reserved seats for their children in institutions of higher education.)

As should be apparent by now, the spatial arrangement of Yanaimangalam is hardly neutral but reflects patterns of rank and power conceived of in an idiom of caste. Much of this study revolves around the way in which caste concepts influence peoples' lives and choices, for caste is part of the reality of the village for those who live there. At the same time, this study is about the pragmatically real power of the gods, about South Indian concepts of action, and, most of all, about how the disenfranchised struggle to define a place in a world of their own making.

PERSPECTIVES

Caste

People in South India, both urban and rural, engage with one another in all sorts of modalities: gendered; class-based; beauty-biased; in friendship; as co-workers, teachers, students, playmates, cricket team members, political rivals, computer experts, cinema lovers, and so on—in as many ways as we imagine ourselves interacting with others around us. For many Tamils, caste too is a modality of interrelating to others. And in Yanaimangalam, caste is never far from peoples' consciousness.

Dirks (2001) warns anthropologists and others away from essentializing caste as a core condition of Indian society. Granted that caste is a historical construction whose contemporary forms are in part outgrowths of colonial and postcolonial processes—and as I will show, Tamils also see their jāti as something alterable through their own actions—it is nevertheless the case that in Yanaimangalam, jāti forms an everyday habit of thought. Streets are named for the jātis who reside there. Jāti titles are used as part of a person's name, and in many cases to avoid the jāti title is to insult the name-bearer. One's jāti has a bearing on the places a person feels comfortable in or is allowed to inhabit, enter, or even sit to rest. And key to this study, jāti is also a trope of power. That is, jāti is the embodied as well as verbal language through which local power relations are expressed and enacted. Jāti has increasingly become the trope for regional if not national political life as well. Political constituencies form along jāti lines, and regional violence between "communities," as the newspapers refer to them, is in fact often violence between groups who identify themselves as members of the same jāti.

Indeed, among the most salient aspects of the given world for residents of Yanaimangalam is an embodied concept of jāti, which is usually glossed in English as "caste" but is more aptly translated as "genus." It is certainly true that local discourse on jāti is not clear cut or without important historical input from colonial and postcolonial state practices. While some village residents clearly embrace jāti as a way of ranking and excluding people on the bases of purity and order, many others in the village eschew these meanings and advocate a much more egalitarian view of society. Some make note of social change that makes caste distinctions less onerous, such as a neighbor who told me that Untouchables are no longer so low because nowadays they are so much "neater" than they used to be. Even when people reject the ranking of castes, however, most still adhere to the idea that jāti is a matter of self, of quality of being, and that different jātis—while *perhaps* equal as human beings—are nonetheless best not mixed through marriage or residence. Caste in India today is a complex, variegated set of discourses. Caste matters at the voting booth and at the temple, just as it matters in many aspects of everyday life. This book offers one look at the multiplex discourse on jāti at the turn of the twenty-first century in rural South India.

Possession and Power

In any village and neighborhood in Tamilnadu where Hindus reside, there too reside gods. But in no two places do the very same gods live. Some gods, such as the universally recognized gods Siva, Visnu, and Krishna (an avatar, or incarnation, of Visnu), and the goddess Kali can be found all over South Asia, in villages, towns, and cities both north and south. Others, such as Yanaimangalam's Vellalakantan or Panaiyatiyan, are unique to one place. Scholars have sometimes described the distinction between universally recognized gods and strictly local ones as a distinction between a "great tradition" and a "little tradition" of Hinduism. But residents of Yanaimangalam have their own set of distinctions. They distinguish among three kinds of gods, what I will gloss here as Brahmanical gods (*pirāmaṅka tēvarkaḷ*), village goddesses (*ūr ammaṉkaḷ*), and fierce gods (*māṭaṉ* or *pēy*, lit. "ghost").

Yanaimangalam's residents compare both castes and gods along several dimensions of contrast. They describe castes as relatively high (*ocanta*) versus relatively low (*taḻnta*), as big (*periya*) versus little (*ciṉṉa*), as pure (cuttam) versus impure (*acuttam*), the latter correlating roughly with vegetarian on the one hand and meat-eating on the other. They describe gods in similar terms, as high to low, big to little, vegetarian to meat-eating and as soft or gentle (*metuvāṉa*) to fierce (*ukkiramāṉa*), a distinction that also corresponds to variables running from cool to hot, "neat" and orderly to chaotic, stable to unstable. Both humans and gods may be further distinguished residentially. Higher, "bigger" (powerful, landowning), and neater castes live in the Big Village while the lower, "little" (landless, service-providing), and chaotic castes live on the peripheries of the village and in the small hamlets out across the fields. Similarly, higher, cooler, and purer gods live in the interiors of the Big Village: in temples on village streets and in alcoves and posters on the walls of residents' houses. Low-ranking, hot, impure, meat-eating fierce gods live outside: out in the fields or the wastelands beyond or outside and facing away from the house in back courtyards.

Given these parallel associations between humans on the one hand and gods on the other, it is certainly easy to see why many scholars have presented structural analyses where the pantheon of ranked gods "symbolizes" ranks among humans and thereby justifies the latter by imbuing them with sacredness. In some contexts, this argument certainly bears out. Tamil temples are critical sites for displaying and constituting dominant social hierarchies. Yet as I argue in Part II, the power of gods does more than merely echo the power of human beings. Gods are not merely cosmological justifications for distinctions in social power among castes. Rather, gods are real sources of power for human beings whether they are struggling for or against domination. It is the lowly fierce gods of Yanaimangalam who empower the powerless through possession of their human hosts.

Dipesh Chakrabarty (1997) describes the difficulty Marxist historians have with reconciling theory to the practices of Indian laborers for whom gods play a role in the productive process. As historians, they translate a local world where laborers treat gods as agents in productive processes into an analytic world where there is no place for a real recognition of the agentive power of gods as anything more than myth, mystification, or epiphenomenon. But as Chakrabarty himself suggests, the question of the "reality" of gods need not boil down to a Cartesian choice between truth and appearance or object and subject. I would suggest that by taking a pragmatic[4] approach to the question, the contradiction disappears, for in such an approach, gods may indeed be understood as "real" historical agents. As tools for human action in the world, gods are conduits for practical human activity. That is, gods assumed to be real by human actors do make those actors act in one way versus another. Things happen that otherwise would not. In this way the gods themselves are by definition real agencies in the making of social life. In this book, I work to show how, by possessing their human hosts, gods are the agents of their devotees' political agendas and as such play a key role in making and remaking the village.

Spirit possession alters the capacities of the persons possessed. In Tamil life, there are two kinds of possession, what Kapadia (2000) calls "malign" and "benign" possessions. In the former, god and host are out of sync and hence violent reactions are possible. The person possessed is considered "grabbed" (*piṭi*) by the god. Often such possessions have been analyzed in psychological terms, as expressive signs of mental illness or social-structural tensions. Nabokov (2000) shows that such possessions often lead persons to do violence to the self by making personal and social compromises that the possessions that fail to address the underlying problems that likely trigger the possessions. This type of possession is very different from "benign," or what I would describe as empowering, possession. In Yanaimangalam, the latter possessions are described as joinings (*cērkkai*) of a god to a prepared host. As Kapadia notes, such possessions, which I describe at length in Part II, are in part political demonstrations of the host community's social power (Kapadia 2000, 186). Possession can make the powerless powerful. It can make the small grow large in power and strength. It can give voice to the voiceless. And when the gods of the voiceless speak, what do they say? Among the messages I heard conveyed were cries for justice in an oppressive world, cries of hopes for a different future. Gods, I argue, are part and parcel of the process through which residents of Yanaimangalam work toward their hopes and bring into reality new feelings and ideas about their humanity.

Self and Society: A View on Human Being

I concur with Jackson (1996) and other phenomenological theorists from a variety of fields (e.g., the anthropologists Kapferer [1997, 194–198] and Munn [1986, 3–20], the philosopher Casey [1996], the psychologist May [1958, 37–71], the pragmaticist Peirce) that the relation between self and world is a productive, dialectical process where actors engage in what is "given" in their lives (the social, historical, and environmental conditions in which they are placed, the contingencies they are thrown) as well as "what is imagined to lie ahead" (Jackson 1996, 11). In that engagement, actors create not only themselves but also possibly new conditions for "existing"; that is, for acting out into the world in a process of growth or, as May (1958, 12) puts it, "becoming." This study both begins from and attempts to demonstrate a dialectical approach to self and society, an approach I argue is consistent with Tamil concepts of person and action and consistent also with some theoretical approaches devised by others working within a phenomenological and existential framework. As I hope to show, such a view of human life, of human "being-in-the-world" accords well with some practical concepts of action held by the Tamils I worked among, concepts of practice and habit (*paḻakkam*), of humans' capacity to create themselves and their world through action, of what might be considered a "karmic" understanding of action as self-, other-, and world-making.

Such a perspective recognizes the capacity of humans to create the world they live in, but as Marx notes, not under conditions that they themselves choose. We inherit a world and live to a great extent in ways given to us. Michael Jackson expresses this when he writes that

> we encounter the world as a fetishized product of previous activity, the work of other lives, an outcome of inscrutable designs. This given world appears to possess a life of its own, and we the living seem to dwell in its shadow. Yet without our consent and labor this sedimented world of ancestral acts and forgone conclusions could not prevail. Its perpetuation is not a matter of inertia but of the vital activity of the living who, in Marx's compelling phrase, force the frozen circumstances to dance by singing to them their own melody. (Cited in Fromm 1973, 83 and Jackson 1998, 27)

So while "history speaks through us in ways we just barely comprehend" (Colapietro 1989, 41), so too do we dance history into action in the here and now. What I hope most of all for this work is that it expresses something about the dance, which I see to be about being human, about the courage it takes to act in the world and possibly hope to change it.

Sometimes the dance is literally a dance. At times, in the midst of pounding out sentences late at night or in quick breaks between teaching classes, I would sometimes lose a sense of the book's importance. I would forget why it mattered that I write this book. To help me remember, I would look at a photograph of a young man, possessed for the first time by a "fierce god" named "Bell Fierce-God" (Cankalimatan) and dancing a god-dance (*cāmiyāṭṭam*) (Figure 1.5). This is meant to be a book about why it matters that a young man was possessed for the first time and danced his god and himself into being-in-the-village and so in the world. This young man fueled his dance not only with the power of a god but also with anger and courage, and he maintained his dance with resolve even as higher-caste youths surrounded his dance and hurled epithets (they could easily have been stones) in his direction. It is not an exaggeration to say that he risked his life for this dance. As Michael Jackson expresses in many ways throughout his work on existential anthropology (1998), what matters for human beings is their capacity to make and to some extent control the social world in which they live; that is, to be able to struggle for a say in the way their world takes shape. This work is in part a chance for me to tell a story about the courage of others who struggle for a future, who struggle to matter in the world at a particular time and place. When the young man danced, he danced within a given world, a world of gods, nations, possessions, bananas, dominance, democracy, oppression. He danced his circumstances on the outskirts of the village, the place where, as outcaste, he belonged. He was singing a familiar melody using given instruments and possibilities, but as he did he also wrote his own song. He danced to remake his world.

What I offer here most generally is an ethnography that in its construction works toward a semeiotic and dialectic (and existentialist) view of culture, a view perhaps most ardently pursued by E. Valentine Daniel (1996,

Figure 1.5. God-dancing, 1990.

121–127, 197–200) and Michael Jackson (1998). Culture, in this view, may be seen as dialogic and as a co-production of many forces and persons, including the anthropologist whose inquiry, as Rabinow (1977) shows, impels informants to rethink their lives in terms the anthropologist can grasp. The heterogeneity of forces and voices that go into the constant creation of culture is not simply a closed universe of discourse in which contestants "agree to disagree" yet ultimately maintain harmony. Rather, as Daniel argues, culture (and life more generally, meaning itself) is "shot through with 'tychasm': that element of chance contained in the 'play of musement'" (1996, 198), contained, that is, in the accidents and unpredictable events that have a role in conditioning our world. Similar concepts include Heidegger's concept of "thrown-ness" and the recognition of the role of "stochastic," random events in evolutionary processes, for "without the random there can be no new thing" (Bateson 1979, 163). And as Appadurai writes of this same process, "[A]s local subjects carry on the continuing task of reproducing their neighborhood, the contingencies of history, environment, and imagination contain the potential for new contexts (material, social, and imaginative) to be produced" (1995, 185). The village can be said to be a living sign precisely to the extent that contingencies of history and society and creative action continue to make the village a critical site of discourse and even discord.

Residents of Yanaimangalam put contingencies—unforeseen events and signs that appear to arise outside a person's agency or a village's arguments—to use in reordering local relations and redefining for themselves their place in the world even as they play a role in shaping that world. But the contingent nature of these outside-coming-in events does not stay contingent for long. Rather, what begins as contingency becomes exigency, becomes part of historical, definitive action by village residents who make use of what comes in from "outside" to change the realities of their lives at home. Among "contingencies" are historical realities and the facts of life in Tamilnadu and India at the time of this research (1988–1990, 2001, and 2003). It is upon these facts and realities—including the colonial past, land reform, bananas, Tamil nationalism and forms of democracy, precolonial idioms of royalty, knowledge of class differences and urban life and migration, Hindu nationalism, Untouchable political movements—that some residents of Yanaimangalam drew as they contested the social and spatial contours of their local lives and their village in a ritual idiom. As villagers apparently extended their alliances beyond the village—connecting to other signs and ideas and political movements—they at the same time reaffirmed the village (*ūr*) as they also reaffirmed their lives as villagers (*ūrmakkaḷ,* lit. "village people"). They bring these ideas home and emplace them in their ūr.

Collocations

Due in large part to the groundbreaking work of Eric Wolf, it is by now a truism in anthropology that there are no peoples, no places, no "localities" that are not in some manner connected to and affected by the wider worlds of which they are a part. Yet the nature of the multiplex process relating local and wider worlds is only partially understood.

The relation between the local and the global, or what I prefer to call the wider world, has been perhaps most often analyzed as a relation of political-economic power, where it is a wider world that has constitutive powers over a "local" one.[5] A second aspect of the relation between the local and the wider world has been, as Gupta and Ferguson point out, inspired in part by the writings of Foucault, de Certeau, and Gramsci on relations among domination, everyday practice, and resistance (1997, 5). This aspect of the process focuses on how local people appropriate wider fields and forms of power and use them to protest or redefine their relation with powerful agents above (e.g., Comaroff and Comaroff 1986; Hebdige

1979; and, for South Asia in particular, Daniel 1993; Dube 1998; Nandy 1983; Haynes and Prakash 1991; Dirks 2001).

In this study, in an effort, in part, to call into question a dichotomous or nested view of the "local" and the "global," I describe a third aspect of the process of relating local and wider worlds by emphasizing how local actors incorporate and use national and other translocal signs, ideologies, and forms to engage in their own local struggles. In Yanaimangalam, regional and national social movements prove in many cases to be a powerful set of contingent ideas and signs village residents draw upon to argue and contest the social and spatial parameters of the village itself.

As phenomenologist Edward Casey argues, humans are "ineluctably place-bound" (1996, 19). That is, as human beings we are always-already emplaced, just as we are always embodied. Our places, as our bodies, are always "ingredients" in our experiences, actions, and perceptions of the world. Furthermore, a place may be said to collocate all the lives and qualities and happenings of its inhabitants and their predecessors as "one arena of common engagement" (ibid., 5). As such, any place is as multiplex as the experiences, actions, consciousness, memories, and agendas of its inhabitants are diverse. It is this heterogeneity that makes places such as villages not just "collocative" or "coadunative" but also deconstructive and changing (ibid., 35–36). Such a perspective allows us to reject both top-down and bottom-up views of the relation of the wide world to the local world. What matters is how the village is both wide world and local world all at once. The wide world can be studied only as it takes shape and grows out of places. The village matters.

Where else is the nation, for example, but in the local material activity of real people who through their actions emplace national ideologies, agendas, and practices? As villagers draw upon and enact regional and nationwide agendas and dramas at home, they are not just demonstrating the nation's existence in their everyday lives in a particular place. They are also constituting their actions, and the meanings of those actions, as already in some respect national even as they are also local. The wide world is in many ways already "home." It is as close as the whitewashed houses bearing party signs in bold colors. It is as close as the Congress Party cow—its owner's party allegiance painted in orange, green, and white on its horns—chomping tender rice shoots in the fields only to be chased off by the irate field owner, who bears his party's black and red stripes on his white waist cloth, which flaps like a flag in the chase. Indeed, as Beth Roy (1995) shows in her work on a village dispute in Bangladesh, even the simplest everyday event—a loose cow eats tender grains growing in a neighbor's field—may be put to use in a struggle to recognize and bring into political reality changes that have occurred in the form of the nation itself.

The process of village-making is also a process of self-making, and I work to show that localizing wider agendas and concepts is part of a more general human process whereby local actors ground and localize the wider world—using whatever forms it might offer—and at the same time create themselves as regional and historical actors, in this instance as villagers (ūrmakkaḷ) and self-aware "peasant cultivators" (*vivacāyi*) who extend, act, and change their own lives and the lives of others and who create the locality (the village) in which they live as they do so. In the ethnography that follows, it will become clear that a critical part of village-making processes are personal hopes for different futures, for bringing into reality something new that is "imagined to lie ahead." As disenfranchised village communities strive for a different future, they are in fact remaking their present as they are also making new conditions for continuing to constitute new futures.

I demonstrate this dialectical, tri-aspectual process of self-, village-, and world-making through a detailed ethnography of political-ritual events centered in temples. These events include argumentative procession routes, possessions by powerful gods, and even simple acts of devotion such as ash-smearing that took place in Yanaimangalam in 1988, 1990, and 2001. Villagers remade the village by drawing on "what was given" in the village, including given relations of dominance, a colonial past enacted if not objectified, a form of democracy, and a ritual language for contesting power. They also drew on imagined futures as these were embodied in present signs of national belonging. The use of national signs in the ritual shows the creative potential of village residents to use and reinvent ritual in order to create new meanings and new contexts—new conditions of possibility—for further action in everyday life. Temples are not the only venue for studying the production of locality in this way, but in South India, because temples remain a key site for the production of power, they practically force themselves to the center of this study.

For residents of Yanaimangalam the village is no simple unit, no bounded harmonious whole. It is, however, a ground of culture. It is the place in which they cultivate not only rice but also their lives, relations, selves, tragedies, and strengths. It is important here to work our way out of the worn and idealized image, found both in prior academic and current popular imaginings, of villages as wondrously harmonious communities, as places that take one back to a retrojected sense of wholeness now perceived as lost in the contemporary world. These idealizations are based in a hopeful nostalgia more than any real understanding of the village as (what I argue to be) a heterogeneous and even heterologic place, a shifting part of world events, power differentials, history, and both the joys and sufferings of human relations.

In order to understand fully the god-dances through which village residents bring their hopes into historical, village-making reality, we need to dig deep and offer up what Geertz would call a thick description of the world of this village. We need to understand peoples' lives in a complex manner, explore the minute meanings and the rich language through which they act, think, and feel. In Part I of this book, I offer a thick description of the social relations of power, of dominance and rank in particular. Only by understanding the ways that Yanaimangalam's residents comprehend and live out their lives (or "dance" to their own melody) can we understand Part II, wherein village residents struggle to redefine and rework—and, for some, maintain—those relations of dominance. As will become clear, I do not intend to set up these two processes, domination and its alternatives, as a simple dichotomous or linear process. Rather, all humans at all times struggle with power in multiple and shifting ways and so make life such a difficult dance.

Part I

DOMINANCE IN THE MAKING

TWO

Who Is the Ūr?

It is well known that in South India, temple rituals are fully entangled in political processes. From precolonial kingship through colonial rule and continuing today in both rural and urban communities, temple rituals have remained a vital means of asserting control over territories, garnering social constituencies, and articulating and contesting relations of rank within communities.[1] The same is true in Yanaimangalam, where temple festivals are arenas for engaging in all kinds of struggles—with gods, family, fellow villagers, and neighbors. In this chapter, I outline village power relations through a detailed discussion of the yearly temple festival for the village goddess. This festival is a venue for asserting and redefining relations of dominance and subordination in an idiom of inclusion and exclusion from the village, the ūr, and as such serves both to exhibit and constitute village power relations. The cases described here serve, also, to illustrate how power, ritual, and place are tied together through temple practices.

Most temple festivals in Yanaimangalam, as all over Tamilnadu's Tirunelveli District, take place in the hot summer months, April to June, when the rice fields turn to bone-dry red earth. Associations of villagers, relatively flush with cash from the harvest, sponsor and produce festivals for gods and goddesses who reside in local temples. In 1990, as also more recently, Yanaimangalam, with only 1,700 people, boasted approximately thirty-five temples and shrines (excluding household shrines). Some of these temples sit snugly among the houses in the village's five residential areas. Others occupy lonely spots in the fields and scrub areas. Some are new, some old, some large, and many are small. Several are relatively impermanent earthen mounds that devotees renew for festival periods but otherwise allow to erode back to red earth with the onset of the monsoon in mid-June. Of the thirty-five temples, sixteen are sites for periodic summer festivals known as *koṭai,* meaning "gift." Most of these temples host a koṭai festival every one to five years, depending on the wealth of sponsors, calendrical opportunity, and community consensus.[2] Festivals mobilize people into groups whose members share a common relationship to a god. These groups, what I call "temple associations," fund their festivals through a head tax levied on association members. Locally, these associations are referred to simply as the "common people" (*potumakkaḷ*) or the "tax-payers" (*varikkāraṅkaḷ*) of their temple. Some temple associations correspond to local caste, or jāti, groupings; others to lineages; and some to residential units, but many associations cut across such categories of person and place to combine jātis, lineages, and residential units of varying power and rank in what prove to be sometimes quite surprising combinations.

Of all the temple associations that organize koṭai festivals, one, and only one, is said to be the temple of the "whole village" (*ūr pūrāvum*). This is the village goddess temple (*ūrammaṉkōyil*). The goddess is named Yanaiyamman. While the goddess stands for the "whole village," as we shall see below, just who belongs to this whole village is passionately contested by village residents and has changed significantly over the last forty years.

THE VILLAGE GODDESS AND THE "WHOLE VILLAGE"

Yanaiyamman's temple sits squarely amid the fields north and east of the Big Ūr. The temple's clean red and white stripes grow straight up like some odd crop among the rice and bananas that green the other small plots (Figure 2.1). Many people make it a habit to swing by this temple on their way home from morning baths at the river. Women come balancing on the narrow paths dividing the fields, wet laundry slung over their shoulders, hair dripping, water pots sloshing from their hips. Some circle the temple before entering, always moving in an auspicious clockwise direction. They then climb the few steps up into the temple and enter into a small but open room with a cool concrete floor and high ceilings that give a feeling of spaciousness. Straight ahead, a small doorway leads into an antechamber large enough for several people to stand. This antechamber is usually reserved for Brahman worshippers only. Beyond this antechamber another small opening leads to a tiny womb-like room, inside of which sits the stone image of the goddess, lit by a dim bulb and the flame of small oil lamps. Most worshippers remain in the larger room. They stand to the side of the inner doorways, peering, bowing, and bending into the goddess's line of vision. They come to "see the goddess," because to see and be seen by her is to partake of her purifying and beneficial qualities (see, e.g., Eck 1981; Fuller 1992, 59–60). In 1990, as he is in more recent years, Subramaniyam, son of the head Brahman priest, was usually somewhere in the

Figure 2.1. Goddess temple in the fields.

vicinity. When worshipers come, he lights a piece of camphor on a small brass lamp, circles the flame in the air in front of the goddess (a practice called *ārati*), then turns and offers the lighted camphor to the worshipers, who place their hands over the flame then scoop the air around it up to their eyes.[3]

Vision is not the only way worshipers partake of the goddess's qualities. Ordinarily, Subramaniyam also doles out pinches of ash (*vipūti*) from the cup that he keeps up near the goddess. The ash distributed liberally in goddess temples, as in any temple to gods associated with Siva, is made of cow dung. A very fine, often scented ash produced in factories and purchased in any local shop, cow dung is considered a beneficial substance in several dimensions. In Hindu ritual as well as myth, ash is "cooling" (Babb 1973; Beck 1969), "pure" (Doniger 1975, 147–149), and "generative." Ash, while produced out of destruction, is also the "seed" of creation that remains to regenerate the cosmos (Shulman 1981, 105). Like all prasad—items given to worshipers only after being transvalued through contact with a deity—ash is thought to transfer the deity's beneficial qualities to the worshipers. By smearing ash on one's body, a person imbibes the goddess's qualities as cool, pure, and generative, and hardly a more common sight can be seen than a clean white horizontal stripe of ash marking a forehead at the start of the day.

Consistent with what Ramanujan and Daniel separately identify as a common Tamil mode of relational thinking that stresses synecdochal and metonymic associations over metaphoric ones (Ramanujan 1967, 1990; Daniel 1984, 106–107), the goddess stands for the "whole" village. That is to say, in the language of literary tropes, the goddess does not merely symbolize the village metaphorically, as a rose might symbolize love. Rather, as synecdoche (a trope in which the qualities of one part of a whole may be said to characterize and suffuse the whole), the goddess is a part which suffuses the whole of the village: her power (*cakti*)—rooted in the earth of the temple grounds—is commonly understood to suffuse the rice-planted soil of the whole village and constitute its fecundity as well as the reproductive potency of all its residents. As metonym (a part which stands for the whole, as wheels for car, hoops for basketball, or press for the entire media), the goddess is also in many ways a part which stands for a whole: her temple association, a mere part of the village population, stands for the "whole village," for the set of people commonly referred to by the encompassing term "the village people" (ūrmakkaḷ); the whole village takes its name from the goddess, as do many village residents. Furthermore, during the yearly temple festivals held for the goddess, residents make several processions which encircle only one part of the village's inhabited areas. Yet these processions are said to encircle the "whole village," the whole ūr.

What is this so-called whole ūr? It certainly does not match the village territory as it appears on the district map, where it is unambiguously bounded with thick black lines. Nor does it include the total census count of the village population. What, then, is it?

A conversation I had one day with Pandi, the headman of the village hamlet called South Ūr (see Figure 1.4) is a good place to begin. Pandi, like most residents of South Ūr, was a Palaiyar, an "S. C." (Scheduled Caste). I asked Pandi about how the village goddess-temple festival was financed. He replied that "all jātis together" (*ellā jātiyum cērntu*) finance the temple through a "tax" (*vari*).

But when I asked him if his jāti—his "caste"—too gave tax to finance the festival, he amended his first answer. "We don't give," he said, but the "big jāti people" (*periya jātikkārańka*) do: Pillaimar, Muppanar, and Thevar.

He named the three jātis (out of fourteen resident in the village) that inhabitants of Yanaimangalam refer to in everyday conversation as the "village people" (ūrmakkaḷ), the politically and economically dominant castes whose members are said to collectively (*potuvāka*) finance the festival for the village goddess Yanaiyamman.[4] In everyday speech, these "big village people" are often referred to as "everyone," as "all jātis," in much the same way that "Man" still refers to all of humanity yet erases women.

During a different interview, this one with Rukmaniyayyar, the Brahman headman (*dharmakkartta*)[5] of the village goddess temple, I again asked who paid tax to the Yanaiyamman temple. He too replied "all the village people," giving me the same exclusive list: Pillaimar, Muppanar, Thevar.

Taken together, these two statements—about just whom the phrases "everyone" and "all jātis" in the village include—point further to the metonymical form of dominance in the village. Just as the goddess is a metonym, a part that stands for the whole ūr, so here is one part of the population of Yanaimangalam, a complex part comprising three jātis (Pillaimar, Muppanar, Thevar) conflated in everyday speech with the entire population of Yanaimangalam, a conflation enunciated in the term "ūrmakkaḷ," "village people." The statements of the S. C. headman, who elided himself and his neighbors from the ūr when he said "everyone" and "not us" in the same breath, reveals the at least partial hegemony of this trope of inclusion.

Continuing my interview with the Brahman headman, Rukmaniyayyar, I asked who receives the benefits or fruits (*palaṉ*) of the goddess-temple festival. In all other temple festivals I studied in Yanaimangalam, people said that the benefits of the festival fell exclusively on the temple-association members, that is, on those who paid a tax to fund the festival in question. In answer to this question regarding the ūr goddess temple, however, Rukmaniyayyar confirmed what others had said when he bellowed out that the benefits of the festival, most generally defined as prosperity and growth for the whole ūr, would fall to everyone in the ūr, not just the taxpayers—those referred to as the ūrmakkaḷ, the village people—but to every person on every street and in every hamlet. Like the S. C. headman Pandi, Rukmaniyayyar too recognized the encompassing hegemony of ūrmakkaḷ dominance. What's good for the dominating part—the "village people"—was good for all the others too. In this way the ūrmakkaḷ, via their goddess, are themselves synecdoche of all the people in the ūr: they are the part that suffuses the whole.

This idealized structure of asymmetrical inclusion is further illustrated by a jāti-based division of labor through which the festival is organized. The tax-paying village people (ūrmakkaḷ) organize, plan, and collect and disburse funds for the festival. But other families from a variety of jātis in the village also have duties to perform for the festival. For example, the village Washerman families are required to bring lengths of white cloth that are used as decorative ceilings for the temple awnings and as a giant placemat for the immense feast offered to the goddess. In addition, they bring cotton to fuel firepots, wicks to light lamps, and oil-soaked cloth torches for the possessed dancers. In return, they receive a share of the feast served to the goddess, grain from ūrmakkaḷ fields at harvest time, and new cloth. The Potter (from a neighboring village) supplies clay pots used in the festival and in return receives a cash salary as well as continued rights over a piece of land in village fields. The Carpenter makes ladles for cooking and serving the feast and in return receives token gifts called *curuḷ* (betel leaf, coconut, and fruit) and *dakṣina* (a small fee paid in coins) as well as a regular share of grain from ūrmakkaḷ fields at harvest. Blacksmiths, Barbers, Garland Makers, Thevars, Kambars (a non-Brahman priest), and Brahman priests also perform obligatory duties and receive shares of the temple and/or village bounty. Similar data have been reported for other South Indian village goddess festivals (e.g., Beck 1972, 118; Brubaker 1979; Good 1985, 149–150; Srinivas 1952, 39–43, 190–194). Even those who do not have formal duties in the temple proceedings are invited to participate—to bring gifts for the goddess, to bring animals for sacrifice, and to receive beneficial leftovers from the rituals. The festival in this way does stretch to include members of the community outside the category of sponsoring ūrmakkaḷ: everyone may, and indeed most appear to, participate and almost everyone receives benefits. Despite the inclusive idiom, however, all participants agree to the structure of inequality the festival reproduces by their very participation. That is to say, in neat Durkheimian fashion, the fact and manner of ūrmakkaḷ and non-ūrmakkaḷ participation in the festival reproduces and affirms the social structure (including inequalities) of "the whole village."

PROCESSIONS

The goddess festival takes place every year in the Tamil month of Cittarai (mid-March to mid-April). The festival lasts for two weeks, though most of the intense festival activity occurs over three central days—the second Monday, Tuesday, and Wednesday of the two-week period. Among the many ritual activities of the festival (some of which are described more fully in Chapter 7) are several processions. I observed these processions over two consecutive years, 1989 and 1990. The processions I observed were said to encircle the "whole village" and further enunciated the metonymic form of dominance explored above: they traversed and encircled specifically that residential *part* of the village in which the big village people live and called it the *whole* village. As the processions moved about the village—up and down all the streets and most bylanes—musicians, dancers possessed by the goddess and her retinue, relatives of the dancers, vowgivers and their affines (in-laws) walked together along the route and with their movement demarcated an interior space from an exterior one, an included inside (*uḷḷē,* or *akam*) from an excluded outside (*veḷiyē,* or *puṟam*). They made interiors and exteriors not only by the paths they walked but also by actions they performed at borders (*ellai*) and crossroads (*cantippu*): they threw eggs, and sometimes pumpkins bloodied with turmeric and lime paste, as sacrifices to feed and appease maleficent beings who linger outside the village and who want to but must not come inside. These actions were in fact border-constituting actions. The inner part of their circle was considered ūr while the outer part was marked as and rendered *kāṭu* (wasteland), the place where demons, ghosts, and certain people, mostly "low-caste" Washermen and S. C., reside.[13]

The four processions were named Milkpot (Pālkuṭam), Coming around the Ūr (Ūraiccuṟṟivarutal), Firepot (Tīcatti), and Chariot (Capparam). The Milkpot Procession started on the busy second Tuesday of the two-week festival period. Early in the morning, the procession started at the riverbank (Figure 2.2), to reach its climax several hours later under the noontime summer sun. Boys, unmarried male youths, and prepubescent girls who had made this vow (or, more often, whose parents did so on their behalf perhaps before they were even born or when, as babies, they were perilously ill) carried pots of milk on their heads through the village. They walked together up and down and around the streets and bylanes, stopping frequently as various relatives brought gifts out to them from houses along the way. Relatives tied new cloth around the devotees' bodies, pinned cash on their clothing, and piled garland after garland around their neck (Figure 2.3). After three or more hours of this, the vow-givers finally wound their way out to the temple, hopefully by this time "possessed" by the goddess, fully united with her beneficent qualities. Sweltering and faint with the sun's heat, the possessing heat of the goddess, and just possibly the heat of all those layers of cloth and garlands, some had to be carried the final leg of their journey by relatives, who stumbled in a broken jog over the clods of scorched fields. Once they reached the temple, the vow-givers circled once around the temple clockwise before entering into the cooler, dark interior to offer their gifts of cooling milk to the goddess. After they offered their milk, the priest returned a little bit back to them as divine leftover, or prasad (*piracātam*), from the goddess. They sipped their prasad, then retreated outside to collapse under the shade of cool neem trees, where their mothers and aunts and uncles and brothers fanned them for a while.

Coming around the Ūr (Ūraiccuṟṟivarutal) was a more subdued procession which took place on Tuesday evening, beginning around five o'clock. The temple god-dancers (numbering about ten and drawn from the three ūrmakkaḷ jātis plus one Brahman), a set of temple assistants, and an "accountant" carrying notebook, pen, and clerkish pouch proceeded around the whole ūr to collect rice and money from individual households—gifts (on top of whatever tax the households have paid) for the temple festival. Many donors also offered the god-dancers (and the goddess possessing them) cooling turmeric water. The donors poured it over the god-dancers' legs and feet and in return received cooling ash prasad to smear on their foreheads (Figure 2.4).

The Firepot (Tīccatti) Procession was a high-charged, slow nocturnal procession that began around midnight that same Tuesday night and finished at dawn on Wednesday. Three god-dancers—one from each of the ūrmakkaḷ

Figure 2.2. (TOP) Preparing milkpots at the riverbank.
Figure 2.3. (BOTTOM) Milkpot vow-givers on procession.

Figure 2.4. God-dancers on procession smear ash on a devotee's forehead.

jātis—carried clay pots around the "whole ūr," hot, flaming, and fueled by oil-soaked cotton provided by the village Washerman (Figure 2.5). They danced the whole way, accompanied by the raucous beats and riffs of drummers and *nataswāram*[6] players and lured on by gaudy cross-dressing dancers hired for the occasion. As the god-dancers flamed through the ūr, they stopped at almost every house en route to pass out divine ash (vipūti) to those watching from their stoops.

Finally, in the Chariot Procession, the goddess's movable form—a bronze image—was placed on a palanquin which in turn was placed on a large cart and wheeled through and around the "whole ūr," then carried by a dense pack of volunteers across the fields to the temple (Figure 2.6). This took place on Wednesday morning and marked a climax and the close of the three central festival days.

All four of these processions are circular. As villagers wind around village streets, they also circumambulate the ūr in a clockwise direction, and as they do so, they accomplish three ends. They effect a unity among the participants (the "village people"), they distinguish an interior from an exterior (inhabitable space from wilderness, ūr from kāṭu), and they protect that interior from negative and harmful influences.

As circular motions, these processions resonate with a whole set of circular motions around bodies and objects that are part of everyday and

Figure 2.5. God-dancer Arunacalam Pillai with firepot.

ritual life in South India, motions that are used to define and protect interiors (body, house, ūr) and to bind or make unions. For example, when devotees circle the goddess temple before entering, they bind themselves to the goddess, just as when groom and bride circle their wedding platform clockwise, their wrists bound together with silk cloth, they become bound (*kaṭṭu*) to one another as husband and wife, an act completed by the "tying of the *tāli*" (*tāli kaṭṭu*), the marriage necklace, around the wife's neck. Such bindings are commonplace. Many people wear protective amulets or strings called *kāppu* ("protection") tied around their wrists. Pregnant women, in their seventh month, undergo a ritual called kāppu (or, more Brahmanically, *cīmantam*), during which they are presented with numerous glass bangles that relatives squeeze over their wrists in order to protect their pregnancy by a kind of associative magic, keeping the fetus bound to them. (When they give birth, the bangles, I am told, break in the struggle of childbirth, the child now cut loose from the womb.) The ūr watchmen go on guard "rounds" along the periphery of the fields to protect them from marauding animals and neighbors. A woman's marriage tāli, a turmeric-stained string

Figure 2.6. Ūrmakkaḷ men rush the goddess back to her temple.

adorned with a gold emblem, must never be cut off except at the death of her husband: to cut the tāli is to cut the relationship, to become a widow. To sever encircling ties that bind and protect is to open one up to danger, to separation, injury, and at any rate to change—whether desired (as the birth of a child) or not. And as we shall see, cutting through procession routes is no exception but is rather explicit political action meant to disrupt, open up, and change the unities that the processions are undertaken to create.

Circular movements do more than protect interiors and bind people together. They may also work to extrude, from bodies or places, negative or harmful substances such as faults (*tōcam*), evils (*pāvam*), disease, and the negative effects of vision, the inaptly named "evil-eye" ("*tiruṣṭi*" means more accurately the harmful effects of eyesight but need not carry any evil intent). Indeed, the "sacrifices" performed on procession routes enact just such an extrusion: they keep offending spirits and ghosts away from the interior places of "civilized" life in the ūr. These procession actions belong to a wider class of "circling rituals" (Kapadia 1995, 107) called ārati that are meant to separate off and expel unwanted substances from protected interiors. For example, in a common practice, the sons of an ill man in Middle Hamlet purchased a lamb and performed what they called ārati by circling it in the air around the body of their gravely ill father. The purpose of this circling was to transfer the illness from their father's body to the lamb's body. They then took the lamb out of the hamlet to a temple, where they sacrificed it. When the lamb was killed, their father's illness, having been transferred to the lamb, was meant to "scatter" (*citaṟu*) with the lamb's dismemberment. On another occasion, a priest circled an egg around an ill Pillaimar man, then took the egg to the edge of the Big Ūr and threw it out into the fields (out of the ūr and into the kāṭu, or wasteland), where it broke. Again, in this manner the fault was transferred from the man and sent out to devouring ghosts, witches, and other such creatures that inhabit the fields at night. Every evening, a young neighbor, Arunacalam (Figure 2.7), asked his mother to circle a piece of camphor around his head three times. He then took the camphor outside the house, set it on the road, and lit it. He sat there watching it burn out, hoping that with the camphor would burn his sad feelings, feelings that his mother thought to be an effect of tiruṣṭi (the evil eye) fixed on this handsome young man.

And as a final example, at a Brahman girl's puberty ritual, female friends and relatives took the girl to the river to bathe after her first period. After she bathed, we all walked back up the path to the village, taking her home. As she walked up the Brahman street, she walked through a gamut of women ready to "pass on the tiruṣṭi" (*tiruṣṭi kaḻi*) that might attach to this now fertile and beautiful young woman. In front of many houses, we paused for another circling ritual. On the street, they waved a blood-red concoction of lime powder, water, and lemon in a circle around her body, and then they dumped it, along with the tiruṣṭi, on the street off to the side of the decorative/auspicious kōlam designs marking the thresholds of their homes (Figure 2.8).[7]

As the community moves in procession through the village, it does more than define a boundary and protect an interior ūr from an exterior, ghost-populated kāṭu. It also lays claim to territory and defines sets of social inclusions and exclusions. For these reasons, whatever a procession's ostensible motivation—to display a god, for example—processions generally have political ramifications. It is no surprise that in the past, in India and elsewhere, processions often instigated clashes, just as they do today.[8]

Processions in Yanaimangalam were potential sources of (and expressions of) conflict and exclusion. They clearly enunciated and even created social distinctions of dominance and subordination—expressed as spatial inclusions and exclusions—in the routes they traversed. Such exclusions may lead to direct conflict, with members of an excluded group including themselves by force, disrupting processual flow, and therewith marking disputes about both the spatial definition of the ūr as well as the social and political definition of the ūr as an exclusionary social unit.[9] As the following examples show, whom the ūr did and did not include was highly con-

Figure 2.7. Arunacalam with grandfather out in a family rice field.

tested at the time of my research and had changed quite dramatically over the previous forty years since Independence and subsequent land reform. It was through a history of processions that I first gleaned something of this history of local dominance.

PROCESSION POLITICS

In 1989, the "whole ūr" that the above-described processions encompassed included five streets and their various bylanes: the four streets of the Big Ūr (the Brahman, Pillaimar, Muppanar, and Thevarmar streets) and then as a fifth street the Thevar section of North Ūr up by the riverbank and out across the fields (Figure 2.9).[10] The musicians, professionals hired from outside, griped about having to cover so much territory—and having to do so thrice in two days—and vowed never to work in Yanaimangalam again. Their griping gave some satisfaction to the people who heard it, for to encompass so much territory signified the extent of the ūr's social-cum-spatial unity and would certainly do wonders for the ūr's *māṉam* (honor/

Figure 2.8. Destroying tiruşţi.

reputation) or *perumai* (greatness/reputation) once word spread around the region.

The following year (1990), the procession route differed: it cut out the fifth street across the fields and constituted an interior "whole ūr" that included only the four streets of the larger settlement (Figure 2.9).

What accounts for the change in route? In 1989, the North Ūr Thevars had been slighted in some of the temple distributions. At the end of any temple festival, food that has been offered to the goddess is redistributed in shares (*paṅku*) among the tax-paying members of the temple association. Receiving shares of the temple distributions not only transfers tangible and beneficial substances from the goddess to her devotees but, as Appadurai and Breckenridge (1976, 197) and Dirks (1987, 285–287) point out, it also reestablishes a person or group as a member of the temple association, often in a particular ranked order. In 1989, the North Ūr Thevars did not receive their share of rice beer (*matuppoṅkal*), one of the most highly charged substances of the entire festival. Matuppoṅkal is a fermented concoction that "boils" over (*poṅku*) from clay pots, the very overflow symbolizing the bounteous potency of field, womb, life, village. When the North Ūr Thevar headman came to collect his community's share, he found it had already been distributed to, and in good measure already consumed by, other—and so it would seem socially more powerful—village men. Denied their

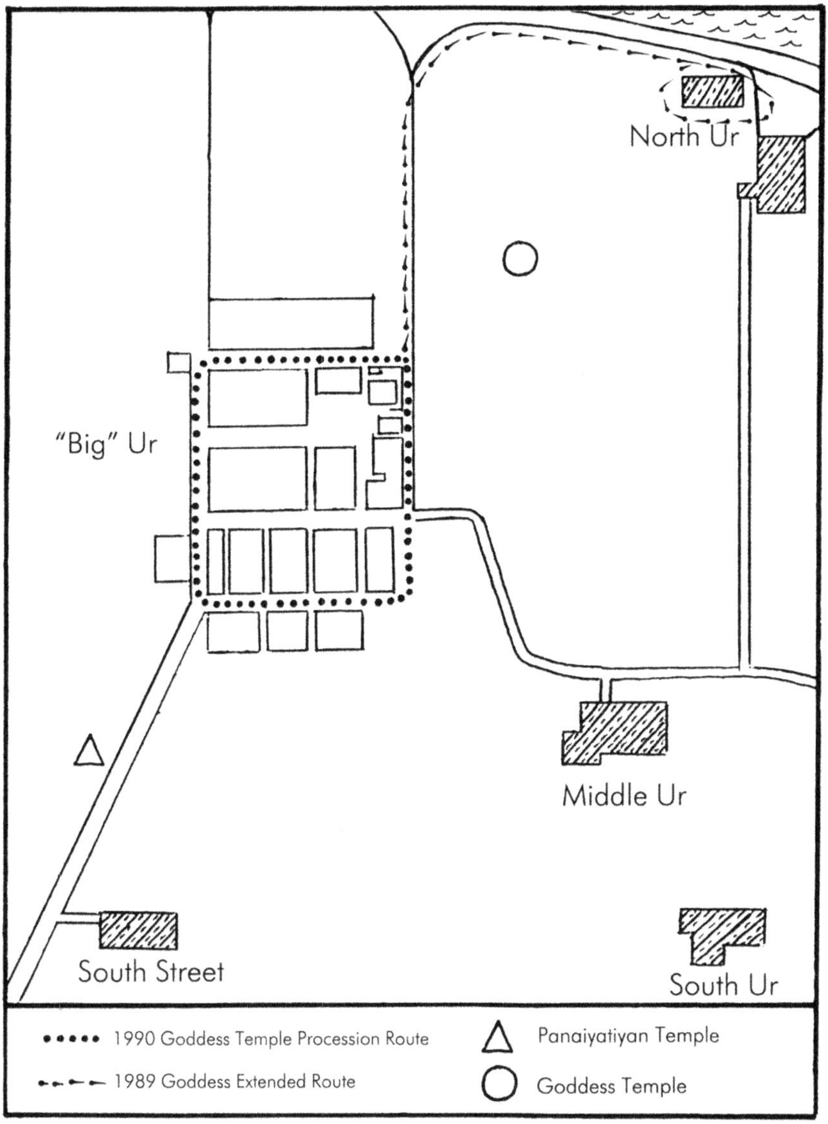

Figure 2.9. Procession routes.

rightful share and effectively dishonored out of the "unity" of the village, North Ūr Thevars were furious. By the beginning of the next festival season in 1990, that anger had boiled over. The first sign of trouble was when North Ūr refused to pay its share of the 1990 temple tax. The second sign came when they asserted rights in the festival nonetheless.

The other big jātis—Pillaimar, Muppanar, and especially the powerful rival lineage of Thevars who lived in the main residential area—used North Ūr's refusal to pay the 1990 temple tax as the justification to exclude the North Ūr Thevars from the "village." North Ūr, a separate hamlet located at an inconvenient distance already, was cut off the procession route and its residents were denied all rights to and shares in temple distributions. As one Big Ūr resident, Ramayya Thevar, put it, "If you don't pay tax [to the goddess temple] you can't be in this village" (*vari koṭukkillainā, inta ūrilē irukkakkūṭātu*).

Yet the North Ūr Thevars did not take their exclusion lying down. They continued to assert their rights as "village people." As a result, the 1990 festival was riddled with incursions. The newly excluded group moved into the center of the festival at every opportunity. One young man, for example, who had been given the right to be the instrument of sacrifice in the previous year's festival (that is, to cut off the heads of goats and roosters offered to the goddess), came up in front of a goddess shrine on the procession route clutching his sharpened sickle. Arm raised, he moved up to the goat tied in front of the goddess, eyeing its neck. He was kept from asserting his previous right by the stronger arms of the main-village Thevars, who pulled and kicked him away from the temple then chased him out of the village—out, that is, of the main residential area, the "Big Ūr."

I was able to trace similar disputes back about thirty years to the time when the goddess temple, which had previously existed as a crude, small structure, was expanded into a proper sculpted temple at great cost to village residents. Narratives I collected about the building of the new temple in 1958, as well as a pamphlet printed and sold for 2 rupees during the 1990 festival, described the new temple's founding as a "collective" or "common" (*potu*) endeavor in which all the village people participated, each contributing a certain percentage of their crops to fund the temple's construction. The pamphlet (composed by the temple's Brahman priests and leading ūrmakkaḷ sponsors) makes frequent reference to these "common village people" (potu ūrmakkaḷ), diplomatically neglecting to name or identify those people and thus eliding thirty-some years of conflict and negotiation centered on the problem of who had the right (*urimai*) to participate in the temple festival, to pay taxes to it, to be included within its procession route, and to receive shares in its distributions—on who were, in short, the "village people."

I traced the history of these conflicts mostly through interviews concerning the history of the festival's processions. As described above, one of the many processions that takes place during the goddess festival features the "firepot dance" (*tīccatti āṭṭam*), during which designated men become possessed by the goddess and carry a clay pot filled with burning oil rags all around the village. These men are usually senior men in lineages which possess the hereditary right to carry the firepot. In 1990, three men carried these pots, one man from each of the three "village people" jātis (Thevarmar, Muppanar, Pillaimar).

One hot afternoon while I sat on my elderly Brahman neighbor Parvathi's veranda discussing firepots and processions, she decided I should interview Arunacalam Piḷḷai, a very old man who carried the firepot for his Pillaimar jāti (Figure 2.5). He lived just up the street a few houses. Parvathi sent a child to call him and he sauntered over and sat slowly down. I asked him how he came to carry that firepot for the goddess.

D. M.: Before you, who took up the firepot?
A. Piḷḷai: That was my older brother.
D. M.: Who before him? Your father?
A. Piḷḷai: Before him, uh, on a street—actually on the Muppanar street—there was a pot. In those days in the village only the Muppanar took up a pot. No one among the other people would take [it up].
D. M.: Really?
A. Piḷḷai: Yes. Then between us [i.e., between Muppanar and Pillaimar] a small dispute arose. During the dispute, we wouldn't join up with them. "Now we'll do it [the festival] on our own (*taṉiyāka*)," [we decided].
D. M.: Really? Then your brother was the first of your jāti?
A. Piḷḷai: The first man, well, we gave a separate festival, and then my brother came and took it.
D. M.: And before that only the Muppanar.
A. Piḷḷai: Before that it was all Muppanar.
Parvathi: Then only after that were there two pots. And then the Thevar also joined.
D. M.: How did they join?
A. Piḷḷai: The Thevar . . . well, when everyone joined and conducted [the festival together], after deciding we mustn't conduct separate festivals and we joined together, the Thevar joined too. The whole village (*ūr pūrāvum*) joined together, and when we spoke about it then we said to the Thevar, "You join in too," and they joined. Ever since then, all the people (*ellā aṭkaḷum*) join for the festival.

In a later conversation on Parvathi's veranda with Arunacalam Piḷḷai and Ramayya Thevar, I learned more details. The dispute that had arisen between the Pillaimar and the Muppanar concerned the content of the *paṭaippu,* the huge heaping meal laid out for the goddess at the festival's climax. The Muppanars wanted to feed the goddess goat meat, but the Pillaimar, being vegetarian, objected. It was then, Ramayya Thevar detailed, that these two jātis split (*piriccuṭṭaṅka*), subsequently holding separate koṭai festivals with separate tax collections at separate times. It was only then that the goddess called on a Pillaimar man to take up her firepot. Furthermore, while Arunacalam Piḷḷai represented the Thevars' entry into the category of ūrmakkaḷ as an invitation bestowed by the Pillaimar and Muppanar, Ramayya Thevar had a different take. He saw his jāti's inclusion as one that was asserted, not bestowed.

THE RISE OF THEVAR DOMINANCE

Indeed, the inclusion of Thevars into the category of Yanaimangalam's "village people" can best be understood through a regional history that goes back at least 150 years, over which period Thevars have been struggling to expand territory and regional dominance. Their inclusion into the category of ūrmakkaḷ came a little later (probably in the late 1970s and 80s), and by 1990, Thevars constituted a plurality of the village population and owned a great deal of land. Three factors involved in the rise of Thevar dominance in Yanaimangalam are land reform, Brahman outmigration to cities, and long-standing strategies of Thevar politics. First, a series of land-tenure reforms legislated at the state level from the 1950s to the 1970s slowly eroded the rights of noncultivating landowners with large holdings in favor of the rights of cultivating tenants to maintain their rights to the products of their labor without fear of usurious rents or eviction (Gough 1989, 20–48). While these reforms did little to help landless S. C. such as the Pallar (Kapadia 1995, 194–195), they did benefit middle-ranking castes in fertile riverine areas, such as Tirunelveli's Thevars (aka Maravars).[11] Thevars were able to gain lands previously held in trust by temples or by Brahman landlords to whom the British had deeded the property at the time of their "settlement" of the district (Settlement Register 1879). These gains were consistent with Thevar efforts to expand their territory in the region, efforts that Ludden (1985, 191–196) shows to have been prevalent at least since the nineteenth century.

Second, these land reforms only hastened a process that Beteille (1965b, 207–210), Singer (1972, 299), and Irschick (1986, 21) have noted was already under way in the first decade of the 1900s; namely, the migration of Brahman landholders away from rural Tirunelveli as they were lured to urban areas by more lucrative economic and political opportunities under colonialism, thus opening up the rural areas for non-Brahman control. Third, Thevars in the region had for over several centuries been competing with other castes for dominance in Tirunelveli District, working to assert their dominance in the manner of "little kings," who, as others have shown (Breckenridge 1977; Price 1996b; Dirks 1987), constituted their power and rank in part through the kind of temple ritual/politics I have outlined here. Thevar interests were further served in the 1960s, when the leading political party in Tamil politics at the time, the DMK, promoted Thevar alliances in electoral politics, allowing Thevars to see themselves as legitimate local representatives of the state's leading political party. I will discuss these processes in more detail below, but for now this brief overview points to the extent to which dominance in Yanaimangalam was already constituted historically by wider regional and state changes in land tenure during the colonial period and shifts through land reform and regional politics later. What I wish to do within the purview of this chapter is highlight the way in which the Thevars living in Yanaimangalam brought these changes home as they asserted and constituted dominance in locally meaningful village rituals such as temple festivals and processions. As Thevar dominance has arisen regionally—in ways that are not part of most local residents' historical consciousness—it has also taken root in Yanaimangalam, legitimized at the lotus feet of the goddess. As recently as 2003, the Thevar headman could often be found discussing matters with his allies on the grounds outside the goddess temple. One informant jokingly referred to this spot as his "office." Thevar dominance is present now not only in ritual acts, but also in marginalization of Brahmans, shifts in ownership of houses and land, the political party colors painted on walls and cattle horns, and in a caution displayed by many in confronting Thevars in local affairs.

The 1990 temple-festival pamphlet mentioned none of this political history but focused solely on the collective and cooperative achievements of the "whole ūr," even though the "whole ūr" was constituted differently in 1990 than it had been in the 1950s, the time the pamphlet describes. According to several people I interviewed, the procession routes also changed along with these different constitutions of the ūrmakkaḷ to encompass more and more streets and bylanes. My neighbor Parvathi expressed the ideology of ūr unity herself when she cited two reasons for the resolution of the dispute between the Muppanars and the Pillaimars in the first place. First, she said that "everyone" had decided that conducting separate festivals was "no good" (*nallāka illē*) for the ūr because it wouldn't please the goddess. Second, she said that other people who knew of the separate festivals made fun (*kēḷi paṇṇa*), and ridicule was no good for the reputation of the ūr (ūr māṉam).

FOLLOW THE MONEY

Procession routes during the goddess festival were not the only way in which the "whole ūr" circumscribed its social boundaries. One other means, already noted above, was the division of labor in the festival, where ūrmakkaḷ fund the festival and other jātis participate by fulfilling ritual obligations under the patronage of the ūrmakkaḷ. Another means—at first not apparently connected with the goddess festival—was the "paddy contract" (*nel kuttakai*). Our "porch talk" (*tiṇṇai pēccu*) on Parvathi's veranda continued:

A. Piḷḷai: Now, on that day [of the aforementioned village meeting], the kuttakai (contract) was set up. It was set for 3,500 rupees, for her [the goddess].
Parvathi (to me): I told you that yesterday night, didn't I? The kuttakai—ūr kuttakai—per person, that is, each one of the ten people, give 350 rupees, didn't I say, when you asked who that money went to?
D. M.: Huh [in agreement].
A. Piḷḷai: We all take that in common for the koṭai. We take that money for the koṭai [festival]. Now it's for everyone in common (*potuvā*). We take it for the koṭai.[12]

What my co-conversers were talking about was the practice of paying ten men, assigned on a yearly basis, a commission of five rupees (in 1990) for every *kōṭṭai* (a measure of approximately 70 kilograms, usually split into two burlap sacks of 35 kilograms each) of paddy that they transported to government-certified mills in the neighboring village during harvest. (This arrangement is allegedly designed to minimize the flow of oxcart traffic from surrounding ūrs into the rice mills and government purchasing centers but also turns out to be a convenient way to regulate prices, thus encouraging midnight trips down the back lanes of the black market.)[13] In 1990, these ten men—mostly but not only from ūrmakkaḷ jātis—had to pay 350 rupees each to receive this contract (of course, if they worked as they should, they stood to make that back plus more with load after load of paddy). The 3,500 rupees that was collected from them went into a common ūr fund (stored in the bank in a nearby town).[14] The communal money was used for communal (potu) purposes. Such purposes included repairs and maintenance of the irrigation system—paths and channels and walls—feeding ūr fields,[15] but by far the major use of this money was the yearly goddess-temple festival and temple upkeep. In other words, money collected by the ūrmakkaḷ to transport the paddy of all landowning villagers—ūrmakkaḷ or not—was used to support a temple festival which only the ūrmakkaḷ control and through which they further demonstrate and establish their own power and dominance, their own centrality, to the exclusion and peripheralization of others, including others who must pay money into the fund.

Who, then, is the village? The ūr is neither a placid nor a static whole. It is, rather, a disputed and changing one, made and remade through the practices of village residents, practices which themselves are in part conditioned by contingent historical events, including colonial and subsequent governmental alterations of land rights. The social dominance or "bigness" (perumai) that permeates everyday social life in Yanaimangalam is displayed, disputed, instantiated, and—under the gaze of the goddess—legitimized.

Through their control over the ritual and spatial processes of the goddess festival, the ūrmakkaḷ, a historically constituted and changing association, demonstrate that they are powerful agents of the goddess they patronize and hence responsible for the productive and reproductive well-being of literally the whole ūr, all its lands and peoples.

Social relations of dominance are embedded in the spatial rendering of the ūr. That is, relations of domination are sociospatial. They are writ publicly in soil of the ūr itself. As Daniel shows, political claims to dominance can literally be inscribed in a handful of soil (*piṭimaṇ*), especially when that soil is inhabited by the qualities—indeed, the very Being—of a goddess who favors a particular group. In Daniel's case, a powerful migrant group proclaimed their essential ties to, and dominance in, a new place by literally plowing their goddess (brought in the soil from their previous ūr) into the soil of their new ūr (1984, 95–102). In Yanaimangalam, political claims are carved out in goddess processions that instantiate and distinguish interiors from exteriors. Even in a procession of children carrying pots of milk, it is the goddess herself who walks and circumscribes sociospatial realities. So just as the goddess validates distinctions of dominant and subordinate by bestowing her prasad on a ranked line of worshipers, so also does she participate in drawing distinctions between ūr and kāṭu, between inhabited area and wasteland, between the place of civilized persons and the place of ghosts and evils.

While processions thunder through and around the "whole ūr," other inhabited areas—North, Middle, and South Ūrs, and South Street—lie quiet across the fields, relegated to the ūr's kāṭu, the place to which pumpkins, eggs, and ash are thrown to appease ghosts and witches. What about residents of these hamlets? How do they see their relation to the ūr that would in some ways exclude them, relegate them to the status of ghost, danger, polluted and wild exterior?

Excluded from paying tax to the goddess temple, cut out of procession routes, and placed outside the ūr borders those routes constitute, many of these peripheralized residents of Yanaimangalam are nonetheless eager, able, and expected—even obligated—to participate in the goddess festival. Their participation ideally—and ideologically—articulates just the kind of unified, functionally integrated community that functionalist ethnographies, paralleling the local rhetoric of village unity, repeat. But not all are so eager and not all comply with their subordination to the ūrmakkaḷ. While the ūrmakkaḷ celebrate their powerful unities, those "out" in the kāṭu experience things differently. To understand these differences, we must delve more deeply into the forms, structures, and pain of subordination in Yanaimangalam.

Let me begin with a true story.

THREE
The Ash Theft

One May morning in 1990, just a couple of weeks or so after the goddess festival, a man from S. C. Middle Ūr went to bathe in the river as he did every day. On his way home, he cut off the broad path from the river and set out across the dry summer fields until he came to the elevated plot where the goddess, enthroned in her temple, presided over her fields. He climbed the few stairs up to the tree-shaded plot and approached the temple doorway. He stopped just short of the threshold and peered inside. No one was there but the goddess herself, far in the back in her small womb-like chamber, illuminated by one dim bulb. She gazed out the door as he peered in. Their eyesight mingled in that tangible, visual exchange called *darśan.*[1] No one else was there, no other worshipers and no Subramaniyam, the young priest on whom the man was counting to come outside and hand him some vipūti, ash prasad from the goddess, to smear on his forehead and complete his morning routine. He waited a minute or two. Then, casting a glance over his shoulder to check for any approaching witnesses, he entered the temple and padded barefoot the length of the cool tile floor. To reach the goddess he not only had to enter the temple and traverse the temple's main room, a space generally reserved for the dominant ūrmakkaḷ ("village people") worshipers; he also had to pass through the small antechamber closest to the goddess, a place where only Brahman worshipers or occasionally outside VIPs were allowed. Perhaps he felt a little nervous—perhaps a little strong—as he walked up against the strong current of rank implied by the temple space. But no one else was there. What rank could there be with just him there all by himself? He prayed a moment, then pinched a little ash from the bowl lying near the goddess's lotus feet, smeared a streak across his forehead, turned, and left the temple. Just as he left and started out across the sunlit fields toward his Middle Ūr home—the ash bright white on his dark forehead—he passed

Subramaniyam and a few ūrmakkaḷ worshipers walking toward the temple. No words passed between them.

A couple of days later, rumor spread that the police were on their way to Middle Ūr. Many of the men in that hamlet were still smarting from the last police visit, when they had been routed out of their houses, bullied, and beaten while the police were looking for a murder suspect. Hoping to avoid more of the same, most of the men suddenly found urgent cause to go visit relatives in other villages for a day or two or to go into town or to inspect some fields or to see what was playing at the tin-roofed, dirt-floored cinema hall in the bigger village a couple of miles down the road. By the time the police arrived on the scene, they were faced with women, children, and a few old men not worth beating.

What were the police there to investigate? According to several witnesses and a few gossips, what happened was this: the Thevar headman—let's call him "Tonti" Thevar after his prodigious "pot-belly," a feature of such eminence as to be rivaled only by his furling mustache—had caught wind of the fact that a certain S. C. Pallar man was seen coming out of the goddess temple. He and his allies went to the nearest police station three miles down the road and accused the man of attempting to steal the brass bell from inside the temple. Surely it was not the young Brahman priest, Subramaniyam, who had squealed. On more than one occasion I saw him, and his father as well, check to see that the coast was clear before signaling an S. C. man or woman into the temple so they could see the goddess better than they could from their usual position standing outside, leaning into the doorway, and peering into the dark from bright sunlight. Besides, when the police questioned witnesses to the alleged crime, Subramaniyam was the first to say that all the man had pinched was some ash to smear across his forehead.

The police concluded their indeterminate case with an injunction. No Middle Ūr person should, for any reason, ever again enter the goddess temple. The injunction was backed by threat of force more than by law, and the S. C. felt compelled to comply. Their exclusion from the temple interior was not necessarily intended to bar their participation in the yearly festival, however, for during the festival, S. C. worshipers were in any case restricted to the sunburned summer fields outside and below the shaded temple plot.

I first learned of this event from Ariraman, a young leader of Middle Ūr. He bitterly denounced the injustice (*anyāyam*) of the whole affair. Hardly a starker insult could be imagined. Temple entry was a hot issue in nationalist politics even before the demise of British rule in India and continues as a widely reported issue throughout India today. Then, as now, the free entry of Untouchables into large well-known temples signaled their inclusion in the nation, just as it signaled the quasi-egalitarian ideals upon which the nation was to be formed. Foremost among the reformers who argued for Untouchable temple entry was Tamilnadu's E. V. Ramaswami Naicker, who battled with Gandhi on this very front (Dirks 2001), the latter eventually himself leading "Harijans" into Hindu temples beginning with the Meenaksi temple in Madurai, a city about 150 kilometers north of Yanaimangalam. Now, decades after temple entry formed part of a nationalist platform that at least gave verbal support to the inclusion of Untouchables in the nation, to be banished from the goddess temple, and therewith effectively from inclusion in the village, surely was at least as painful as a police lathi stick searing the skin.

After Ariraman finished telling me the story of the ash incident, he made a bold claim. He claimed that it was his own jāti that had the primary connection to the goddess. Not the ūrmakkaḷ, as they claimed. The ūrmakkaḷ were relative newcomers, according to Ariraman. But the S. C.? They had always been there, he told me. Weren't they called the "Original Dravidians"?

Here Ariraman localized a broader sociopolitical discourse on Untouchability by drawing on a Tamil nationalist term, "Original Dravidian," "Ati Tiravita." Dravidian is a cultural and linguistic category (formerly a common "racial" one as well) that identifies South Indians, including Tamils, as historically distinct from North Indians, whose cultural and linguistic origins are understood to be Indo-European or "Aryan." The term "Original Dravidian" came into general use beginning in the 1920s, when E. V. Ramaswami Naicker led the well-known Self-Respect (*cuya mariyātai*) Movement in Tamilnadu. This progressive political movement campaigned for social and political reform, denouncing a constellation of social facts that many Tamil politicians and social reformers saw as signs of North Indian and Brahmanical hegemony imposed on an indigenous South Indian life. These signs included the Hindi language, Sanskritic elements in Tamil language and culture, caste inequities, and, what was important, the restrictions on temple entry that came to represent those inequities to the nation. Dirks (2001) argues that this Tamil nationalist platform had even deeper roots in the colonial project, for the origins of the anti-Brahman movement can be traced to colonial missionaries, especially to Robert Caldwell, who himself found Brahmanical "Aryan" ideas of caste to be inimical to the conversion of Dravidians to Christianity and so launched his own anti-Brahman movement to further his colonizing/missionizing goals. Whether or not Ariraman was aware of the details of the history of Tamil nationalism in relation to colonialism I do not know, but what he understood quite well was that the term "Ati Tiravita" connotes the primacy of an Original Dravidian culture over the "Aryan"- and Sanskritic-influenced northern culture. Moreover, in his deployment of the term, he constructed S. C. Pallar in particular as the truly original Dravidians and, as such, full citizens deserving a central place in the definition of Tamil culture and social life. Even more urgently and locally, by skewing the category of the Aryan other to include all ūrmakkaḷ, and Thevars in particular, Ariraman also constructed a mythologized alternative primacy for his own community as the original inhabitants of Yanaimangalam.

The story Ariraman was weaving, then, was that the alleged thief had in fact acted appropriately as a true, proper, and original (thus rightful) devotee of the goddess. But from the point of view of the Thevar headman and several other ūrmakkaḷ with whom I spoke, the man was doing something quite different. He was testing social limits. He was trespassing. He was asserting a freedom of movement within the temple that even most ūrmakkaḷ would not assert—the freedom to walk all the way up to the goddess herself and take ash from her shrine without mediation by the Brahman priest. Some implied that his act had nothing to do with devotion at all but was intended as pure provocation. However they read his intentions—whether as devotion or subversion—almost all ūrmakkaḷ agreed that he was wrong to go into the temple and take his own ash. Tonti Thevar's recourse to false charges and police threats was unfortunate, some thought, but most concurred that his aim was true: to put things back in proper order (*muṟai,* or *oḻuṅku*); in other words, to put the disruptive S. C. back out on the periphery of the temple and, by metonymic extension, the periphery of the orderly "Big Ūr"; that is, the ever-shifting ūr of the ūrmakkaḷ.

Ariraman was not yet finished. Even if the falsely accused "thief's" act was a simple act of devotion with no subversive intent, Middle Ūr's response to the accusation and banishment was, by contrast, clearly intended to subvert: Ariraman stated that Middle Ūr would no longer participate in the goddess-temple festival. That is, next year, for the first time, Middle Ūr residents would not pool their money to buy a ram for the sacrifices that take place at the festival's climax. They would not attend at all. They would not see the goddess or receive even one speck of ash as prasad. From now on, Ariraman contended, they would be satisfied with their own image of the goddess, who resided in a small temple in their own hamlet, their own "ūr," as he put it. They would boycott the big goddess temple. "And that was that"—*avvaḷavu tāṉ*!

So, in a neat turnabout, Middle Ūr seized the ūrmakkaḷ's injunction and appropriated it. They turned banishment into boycott. I heard no plans for overt protest marches or sit-ins. No one would carry banners. They simply planned to stay away, to withdraw the usual ram they give for sacrifice. Given the silent, or what James Scott (1990) might call "hidden," nature of their planned boycott, it is fair to ask if such a protest would amount to anything more than reflexive rhetoric, anything more than a soothing psychological tactic to placate the sting of exclusion. Were Ariraman and the rest of his community really just fooling themselves by turning the terms of their punishment into the very terms of their protest?

My argument is no. On the contrary, they were deliberately critiquing the local structure of domination by drawing on phrases from nationalist discourses and on a familiar technique of labor resistance, not to mention Gandhi's anti-British tactic; namely, the boycott. By turning forced exclusion into a plan for a determinate boycott, the community would do something striking: they would refuse to participate in the reproduction of their own peripherality, smallness, and subordination as Untouchable "Pallars" in relation to the dominant ūrmakkaḷ.

Everyday acts may invoke the large life of our social and cultural worlds. In this case, a pinch of ash entails, as it also invites us to explore, a complex set of structures, meanings, histories, and ideals used by residents of Yanaimangalam in 1990, when the "ash theft" occurred. In order to more deeply understand why the pinch of ash mattered so much that it resulted in banishments and boycotts, it is important to understand just what the discourse on "caste" was in Yanaimangalam in 1990. This discourse included an awareness of historical changes that marginalized Brahmans, promoted Thevar power, and gave S. C. a language with which to dissent. And while these factors are critical to our understanding of the dispute, equally if not more important in local discourse is an intricate understanding of how everyday caste relations were understood and how these understandings contributed to structures of domination and subordination in social life. This chapter and the next will offer a thick description of the event by teasing out the complexities of local meanings of caste from the points of view both of those who dominate and those who are subordinate. This inquiry will appear to take us away from the ash incident, but in fact it will provide a deeper understanding of the multiple meanings involved in the dispute, as it also will explicate ethnographically some of the lived meanings of caste in the late twentieth century in this part of rural South India. I will delve most deeply into two aspects of interpersonal and interfamilial relations that are at the same time pervaded by embodied caste realities. In this chapter, I focus on a set of relations called *kuṭimai,* a complex idiom of interfamilial economic and ritual ties that also implicate jāti dominance, subordination, and interdependence. In Chapter 4, I focus on *mariyātai,* a generalized Tamil idiom of rank and distinction.

Before continuing, it is important to note that these two aspects of caste relations are not intended to mark the limits or parameters of a structure or "system" in which we can contain the meaning of caste. That is, I am not working here to provide a neat, clean, and fixed description of "the caste system." As many others have demonstrated before me, albeit in different ways, no such description is possible. There is simply no singular overarching or static *system* to be so described. As Cohn (1987) and Dirks (2001) have argued, the "system" aspect of caste as it is often described is partially (Dirks might say completely) a colonial and anthropological construction. Indeed, the impact of colonial anthropological accounts and colonial practices on Indians' own perceptions of caste is quite significant and not without relevance for Yanaimangalam. But for residents of Yanaimangalam, caste is understood by most, without direct recourse to historical arguments, to be an embodied as well as socially produced aspect of their social worlds and an enabling and inhibiting aspect of their outreaching selves. This does not mean, however, that residents agree on the implications of caste for their social and personal life, for their capacity for action and self- or community-making potential. Like the village itself, caste in Yanaimangalam may be understood as what V. N. Volosinov calls a "multi-accentual" sign (1986, 23).

To parse that phrase, first of all "jāti" is a "sign"; that is, it is a concept as well as a material reality (here, an embodied one) that has specific meanings to people. Second, to say that this sign is "multi-accentual" is to say that its meaning is "refracted," as Volosinov puts it, through different social lenses and existential orientations. Volosinov, a Marxist linguist, saw these refractions as directly related to class struggle, but we can broaden that to mean any sort of struggle that comes from persons and groups that have different positions in a socially differentiated arena, particularly one characterized by different access to power. Ariraman's political narrative about the "Original Dravidians" certainly illustrates the "accent" of his disempowered social position in relation to a more dominant one. Third, jāti is a living sign. For residents of Yanaimangalam, its meaning and significance are still argued, still part of living discourse about what it is to be human. Jāti is an aspect of everyday life, of yearly political-ritual events, and of political alliances that connect residents of the village to wider organizations and electoral politics. That is, jāti matters to self and village as well as to regional and state politics, where "caste associations" formed around constituents' interests influence peoples' choices in the voting booth. While it may seem unfashionable now to dwell on meanings of caste in villages, for Yanaimangalam's residents caste nonetheless remains a critical aspect of their struggle to define social relations and their place in the world.

To say that jāti matters deeply for everyday life is not to say that its meanings are unchanging. The struggle to belong in the village is exactly part of a broad struggle to change the meaning of caste. Jāti is a sign not only because it has meaning to people but because, and this is important, it is put into use in struggles of growth. That is, in Peircian terms, jāti is a material reality—a sign—that is fully engaged in semeiosis—the growth of the sign. Caste, in other words, is not just an everyday form of domination reinforced through ritual. Caste is also a material semeiotic resource for contesting, subverting, and posing the alternative structural formulations of the ūr that play out not only in this ash incident but also in other events. It is not just ritual language but, and perhaps this is more important, some of the everyday language (in a grammar of exchanges and gestures and pronouns) of jāti rank and village domination that proves also to be the language of reversal, irony, boycott, and change.

KUṬIMAI: DOMINANCE AND SUBORDINATION IN AN IDIOM OF RECIPROCAL SERVICE

Dictionary definitions of kuṭimai include allegiance, homage (as of subjects to their sovereign), domestic economy, slavery, servitude, and feudal dependence (*Tamil Lexicon* 1982, 971). The root word, *kuṭi,* means family, inhabitant, subject (or citizen), a hut, tenancy, class, a residential area, the body (Fabricius 1972, 255; *Cre-A's Dictionary of Contemporary Tamil* 1992, 317; *Tamil Lexicon* 1982, 968). In Yanaimangalam, both words—kuṭi and kuṭimai (the state of being kuṭi)—connote personal attachment (as of a person to a house or family or landlord) as well as dependent subordination (as in servitude, tenancy, subject).

In Yanaimangalam, kuṭi connotes hamlets, huts, and laborers. Many ūrmakkaḷ commonly use the word "kuṭi" coupled with a caste name to denote the residential areas where the S. C. live. Hence they refer to North Ūr, Middle Ūr, and South Street (see Figure 1.3) as North Pallar kuṭi, Middle Pallar kuṭi, and Iruva (a less respectful name for what I otherwise call Illuttuppillai) kuṭi, respectively. The S. C. inhabitants of these residential areas consider these names to be derogatory, lacking in respect (mariyātai). "Kuṭi" is the root of the word *kuṭicai,* meaning a mud-and-thatch hut that remains the common house type of many poorer hamlet (kuṭi) residents. (Most ūrmakkaḷ live in white-washed or pastel-colored houses made of brick and concrete, topped with red tile roofs.) "Kuṭi" is also the root of *kuṭimakaṉ,* "child" (lit. "son") of the kuṭi. Many ūrmakkaḷ use this term to refer to their laborers and to their tenants, the persons more likely to dwell in such huts and hamlets (kuṭi).

The term "kuṭimakaṉ" (or *kuṭimakkaḷ,* "kuṭi people," in the plural form) denotes not only S. C. laborers[2] but also denotes more specifically a marked set of service-providing families whose jāti names correspond to their occupations, such as Washermen, Barbers, Potters, Carpenters, and Blacksmiths. In Yanaimangalam, some members of these jātis were related to ūrmakkaḷ through a kind of subordinate inclusion in an idiom of hereditary service attachment as "sons" and "daughters" to the ūrmakkaḷ families they served. Landlords referred to some of their kuṭimakkaḷ as *contam*;

that is, as part of the category of one's "own people," one's family, joined in kinship through long-standing service ties and through the sharing of food and sometimes other substances. This kinship is not merely metaphorical, as we shall see below. Rather, it is considered to be materially real, defined through the sharing of bodily substance.

The kinship between ūrmakkaḷ and "their own" kuṭimakkaḷ is asymmetrical. Kuṭimakkaḷ take in "gross" substances of their landlords through food, soiled clothing, and other items that are understood to carry the bodily substances of the givers. In return, landlords receive nontransformative "subtle" returns in the form of work, service, and obedience. As many ethnographers have shown, in a wide range of South Asian contexts actors understand their bodily transactions with other persons (Marriott 1976; Inden and Nicholas 1977, 17–18; Trawick 1990, 99; Lamb 2000, 30–37; Parry 1994, 114, 169–170), deities (Nabokov 2000; Eck 1981; Fuller 1989, 74), places (Daniel 1984; Parish 1996; Kakar 1982, 228; Zimmerman 1987, 24–31), and even seasons (Zimmermann 1980; Hart 2000; Selby 2000) to be potentially transformative. That is, one may take on or become more like the qualities of the people, places, and times in which they live. As formulated by Inden and Marriott (1977), these qualities may be either "gross" or "subtle" in nature. Gross substances, such as boiled food (which, due to the catalyst of heat, has taken on qualities of the cook), blood, hair, saliva, and other bodily wastes are more potently transformative than subtle ones, such as uncooked grains, words, gestures of respect. Here, in a well-known principle, taking in certain cooked food items, especially boiled foods such as rice, is a means of taking in the bodily substances of the giver. In this context, kuṭimakkaḷ may consume the cooked food of ūrmakkaḷ but not vice versa. Kuṭimakkaḷ may also take in through touch other gross heating substances such as the blood and other bodily fluids (sweat, urine, blood, hair, shit) in dirty clothing that Washermen wash and that Barbers contact in their work. Such one-way substance transfers, where ūrmakkaḷ send their grosser substances literally "out" to kuṭimakkaḷ, help create such intimate, yet asymmetrical, connections. In cases where such exchanges are asymmetrical, as here, it is the giver who ranks higher than the receiver. The giver becomes part of the receiver, "marks" the receiver, in a sense (Marriott 1990, 18–21), hence encompassing the receiver within an asymmetrical kinship idiom where receivers may be seen to be more related to givers than vice versa simply because they receive more transformative substances from "above," while those on the giving end of the transaction receive little or no transforming substances from the kuṭimakkaḷ (see also Mines 1990, 112–117).

Putting this all together, we can say that the kuṭimakkaḷ of Yanaimangalam are the people (*makkaḷ*) who live in hamlets (kuṭi) and often in huts (kuṭicai) who are—whether as laborers, servants, or tenants—subjects (kuṭi) of the ūrmakkaḷ, attached to them through contractual (as is the case with tenants and laborers) or hereditary (as is the case with Washermen, Barbers, etc.) service rights and obligations, some of which center on specific agricultural practices, others on ritual and everyday services such as washing clothes, doing carpentry, and so forth. "Kuṭi" is thus on many levels a semantic complement to "ūr," as "kuṭimakkaḷ" is the complement to "ūrmakkaḷ." The term "kuṭi" denotes the relatively subordinate and dependent status of both the hamlets (kuṭi) and their residents (kuṭimakkaḷ) to the dominant ūr and its ūrmakkaḷ (see Pfaffenberger 1982 for an elaborate analysis of kuṭimai relations in Tamil areas of Sri Lanka). Furthermore, by engaging in these relations over time, kuṭimai grows into a kind of kinship based on the asymmetrical sharing of bodily substances (in food, blood, saliva, and shit) from ūrmakkaḷ to kuṭimakkaḷ, from landlords to laborers, as from parents to children.[3] Aruna explained this kinship to me once. As we were walking across the fields one day, she greeted an older man. After he passed, I asked her who he was. She replied, "contam," meaning literally "one's own," or "family." I asked how he was related. She explained that he wasn't actually an uncle or anything like that. He was an S. C. man who had worked for her father-in-law for a long time . . . that's how he was family.

As you read on, bear in mind that the version of jāti relations you are reading about now—familiar to and to an extent practiced by village residents of all jātis—is a far cry from Ariraman's claims to primacy, justice, and autonomy. The discussion of interjāti relations that follows represents instead the idealized point of view, or what Volosinov would call the "accent," of many ūrmakkaḷ.

KUṬIMAKKAḶ IN YANAIMANGALAM

The *Tamil Lexicon* lists—albeit rather archaically[4]—eighteen different jātis under the entry "kuṭimakkaḷ" (see also Pfaffenberger 1982, 35):

> Washerman (*vaṇṇāṉ*), Barber (*nāvitaṉ* or *nācavaṉ*), Potter (*kuyavaṉ*), Goldsmith (*taṭṭāṉ*), Brazier or Bell Metalsmith (*kaṉṉāṉ*), Stonecutter (*kaṟṟaccaṉ*), Blacksmith (*kolaṉ*), Carpenter (*taccaṉ*), Oil Presser (*enneyvaṇiyaṉ*), Salt Merchant (*uppuvaṇiyaṉ*), Betel-Leaf and Vegetable Vendor (*ilaiyavaṇiyaṉ*), Village Guardian (*paḷḷi*), Garland Maker (*pūmālaikkāraṉ*), Drummer (*paḻaiyaṉ*), Cowherd (*kōvirkuṭiyāṉ*), Sacrificer to the Goddess (*occaṉ*), Fisherman/Hunter (*valaiyaṉ*), Tailor (*pāṇaṉ*).

Nine families working or living in Yanaimangalam belonged to kuṭimakkaḷ jātis listed here. Some of them practiced their customary labor (*toḻil*). Some of them did not. Some of them resided in Yanaimangalam. Others lived in nearby villages. These are the nine: Washerman, Barber, Potter, Metalworker,

Blacksmith, Carpenter, Garland Maker (also a non-Brahman priest caste, singers to the goddess), Drummer, and Betel-Leaf Vendor.

But like any list of identities which freezes a changing and shifting reality, this list too distorts human reality. We have seen already, for example, that the Barber jāti in Yanaimangalam does no barbering at all. The "Betel-Leaf Vendors" are no such thing. They go by the title "Muppanar," meaning elder or dignitary. They eschew the less honorable (because it connotes kuṭimai) jāti name of Ilaiyavaniyan and have nothing to do with raising or selling betel leaves, though they consume them as often as anyone. They grow rice and, increasingly, bananas. Furthermore, while their jāti is listed in the dictionary as a kuṭimakkaḷ jāti, in Yanaimangalam today they belong squarely among the ūrmakkaḷ. And who in Yanaimangalam serves the "kuṭimai" functions of sacrificing animals and guarding the ūr? The ūrmakkaḷ Thevars, that's who. The Metalworker in Yanaimangalam is, indeed, a Metalworker jāti, yet he works solely for wages and has no hereditary rights in Yanaimangalam. He is a recent immigrant to the village. The "Drummers" (S. C. Palaiyar) do no drumming. Like most S. C. in the village, they mostly labor on the land of others. A few S. C. lease or own their own lands. Others work in town in the civil service. Many young men and women go to college. By the end of my first stay there in 1990, only a few—particularly some of the older S. C. men and women—were still attached to ūrmakkaḷ families in relations of formalized servitude (*paṇṇaiyāḷ*) as semibonded laborers, and just one family from this jāti performed kuṭimai-linked funerary functions for the ūrmakkaḷ.

Some of the old-timer Brahmans did wax nostalgic for the "old days" when, according to them, more kuṭimakkaḷ practiced their traditional art. Oil Pressers and Goldsmiths were also local, they told me, and the Palaiyars still played the drums when called. In those days, Brahmans were dominant[5] and the rest of the villagers were their kuṭi; that is, their dependent tenants, workers, and service jātis. In fact, my Brahman neighbor Parvathi sometimes slipped and referred to the ūrmakkaḷ as "kuṭimakkaḷ," a mistake that she would quickly correct to "ūrmakkaḷ." Whether these are idealized memories or historical facts, one thing is clear: static models of intercaste relations are distortions of fluid historical realities.

THE JAJMĀNI SYSTEM?

Armed with imminent criticism or warmed with a sense of nostalgic familiarity, readers familiar with India may be thinking, "Ah, here is what I've been waiting for! The traditional caste system still operating—albeit imperfectly now—in The Indian Village." To respond to such a thought, I must digress for a few pages and discuss the connection between two problematic concepts: "the *jajmāni* system" and the "traditional Indian village." As Fuller (1989, 52–57) has argued, the two concepts are interlinked, because the way that some researchers—including anthropologists—have in the past depicted intercaste, village-level exchanges ("the jajmāni system") has unwittingly contributed to a false view of villages in India as somehow "traditional" and static timeless wholes.

In 1936, William Wiser first coined the term "jajmāni system" to describe a pattern of nonmonetary, nonmarket exchange he found at work in a North Indian village. He found that the non-Brahman landholders (called *jajmān*) in this village gave shares of their grain harvest as well as cooked food and other goods to other occupational jātis such as Barbers, Potters, Washermen, Carpenters, and Blacksmiths in return for long-term service. Wiser characterized these exchanges as "mutual" or "symmetrical." That is, Wiser saw the jajmāni system as a division of labor where landholding castes exchanged grain for the services of the other jātis tit for tat, exchanges that apparently worked for the mutual benefit of all those involved (see also Dube 1955).

As Kolenda (1963) explains, other researchers working in India took issue with Wiser's characterization of these relations as mutual, seeing them as coerced and asymmetrical, where services were given to the powerful landholders who then redistributed grain in return. That is, while Wiser saw the landholders engaged in reciprocal, tit-for-tat relations with occupational service castes, others took into account that the landholders were politically and economically powerful groups with privileged access to the food supply who controlled these exchanges using their power as the "dominant" castes (e.g., Harper 1959a; Gould 1958; Beidelman 1959; Bronger 1975).

Whether they viewed these "jajmāni" relations as mutual or asymmetrical,[6] all of these researchers painted a picture of the jajmāni system as a more or less bounded, interdependent, and self-sufficient village exchange network among permanent hereditary occupational groups, or "castes." Such accounts evoke an even earlier picture of the allegedly self-sufficient village political-economic system whose systematicity as well as "self-sufficiency" was, as both Fuller and Inden show, admired, idealized, and, to an extent, imagined by nineteenth-century scholars such as Maine, Baden-Powell, and Marx as well as by many British civil servants (Inden 1990, 143–148; Fuller 1989). The view that such writers offered of the self-sufficient village community has, in fact, rarely been reproduced by contemporary ethnographers, yet it remains a popular stereotype, one that even some residents (Brahmans, in particular) of Yanaimangalam, as well as many Indian urban dwellers (Nandy 2001), look "back on" with nostalgia.

Because the kuṭimai relations I have described above—and will continue to depict below—resonate so strongly with the image of the jajmāni system, I would like to briefly review some of the problems that arise with that image. Fuller (1989) has demonstrated that the allegedly "self-sufficient village economy" was probably never so closed, self-sufficient, "systematic," or universal as colonial, anthropological, or even Indian nostalgic accounts have imagined or represented it. Rather, jajmāni relations, where they existed, were always part of wider relations in political-economic systems of patronage, kingship, and trade (even global trade; Greek, Arab, Jewish, and Chinese traders resided in South Indian coastal towns as long as 2,000 years ago). Villages in India have been parts of shifting kingly states for hundreds, indeed thousands, of years and as such have been linked to greater economic and political networks and centers (see, for example, Cohn and Marriott 1958), as most Indian village ethnographies acknowledge and as many have emphasized.[7] Indeed, there is no "traditional village," if that term refers to an essentially unchanging, closed, perhaps religious and ahistorical isolate that modernity has only recently altered in the last few centuries. Moreover, as Dube (1998) demonstrates, local peasants were always "entangled" with broader political-economic processes, and some precolonial land tenure systems provided significant flexibility for lower castes to bow out of relations with unforgiving landlords and strike out on their own into frontier lands available for cultivation (see also Ludden 1985, 81–85). Colonialism played a large role in solidifying relations that were previously more flexible.

Yanaimangalam was most likely founded at least 600 years ago by regional kings as a brahmadeya (see Ludden 1985, 36–37; Araṅkācāri n.d.), a community donated for the support of Brahmans. Kings as well as local "dominant caste" Veḷḷāḷas (peasant farming groups) supported communities of Brahmans by providing shares of the harvest and other financial support for their upkeep. Residents of Yanaimangalam are reminded of these former royal linkages with every trip to the river, for the names of kings and those to whom the kings conferred local rights in temple affairs over the last 600 years are inscribed in three different languages in the stone walls of the riverside Visnu temple. Three-hundred-year-old inscriptions in the Siva temple suggest a subsequent change in political and religious affiliation connected to regional changes in kingship. And certainly since colonialism, the village has changed even more. Older Brahman residents link their current marginalization in part to what they perceive as the loss of British rule, though they are not quite so conscious of the role colonialism played in establishing their local hegemony to begin with (they were granted ownership of most lands in Yanaimangalam in the late nineteenth century). And certainly the fact that Thevars are now the dominant ūrmakkaḷ in Yanaimangalam and the fact that Ariraman invoked an Ati

Dravida identification are examples best understood historically in the context of colonial and postcolonial land reform, regional social change, and state political processes.

What distinguishes today's village life from earlier times, then, is not so much the presence versus the absence of connections with the wider world, but (as is true for all of us) the number and intensity and breadth of those connections. Today village residents remain fully involved in regional and global political economies through such practices as buying and selling grain, applying for bank loans, paying taxes, using pesticides, exporting bananas to Dubai, migrating to Bombay for labor, working for and initiating capitalist enterprises, laboring in textile mills that export cotton to Russia, watching TV, reading the newspaper, traveling on business, marrying children off to families in distant places, voting in national elections, talking to anthropologists, moving to the United States and asking village priests to send them temple prasad by airmail (in orange envelopes), remembering life on the line at the British-owned textile mill several miles west, remembering a father imprisoned for resisting British rule, wearing clothes striped in the colors of a political party, painting the horns of goats and oxen in those same party colors, splurging on a bar of Dove soap or Cadbury chocolate, brushing with Colgate toothpaste, buying factory-made ash to pinch and smear, and so many other quotidian practices.

The village resembles nothing like (nor did it ever resemble) a closed system based purely on nonmonetary forms of reciprocal and redistributive exchange. On the other hand, Good perhaps goes too far in dismissing the relevance of the concept of jajmāni for understanding South Indian realities, simply because neither the term nor the concept is "indigenous" to Tamil usage (1982, 32). While the kinds of relations associated with the jajmāni system may not be prevalent in all South Indian villages (for there are many types of villages), the general concept of the jajmān—the central landlord who protects the well-being of the whole village that has organized around him—does resonate with both popular images and contemporary local practices in at least wetland—that is, amply irrigated—villages such as Yanaimangalam. Popularly, the image and idea of the "jajmān" is propagated in such hit films as *Ejjaman* (jajmān) (2000). In this film, star Rajnikant plays the adored dominant landowner in a village, who is surrounded by happy, dancing, and singing kuṭimakkaḷ. And *Mutal Mariyātai* (1985), starring Sivaji Ganesan, depicts an honorable landlord/jajmān who falls in love with a low-caste kuṭimakkaḷ woman. Together they heroically but tragically defy caste injustices while singing many fine duets.

Furthermore, the concept of a dominant landowning-caste group (jajmāns) receiving services from occupationally named kuṭimakkaḷ is frequently cited in South Indian ethnographies.[8] What's more, as the data presented below show in detail, these relations do serve some of the ritual functions that, according to Raheja (1988), also characterize jajmāni-type exchanges in north India.

Longitudinal ethnographic studies have demonstrated that in many parts of rural South India, an expanded cash economy, changes in land tenure, and the stigma of being a kuṭimakaṉ, coupled with increasing educational and non–rural-based job opportunities, have contributed to the attenuation of some of these relations.[9] Based on my informants' accounts, the same is probably true for Yanaimangalam. However, even though many Indians themselves participate in this construction of the rural as traditional and the urban as modern (Nandy 2001; Pigg 1992), these changes should not be interpreted as a move from an unchanging ahistorical caste-bound "tradition" to a historical "modernity" that is becoming casteless. Historical research has shown that relations among economic units in villages have shifted, changed, and varied throughout India's history—not just in "modern times" (see, for example, Ludden 1985, Dirks 2001, Inden 1990, Fuller 1989, and Dube 1998). The purpose of my use of the term "collocation" is a desire to acknowledge that villages are always-already defined through such historical, political, and social processes. Those processes are already "there" in the village, and even though most village residents do not frame their own daily lives with conscious historical discourse, they do bring these broader processes into existence through their actions.

What is easy to assert is that at the turn of the twenty-first century, in conjunction with other social and economic relations, there existed a limited but vital sphere of partly nonmonetary and mostly local exchange relations surrounding rice agriculture and implicating wider relations between landowners and the families of kuṭimakkaḷ who provided services to them. While these kuṭimai relations were vital for the economic livelihood of some and for the convenience of others, they were also salient for the social capital of many ūrmakkaḷ, who built and maintained local power and their own well-being in part through sustaining these relations. Kuṭimai was the stuff of local dominance, and it played into how the ūr (big and small) defined itself socially and spatially. This is the aspect of kuṭimai that interests us here: the idiom of dominance it entails.

Two aspects of kuṭimai relations are pertinent for our deeper understanding of Middle Ūr's intended boycott of the goddess temple after the "ash theft." Both aspects of kuṭimai relations pertain to the kinds of exchanges that take place between patron ūrmakkaḷ families and kuṭimakkaḷ. The first aspect matches what Wiser and then Raheja (1988) described as reciprocal "mutual" transactions where service was rendered into grain at harvest. The second aspect, which I call "exteriority," foregrounds the social asymmetries, which are also spatial asymmetries, implicated in such exchanges. These asymmetries may be seen from two points of view. First, they may be seen as a perceived difference in embodied morality where dominant ūrmakkaḷ jātis maintain their order and coherence (muṟai) by sending negative moral substances out to dependent kuṭimakkaḷ. The second point of view on asymmetries concerns the patron-client aspect of ūrmakkaḷ-kuṭimakkaḷ relations, where patrons view their dominance as patronage requiring them to act as protectors and affectionate superiors to the kkuṭimakkaḷunder their care.

Mutuality: Kuṭimai as Division of Labor

The first aspect of kuṭimai resembles what Wiser (1936) and Raheja (1988) perceived as "mutuality" in two northern Indian multicaste agricultural villages, as reciprocal transactions where kuṭimakkaḷ—including Middle Ūr field laborers—provide service and particular kinds of specialized labor (toḻil) to land-controlling families (ūrmakkaḷ) in return for cash wages and specified shares of the grain harvest. Services may include agricultural, household, or ritual work during life crises as well as temple rituals. In Yanaimangalam, harvest shares have different names depending on context and recipient, but one general term used to denote such prestations from ūrmakkaḷ to kuṭimakkaḷ is *cutantiram.* "Cutantiram" is a polyvalent term that can be translated in this context simply as hereditary or customary right (Fabricius 1972, 414, *Tamil Lexicon* 1982, 1513). In Yanaimangalam, villagers refer to the givers of cutantiram, generally ūrmakkaḷ jātis, as the *cutantirakkāraṅkaḷ* of their kuṭimakkaḷ; that is, as the cutantiram "doers."

Take, for example, Yanaimangalam's two families of Carpenters. Each is "attached" or "tied" (kaṭṭu) to certain ūrmakkaḷ families, and they have the following responsibilities (*kaṭṭāyam,* or *poṟuppu*) that they must fulfill as kuṭimakkaḷ to those families or, in some cases, to the ūr as a "whole." They must repair on demand the plows and other agricultural tools—such as carts, yokes, and sickle handles—owned by their ūrmakkaḷ families. They might also be called in to repair a house door or build a shelf. In return for any particular act of labor (toḻil), the Carpenters *may* receive some small salary or wage (*campaḷam*). In addition to a wage, they receive as cutantiram (that is, as their customary right) specified shares of grain from the rice fields of the ūrmakkaḷ they serve. They receive these shares regardless of whether they have worked for the landlord in the period leading up to that harvest or not. That is, they receive cutantiram as a right (urimai), not as a return for any specific instance of service rendered. In 1990, the Carpenters in Yanaimangalam received 8 to 10 *paṭi* of grain (a measure of approximately 1.5 kilograms) per crop (of which there are two per year) per landlord.

Similar prestations of grain are due to Barbers (who come from the next village south, since Yanaimangalam's Barbers have moved on to other professions), Washermen, Blacksmiths, Priests, and Garland Makers (they also live in the next village). Each of these kuṭimakkaḷ families also perform regular services for the ūrmakkaḷ. Barbers cut hair and shave their patrons. Washermen and women wash clothes. Though by 2003, tractors were starting to outnumber ox-drawn plows, still Blacksmiths make plow tips, wright wheels, and do other ironwork, and Garland Makers make garlands for temple rituals and deliver strings of white jasmine every morning by bicycle for daily domestic rituals and for women and girls to adorn their thick braids. Brahman temple priests also receive grain at harvest from the ūrmakkaḷ. Their share is not called cutantiram, probably because it does not go to them directly but rather comes to them via the "donations" of first harvest grain (*nāḷkatir*) that landowners make to the temples these priests serve. In addition, Brahman priests who work in the Siva and Visnu temples receive a small—very small—government stipend (campaḷam) as well as coins that worshipers donate during temple rituals. All of these service jātis also provide service at life-crisis rituals in ūrmakkaḷ homes (Figure 3.1).

The Potters, who make clay pots for domestic and temple use and who also serve as priests in the local temple for a deity named Sasta, do not receive their shares in the form of cutantiram on the threshing floor. Rather, they retain a field that was granted to them by the ūrmakkaḷ. Such land grants are called *māṉiyam,* or kuṭimakkaḷ māṉiyam. Land grants were common before British land "settlements" of the territory in the late 1800s. As Dirks shows, māṉiyams were commonly granted and administered through state offices, through hierarchies of control linking villages to kingship (Dirks 1987, 120–121; see also Ludden 1985, 77–78). While there are no longer kings or their underlings to make and administer such grants, locally dominant ūrmakkaḷ make use of many of the idioms of kingship when they assert their dominance. Still, they may get together and grant portions of their own lands to public causes. Residents of Yanaimangalam assert that the present lands held by Potters, and previously by others such as the non-Brahman Kambar priests, Blacksmiths, and Carpenters, were gifted by the Brahmans of the village at the time when they were in control of the majority of the land. These lands were assigned for the use of kuṭimakkaḷ by their Brahman patrons, free of rent. By my first visit to Yanaimangalam in 1988, only the Potters retained their māṉiyam. Others are said to have sold their holdings after attaining a deed, while some lost their rights to the land, such as a priestly Kambar family whose land was reclaimed in the courts (as well as outside the courts by force) by the ūrmakkaḷ for the construction of the new goddess temple.

Figure 3.1. The Barber gives a Pillaimar boy his first haircut.

In Yanaimangalam, field laborers working for daily wages receive some obligatory prestations of grain on the threshing floor. Ariraman from Middle Ūr, for example, labors on the fields of Gurusamipillai. These are some of his jobs: plowing, fertilizing with manure, harvesting and threshing paddy, and filling burlap bags with grain. His wife also works in these fields: she plants, transplants, weeds, and harvests (Figure 3.2). Workers may be paid in cash or kind or both. Gurusamipillai said that for his regular workers, he pays only in grain at the end of harvest. He pays them somewhat less than one kōṭṭai (approximately 70 kilograms) per acre of paddy (my associate Aruna's husband added that the wage in kind that he pays varies according to the yield of the field in a given season). In addition, workers receive daily shares of grain during harvest as cutantiram. These are of two kinds, according to Aruna's husband Murukan: *aṭikkiratukku nel* ("paddy for beating") and *katirkaṭṭu* ("bundle of grain").

The first, aṭikkiratukku nel, are daily measures of grain that the workers take from the grain heap. At the time of this research, Murukan said that each male laborer received two *marakkāls* (approximately eight liters) and each woman received one paṭi (about one liter) per day. The second type of payment, katirkaṭṭu, is a token share of the cut grains that serves almost as a little extra, like a tip. There are two kinds of katirkaṭṭu: *talaikaṭṭu* ("head bundle"), which is also called *arivalāḷkaṭṭu* ("sickle bundle"), and *piḷḷaikaṭṭu* ("child bundle"). Each worker receives the former, and the latter goes only to women with very young children who are still nursing. Each of these "bundles" is literally the amount of grain a person can cut and gather with a single swipe of their sickle. This grain must be thrashed, husked, and winnowed before it can be eaten. Workers often use their daily shares of grain for food during harvest. Thus, after working the fields, some laborers return home (or if they are migrant laborers they return to their camp) and begin the work of processing the grain for the next day's meal. For work other than harvesting (plowing, weeding, transplanting, fertilizing), both farmers I interviewed pay a daily cash wage. In 1990, the daily minimum wage was 20 rupees per day for a man and 10 rupees for a woman (at the time these wages were equivalent to approximately $1.10 per day for men and fifty-five cents for women).

When workers speak of cutantiram as shares collected on the threshing floor from heaps of newly harvested grain, the sense they convey is that their share is a right they receive in simple reciprocation for labor performed, a "mutual" transaction. However, there are other kinds of and occasions for ūrmakkaḷ to give cutantiram as a prestation in return for services where the meaning of the prestation carries added weight. In particular, the cutantiram, (customary payment) that ūrmakkaḷ give in return for services kuṭimakkaḷ provide on ritual occasions—especially life-crisis rituals from births to deaths—is said to "pass on" (kaḻi) negatively valued, harmful substances from the givers to the receivers. These transactions are thought to have lasting biological-moral affects on both givers and receivers. They also feed into spatial distinctions of interior and exterior, of ūr and kāṭu, and condition some of the everyday and ritual exclusions kuṭimakkaḷ still face in relation to dominant ūrmakkaḷ.

Exteriority: Kuṭimai as Sociospatial Asymmetry

Substances used and transformed in the performance of life-crisis rituals are passed on to kuṭimakkaḷ, as well as to Brahman priests, as cutantiram. Some kinds of cutantiram transacted at life-crisis rituals come to their recipients transvalued: they contain more than their visible form, having been "marked" through ritual procedures by the donors' unwanted, negatively valued substances—their "bad karma," in a sense.[10] These kinds of cutantiram transfer, thus, not only the visible objects from ūrmakkaḷ donors to kuṭimakkaḷ but also parts of the former's negatively valued biological-moral substance. In particular, such objects most often are thought to transfer either evils (pāvam), which are the embodied negative results of previous immoral acts, or tiruṣṭi, the embodied negative effects of emotion-laden visual contact sometimes translated as "evil eye." By taking in these varied negative substances and qualities, kuṭimakkaḷ continue to re-

Figure 3.2. Transplanting rice seedlings.

inforce what many see as their own negative bodily and moral qualities. Kuṭimakkaḷ are seen as rough, chaotic, messy, and sinful, not unlike the kāṭu, the "wilderness," they inhabit.

Some informants refer to these prestations not by the general term "cutantiram" (a term that foregrounds their reciprocal aspect, or mutuality) but more specifically as *tāṉam,* a term that lexically links intercaste dynamics in Yanaimangalam to that aspect or pattern of caste relations Raheja discussed in depth as "centrality." Raheja shows that in Pahansu, a North Indian village in Uttar Pradesh, the dominant landowning Gujars transfer "inauspiciousness" from themselves out to others. Some of the transfers are effected through simple ritual procedures by now familiar to us, such as circling an object around a person's body to remove an illness or other negative quality and then transferring it to another person or place (Raheja 1988, 85–86; Kapadia 1995, 107–111; Shulman 1985, 104; Mines 1997b). Gujars in Pahansu gave *dān* (the root of the Tamil tāṉam) "out" to Brahman priests and service jātis (called *kamīn* in Hindi), including Washermen, Barbers, and Untouchable "Sweepers." By giving *dān,* Gujars transfer what Raheja glosses as "inauspiciousness" (be it faults, evils, or other afflictions) from a person, a family, or the village as a whole out to specific appropriate recipients. Raheja demonstrates that the regular movement of evil (*pāp* in Hindi; pāvam in Tamil) and other kinds of inauspiciousness from centers (interiors such as person, home, and village) out to appropriate others who take it away is necessary to the well-being not only of the Gujar patrons but also of the whole village. The others depend upon the landowning Gujars' success and prosperity for their own well-being. Barbers, Dhobis, "Untouchable" Sweepers, and higher-caste Brahmans are said in Pahansu to be "appropriate" others who are capable of digesting their patron's evils without endangering their own bodily-cum-moral makeup (Raheja 1988, 201–202; see also Parry 1980, 89 and Parish 1996, 28). As Parry notes, however, the danger to a receiver's biological-moral makeup may be more perilous than Raheja's informants liked to admit (1989, 75–76).

In Yanaimangalam, kuṭimakkaḷ—especially Washermen and Barbers—and Brahman priests are called upon to perform certain functions at the life-crisis rituals of ūrmakkaḷ families to whom they are bound. I found that during life-crisis rituals, prestations called variously tānam or cutantiram are routinely said to "dispose of" or to "pass on" (*kaḻi*) negative substances from giver to receiver, from ūrmakkaḷ patron to kuṭimakaṉ or a Brahman priest. Kapadia (1995, 120–123) finds similar processes operating in Tamilnadu, as do Brubaker (1979, 133–134), Inglis (1985, 99), Good (1991), and, in historical accounts of South Indian kingship, Shulman (1985, 101–105). As the following examples show, Yanaimangalam's residents say that tānam and cutantiram may transfer faults (tōcam), evil (pāvam), the "evil eye" (tiruṣṭi), and, in some cases, impurity (*tīṭṭu*).[11] These prestations transfer negative substances out to appropriate others (usually either kuṭimakkaḷ or Brahman priests) or to exterior places, places outside the ūr. Like the processions detailed in Chapter 2, these exteriorizing practices also constitute the distinction between ūr and kāṭu. Ūr and ūrmakkaḷ pass their own negative and hindering qualities out to kuṭimakkaḷ and kāṭu, hence rendering themselves dharmic or orderly while also rendering kuṭimakkaḷ and kāṭu adharmic or chaotic. Such negative qualities, people, and places are best kept separate from the interior places of ūrmakkaḷ life, places which include not only ūr but also house, kitchen, and body. It is interesting, however, that the highly pure Brahmans too may be recipients of these negative qualities, as the following example illustrates.

Passing on Evils[12]

The first time I heard evils (pāvam) discussed in Yanaimangalam was about three months into my stay when I attended a funeral ritual (*titi,* or *sraddha*). This titi took place at Arumukam Pillai's house for the senior of his two wives one year after her death. The elaborate ritual was designed to accomplish two related ends: first, to finally remove any evils (pāvam) that might remain attached to the deceased's soul (the soul is thought to hover close to the living for a year, being unable to give up family attachments) and second, to hasten her arrival in the realm of the ancestors. The ritual was elaborate and I will not describe it in full; my focus here is on the disposal of evils via prestations to the priests, prestations that Arumukam Pillai referred to as tānam.

For two hours, two Brahman priests sat cross-legged in front of the shrine wall in the main room of Arumukam Pillai's small house, reciting numerous Sanskrit mantras while family members bustled about the house on various ritual missions. As they recited mantras, the priests piled uncooked foodstuffs, one after another, onto a set of wide banana leaves they had laid out in front of them. Periodically they switched into Tamil and called out for someone to fetch a missing item. One after another, they heaped onto the pile jaggary, ginger, chickpeas, green gram, black gram, red gram, tamarind, green bananas, raw rice, paddy, snake gourd, pumpkin, potato, sugarcane, banana flower, carrots, green mangoes, green beans, limes, eggplant, okra, betel leaf, and areca nuts. They also formed several *piṇṭams* ("fetuses," or "bodies"), rice balls that represented male and female ancestors reaching back three generations. The mantras they recited effected several transformations, chief among these being (1) the creation of a "subtle body" for the deceased to use on her journey to the realm of ancestors and (2) the transfer of her soul's clinging evils to the foodstuffs before them. When these actions were complete, the priests ceremoniously sent the deceased's sons to the river with all of the piṇṭams, the rice-ball subtle bodies of the ancestors including the deceased, which they were to release into the river (her route to heaven and the world of the ancestors). As soon as the sons left the house, the priests, their ritual work done, popped some betel nut in their mouths, reached behind them, and pulled out several cloth bags, which they promptly began to stuff full of the raw foods before them. The priests also wrapped into the top folds of their veṣtis the dozens of one-rupee coins that had been placed on top of betel leaves and on top of one of the piṇṭams, the one representing the deceased, during the ritual.

I asked Arumukam Pillai, the widower, why they took all these things home. He replied "That's for eating the evils. That way, the evils will be removed. It's a kind of tāṉam" (*Atu pāvattaic cāppiṭutiṟkkāka. Appaṭi pāvam pōkum. Atu oru mātiri tāṉam*). Then, much to my delight (I had been hoping to elicit such a statement, having gone to India with the findings of Raheja and Parry much on my mind), he added almost as an afterthought that the priests eat the evils and digest (*ceri*) them. Once digested—it's an easy inference—the evils would move even further out into the wastelands (kāṭu) where people euphemistically "go outside" (*veḷiyē pōka*) to defecate.

Brahman priests who take in tāṉam are thought to have both the bodily and ritual capacity to cleanse themselves of the evils of others. That is, their purity and orderliness is the very reason they can take on and then digest and rid themselves of the sins of others. But Brahmans are not the only recipients of evils and other negatives. In Yanaimangalam, Washermen and Barbers were frequently direct recipients of ūrmakkaḷ negatives, performing services and receiving cutantiram and tāṉam at life-crisis rituals, paramount among them funerals, where ridding the deceased of evils is a crucial step in easing their journey into the afterlife. Washermen and Washerwomen, for example, provided cloth for tying the corpse securely onto the funeral-procession bier and for decorating the funeral shed erected just outside the house of the deceased. They provided wicks for the household lamp, which during the course of the ritual needs to be renewed. At Thevar funerals, the Washerman is also responsible for bringing a long length of cloth, upon which the chief mourner must tread as he makes his way from the river, where he undergoes ritual preparations such as a head-shaving, back to the house where the corpse is being prepared. This way, the feet of the death-polluted mourner do not touch and pollute the ūr through contact with its soil. Barbers make the funeral bier out of coconut fronds. They shave the chief mourners (that is, the sons of the deceased). They blow the conch during funeral processions and provide mango leaves for decorating the pot of river water used to bathe the corpse. At some funerals, Barbers participate in providing the *vāykkaraci*, "rice for the mouth." Here the female Barber prepares paddy from the house of the deceased. She pounds it, husks it, winnows it, soaks it in water, and then puts the rice in a small pot and passes it around to all the relatives, who are to take a few grains to feed the corpse by literally putting the rice in the mouth of the corpse. In return, the Barber receives coins as cutantiram. Aruna told me sometimes rich people will make "rice grains" out of gold. Mourners will feed this gold to the corpse, and the Barbers are to remove the gold rice and take it as cutantiram. In return for their services, Barbers and Dhobis receive various foodstuffs, including paddy, as cutantiram. Both Andi Muppanar, a local ritual expert, and the Barber who works for Aruna's family, said that taking cutantiram from rituals such as these was a way to transfer pāvam, evils, from the deceased. But while Brahmans are thought capable of ridding themselves of such evils, Barbers and Washermen are thought to simply take them on and live with them. This, in part, is the logic for their residential marginalization. Their task is to remove negatives from the ūr and the ūrmakkaḷ. Since they embody those negative qualities, they must remove themselves from the ūr as well. Hence, they live on the edges of the ūr, and many ūrmakkaḷ to this day do not allow them to enter farther than the exterior courtyard of their houses.

Passing on Harmful Gazes and Other Faults

Most village residents did not articulate such a learned point of view as the religious and literate Arumukam Pillai, whose Tamil words and concerns echoed Sanskrit texts such as the Laws of Manu (e.g., IV.185). Nevertheless, the idea that negative moral qualities can be transferred from persons to objects and then on to other persons and outside places is common throughout the village. One of the most common negatives transferred through the cutantiram given at life-crisis rituals is tiruṣṭi. Like the word pāvam, which can refer both to the act (an evil deed) and the material remainder of the act (evil stuck to the soul), so too tiruṣṭi refers both to seeing and to the negative residues that may stick to the object of emotion-laden gazes. Tiruṣṭi removal figures centrally in weddings and in girls' puberty rituals, where the ritual subjects are especially vulnerable to the penetrating gaze of all those gathered. They are vulnerable in part because they are beautifully adorned and hence attractive foci of attention and sometimes envy and in part because they are more open to outside influences because of their own open and heated ritual condition.

One of the tiruṣṭi-removing procedures common at non-Brahman girls' puberty rituals is called *ēṟṟiyeṭuttal,* "raising and taking [away]." In this ritual action, two women kin of the girl (preferably affines or in-laws classified as *attai*; e.g., father's sister or mother's brother's wife)[13] post themselves on either side of the girl, facing one another. They take three sets of different substances in turn and wave each three times in synchronous arcs in the air on either side of the girl.[14] The specific substances used often include first, *kumkumam* and sandalwood paste; second, a kind of sweet-rice pancake (*appam*); and third, a coconut and a small container of cow urine (the same container from which urine would have earlier been scattered about the house to purify it). Subsequent to this "raising" of the substances, the women circle puffed rice and a sweet rice around the girl's head or front, then set these substances down in each of the four directions outside the arced space they made with their arm gestures. I asked on several different occasions what these activities accomplished. Those in the know invariably replied it was to "pass on or destroy the tiruṣṭi." These movements transferred tiruṣṭi from the girl to the place outside her protective circle created by the arcs. Moreover, in several cases, some of these substances (especially the appam and puffed and sweetened rices), were given away as cutantiram to the Washerwoman, who took it to her home on the outskirts of the ūr, where her family ate it.

Weddings are another occasion requiring the disposal of tiruṣṭi through prestations of cutantiram. I watched at Kutti Thevar's wedding as the Brahman priest tied protective amulets (kāppu) around the wrists of the groom and then, separately, the bride, as the first phase of the wedding ritual. The amulets are put together with a piece of cooling turmeric root, a rolled betel leaf, and a piece of iron, which is said to absorb tiruṣṭi, all tied into a bracelet of turmeric-stained string. In the first step of this amulet-tying ritual, the priest places a tray of raw rice between the groom and his mother's brother. The latter, instructed by the priest, puts a dab of sandalwood paste onto a whole raw coconut that sits on the rice. The groom picks up this coconut in his cupped hands as the priest hands the amulet to the mother's brother, who ties in onto the right wrist of the groom (Figure 3.3). The groom sets the coconut back down on the tray of rice, and the priest then puts both the rice and coconut into a bag which, according to some, is later given as cutantiram to the family Barber or, according to others, taken home by the priest himself. The same procedure is repeated with the bride (her mother's brother ties the amulet onto her left wrist). The coconut and rice absorb both generalized faults (tōcam) and tiruṣṭi from the ritual subjects, and the amulet protects them during the course of the ritual by absorbing any tiruṣṭi they may be subject to during the wedding. After the wedding is over, the amulet is either thrown out into the kāṭu (wasteland) or it is given, along with the rice and coconut, to the family Barber.

TOḺIL: PRIVILEGE OR CURSE?

The preceding examples clearly illustrate that prestations such as tāṉam and various kinds of cutantiram effect transferals of negatively valued substances. The receivers are kuṭimakkaḷ, Brahman priests, exterior places (kāṭu, the street), and sometimes temples. I asked several different people why anyone would take on such negatives. Wouldn't they be adversely affected by doing so? Andi Muppanar, a prominent man in Yanaimangalam who is considered a local expert on religious matters (and someone we shall meet up with again), explained to me that Barbers and Washermen as well as Brahmans, because of their important toḻil, their labor functions and capacities, all have a certain kind of authority (*talaimai,* lit. "headness") at rituals such as these. Hocart (1950, 7–14) argued much the same thing when he referred to the priest-like qualities of Barbers, Washermen, and artisan jātis such as Potters. Others working among Tamils have also noted that service jātis such as these have special capacities to absorb or take on impurities (Pfaffenberger 1982, 40; Brubaker 1979; Inglis 1985, 99). In Yanaimangalam, village residents such as Andi Muppanar, Parvathi, and several others with whom I spoke on the matter insisted that taking in these dangerous substances does not harm the receivers.

Their statements are consistent with other general principles of personhood in South Asia, where acts and substances that are harmful for one

Figure 3.3. Coconut ritual at Thevar wedding.

person may not be so for another, based on a "principle of appropriateness" (Zimmermann 1980) common to many Indian understandings (see also Raheja 1988, 91, 201–202; Daniel 1984, 79–95, 184–188). My associate Aruna explained to me that people consider it both dangerous and polluting for a woman to wash her own menstrual clothing (though many do it). To do so means that the pollution (tīṭṭu) of menstrual blood stays in the household. This is said to endanger a household's capacity for growth and production (*virutti*). A female Dhobi, a woman of the Washerman jāti, however, is an appropriate cleaner of such clothing: she may wash anyone's soiled (tīṭṭu) clothing and, as one woman told me, "she won't know [experience] a thing" (*avaḷakku oṉṉum teṟiyātu*). Likewise, a Barber or a Dhobi or a Brahman priest who takes tāṉam or cutantiram need not worry about the faults and evils of the donors they take in. I was told, in so many terms, that evils "will not stick to," "will not be enough," "will not accrue in," "will not strike" (*oṭṭātu, pattātu, kiṭṭātu, takkātu*) these recipients. It is their special labor (toḻil), their capacity/skill *(cāmarttiyam)*, or even their "function" (as some dictionaries gloss "toḻil").

Brahmans, because they know the precise verbal formulas (mantras) and are aided by a relatively light and subtle bodily quality (*kuṇam*), are able to "digest" evils and other negatives. They process them through their superior bodies and out, finally, to the wastelands. For kuṭimakkaḷ, as Andi Muppanar, Aruna, and others expressed it, negative substances are seen to cause no harm because their bodies always-already partake of a more chaotic, mixed, and hot nature that matches the negatives they take in. In some ways, these kuṭimakkaḷ are, then, ritual specialists; thus, their specialty is raised to privilege.

While the givers of cutantiram are eager to send their negative qualities out to others and/or out to the wild wasteland, not all of the receivers of cutantiram are quite so philosophical or sanguine about the effects that accepting these prestations may have on them. Indeed, what the respected elder Andi Muppanar (as well as Hocart and Brubaker) turned into a kind of privilege, others call *cāpattīṭu*, "the disastrous affects of a curse" levied by god (*kaṭavuḷ*) on those who are born into the families of Barbers and Washermen. And as Jonathan Parry has shown, Brahmans too may not always be so sanguine about their capacity to digest the evils of others. Brahman funeral priests in Banaras find their capacity to digest others' evils to be impeded. They take in more than they can digest and they are often uneducated in the rituals needed to digest these evils. Because they accumulate the evils of others but do not digest them all, they describe themselves as the "cess-pit[s] for the wickedness of the cosmos" and predict for themselves an unfortunate fate (Parry 1980, 89).

Residents of Middle Ūr (the neighborhood of the ash "thief") have their own place in the sets of kuṭimai relations. First, Middle Ūr residents clearly engage in the "mutual" transactions depicted above. In return for their field labor, they receive grain as cutantiram in addition to a daily wage. Second, as residents of the exteriorized kuṭis (hamlets), Middle Ūr (kuṭi) residents may be said to partake of the chaotic disordering qualities of place that characterize the exterior, the wasteland, the kāṭu, the place to which evils, faults, and other morally disruptive substances are sent.

Indeed, it is just such qualities that led a few older Brahman residents to contrast these days of chickens and goats with a more fondly remembered time when S. C. kuṭimakkaḷ, and to a lesser extent Thevars as well, would not enter the Brahman street at all but would approach houses from side lanes or backyards and shout out their business or needs. The fact that they take more liberties today was, to some Brahman residents in particular, a sign of the village's moral deterioration. Even today, despite the attenuation of many of these restrictions of entry into ūr or house, some residents will not allow S. C. into their houses, at least not beyond the exterior portions of the house—the outer veranda or courtyard. Many consider S. C. to be impure (acuttam) as well as disorderly (*muṟai illāmal*), and their very presence would bring those qualities into the more pure and orderly interiors of ūrmakkaḷ and Brahman lives. Others voiced a different thought, explaining that the qualities of people themselves have changed. The S. C. have become much "neater," as Pichaiya Pillai explained, using the English word.

CUTANTIRAM WITH A KUṬIMAKKAḶ ACCENT

The term "cutantiram" has a double meaning in Tamil. On the one hand, it refers to those evil-bearing gifts that free ūrmakkaḷ of their moral burdens for a time and that taint the kāṭu and kuṭimakkaḷ with disorderly qualities. From the ūrmakkaḷ's point of view, this function is critical not only for their household's well-being and growth (virutti) but also for the well-being and productivity of the whole rice-growing ūr. Just as Raheja (1988) reports for Pahansu and Wadley and Derr report for Karimpur (1989), in Yanaimangalam as well, the well-being of the whole village depends on the productive capacity of the landowners, which in turn depends upon the proper disposal of production-hindering negatives, be they evils (pāvam), tiruṣṭi, or other faults. An ūrmakkaḷ overwhelmed with faults and evils would threaten the well-being of that "whole" they synechdochally suffuse.

On the other hand, "cutantiram" means independence, including the freedom for national self-determination celebrated as Indian Independence Day on August 15 (Cutantiranal). For many kuṭimakkaḷ, these two meanings are irreconcilable. Abiding by one means rejecting the other. Either they help ūrmakkaḷ and the ūr remain free of evils by becoming receptacles and channels of negative substances, thus consenting to their own bound position of subordination, or they free themselves from those ties and achieve their own independence. Though many kuṭimakkaḷ who served ūrmakkaḷ of Yanaimangalam were deeply tied to their service relations—and some not without genuine and mutual affection and care—others resented those service relations and were working to attenuate them. They did not consent to the exterior and inferior moral position kuṭimai offers them, nor did they consent to the system of meaning that suggests that their failure to embody their landlords' moral failings will lead ultimately to their own downfall as dependent members of the ūr.

Two strategies available for achieving freedom from subordination in an idiom of kuṭimai were (1) leaving the village altogether and entering into a more class-based political economy available in nonagricultural labor and (2) staying at home and struggling to attenuate or reframe certain aspects of interjāti relations in a subtle politics of meaning.

Leaving

Many residents of Yanaimangalam, convinced, like Aruna, that "this village never changes," see their only hope for freedom from domination in relocation to other, bigger towns where, as one older S.C. couple who had made the move put it, "caste differences don't matter" (*jāti vityācam teriyātu*). Some have achieved this relocation through migration for work, mostly factory labor. Other families invest in their children's education, which they hope will enable at least the children to find employment elsewhere. The kids study Internet technology, computer applications, engineering, and education in search not only for a new place to work but also for a rise in class status and the trappings that status entails (motorbikes, refrigerators, VCRs, imported goods, marriages into a higher class, etc.). For most kuṭimakkaḷ families, this education is possible only by securing usurious loans with annual interest rates of up to 120 percent, loans that further imperil the family's ultimate quest for a better life. And many of those village youths who have achieved their B.A.s and M.A.s still lack the cultural capital to find employment and end up back in the village working alongside their parents in the fields again.

This dream for a better life was poignantly depicted by Muppatati, a 13-year-old girl from South Ūr, who both before and after school each day worked as a servant for a high-caste family in a neighboring village for little more than food and clothes. Muppatati's goal was to finish the tenth grade and then enter the police academy to become a "woman police." Other kids, such as Aruna's son Joti, went to college to study science, determined to become engineers. Aruna too dreamed of a better life through education. When I first knew her in 1988, she was about 30 years old and was busily taking a correspondence course in secretarial skills. Later she secured an M.A. in social work, also by correspondence. Yet still she could find no work other than the development work she performed day in and day out for a pittance. By 2003, students were pinning their dreams on Internet technology. But many of these students, such as Raja of Middle Ūr, were disappointed. Raja, like many eager college students, could not find employment and has had to return to field labor at home, and returning home presents its own dangers.

Many educated young men from kuṭimakkaḷ families fear for their safety if they stay in the village, for some ūrmakkaḷ youths turn to that age-old method of keeping people in their place: violence. By 2001, Aruna's son Joti had studied all the way to his M.S. in chemistry. Unemployed and looking for work, Joti was staying at his mother's sister's house in a larger town about twenty miles away for fear of being beaten up at home. By 2003, he had a low-paying teaching position in a polytechnic (barely enough to live on at 2,000 rupees per month, about 50 dollars), and his parents, who had accrued thousands in usurious loans, were struggling just to keep up with the monthly interest.

Commodities presented to village residents by relatives who have migrated (saffron from Dubai, a rechargeable flashlight, a motorbike, a VCR, or fashionable clothes) often stand as fetishized signs of a better life. Those who do migrate return home periodically with tales of neighborhoods where people of all jātis live next door to one another without a thought. I heard this refrain so frequently in conversations with S. C. residents of Yanaimangalam that it was clearly a common point of discussion. So the migrants bring home a discourse that feeds egalitarian dreams and leave some village residents speaking of their own village as a backward isolated place, a hick village (*paṭṭikkāṭu*) where "nothing ever changes." Of course, what they do not notice is that the presence of such a discourse of disillusionment relative to the idealization of a commodified class-based urban life is itself a change.

Staying

Those who remain behind in Yanaimangalam use other, more subtle, means of declaring dignity. The ways in which kuṭimakkaḷ understood, as well as worked to redefine or limit, the meanings of kuṭimakkaḷ-ūrmakkaḷ relations can be seen in several sorts of everyday acts, beginning with utterances that name things. The use of jāti names is one arena of political discourse about rank and privilege, on the one hand, and egalitarian expression, on the other. Specific kuṭimakkaḷ jāti names function pragmatically to create contexts of subordination, whether of kuṭi to ūr, hut to house, or kuṭimakaṉ to landlord. A preferred alternative exists for every kuṭimakkaḷ jāti name. "Pallar" and "Palaiyar" prefer S. C.—though for some the more national, political term "Dalit" has come into use in more recent years—and the Iluvar preferred "Illuttuppillai." Washermen find their Tamil name, "Vaṇṇāṉ," degrading and hence prefer the more neutral (in Tamilnadu) Hindi term "Dhobi." The nonbarbering Barbers (Nacāvan) simply claimed to be Thevars to strangers such as myself. The old kuṭimakkaḷ jāti names are used almost exclusively by ūrmakkaḷ and not even by them if they wish to display an egalitarian ideology, such as that supported and disseminated by many development projects, some of which are at work in Yanaimangalam. Even the word "kuṭimakaṉ" is not a term that those to whom it applies choose for themselves unless they are looking for protection or are poor enough to need patronage, as is the Washerman from North Hamlet who came every day to the Big Ūr to collect scraps of leftover food from the families he served.

Pronouns, it is well known, also function pragmatically. It is common for Tamils to use the nonhonorific form of the Tamil second-person pronoun (*nī*) when referring to anyone ranking lower than they, whether by age, gender, or jāti. Conversely, those who rank lower (younger siblings, wives, or kuṭimakkaḷ) use the honorific second-person pronoun (*nīṅkaḷ*) when addressing higher-ranking people (older siblings, husbands, or ūrmakkaḷ). The use of reciprocal honorifics is complicated. As Levinson notes, it can serve to acknowledge equality, what village residents would call *camam*. But it can also connote a "lack of affection" and so create hurt feelings, as I demonstrate in Chapter 4. However, when used among adults, it usually connotes "mutual respect." Part of Aruna's World Bank–project job was to visit each house in the village where an infant or small child lived, weigh the child, and provide nutritional counseling and supplements when required. She was instructed by her employers to address all adults (usually she dealt with mothers) of all jātis of whatever location or rank using the honorific second-person pronoun *nīṅkaḷ*. Her compliance with this regulation led members of her own street to poke fun at her for addressing S. C. women honorifically, yet it also brought into reality a daily practice of egalitarian ideology and so reconstituted the shape of relations possible between Aruna and S. C. hamlet residents while also inviting discourse on egalitarian practice.

Many kuṭimakkaḷ foregrounded or maintained that aspect of their relationship to ūrmakkaḷ landlords that can be construed as "mutual"—that is, as transactions of service for grain—while foregoing or attenuating the second aspect that connotes subordination and/or the transfer of negatives. Some may even choose to refuse certain kinds of "gifts" from ūrmakkaḷ and thereby attenuate some of the, in their eyes, more degrading aspects of their responsibilities to the ūrmakkaḷ. For example, one of the Carpenter families in Yanaimangalam stopped accepting certain kinds of items from their landlords. They stopped accepting a cutantiram known more specifically as *Poṅkal paṭi*. Poṅkal paṭi, a small token usually consisting of a rupee coin or two, or sometimes, following more customary practices, a paṭi measure of rice (about 1.5 kilograms), is given to kuṭimakkaḷ on the occasion of Tai Poṅkal, an annual agricultural ritual. In conducting a survey on who received what as cutantiram, I asked the Carpenter family if they received Poṅkal paṭi. They said no. Later I learned that one of the Carpenter's kuṭimakkaḷ duties was to provide their ūrmakkaḷ patron with a wooden ladle for making poṅkal—the special rice dish for which the holiday is named. And when I asked one ūrmakkaḷ neighbor why they didn't then give Carpenters paṭi for that service, she countered, "Oh, but we do!" She suggested that the Carpenter had lied to me, that she had seen for herself last year that the Carpenter had come around collecting paṭi from houses he served.

Next time I visited the Carpenters, who lived over on the outer edge of Thevar Street, I pestered them again and asked if they had ever, perhaps in the past, received Poṅkal paṭi. The Carpenter's wife admitted that they used to collect paṭi. I asked why they stopped. She said they did not like going around from house to house like beggars, standing out on the street and waiting for handouts.

Like Middle Ūr's planned boycott of the goddess temple, this refusal to collect certain kinds of cutantiram may be seen as a way to separate from the subordination and shame (*veṭkam*) that kuṭimakkaḷ-ūrmakkaḷ relations entail. Some kuṭimakkaḷ, such as the Barbers, have been able to stop all such giving and receiving with ūrmakkaḷ. Structural changes have in recent years also helped many S. C. attenuate some of their labor dependence on ūrmakkaḷ. In particular, most farmers in Yanaimangalam have converted many of their fields from rice to bananas, which fetch a much better price. Unlike rice, the banana harvest is organized not by the farmer but in most cases by middlemen, exporters who come with their trucks to load bananas that they then transport for shipment overseas, mostly to the Middle East. These men contract for labor independently of the field owner and in 2003 were paying a cash wage of 100 rupees per day, plus meals, to S. C. and other laborers. This alienated labor frees kuṭimakkaḷ from the denigrating attachments that permeate the rice harvest.

Middle Ūr is a place where people dream of a better future. Indeed, it was in Middle Ūr and the other S. C. hamlets where I heard such discourse most of all. So when Middle Ūr residents were stung by an explicit exclusionary power play in the wake of a man taking a pinch of ash, that event came to signify everything about "what never changes" as against what could be. But before returning to analyze the ash theft, we must consider another aspect of interjāti and, more broadly, interpersonal relations that also lends meaning to the ash incident, namely mariyātai.

FOUR

Making Social Distinctions

"Mariyātai" means "distinction." It is the most prevalent idiom of rank and social differentiation in Tamilnadu. Most transactions, from greetings to commodity transactions to ash smearings, signify multivocalically, and one meaningful outcome of most actions in Tamilnadu is mariyātai or its lack. To "give mariyātai" (*mariyātai koṭu*) is to enunciate and create social distinctions among interacting and transacting persons. Mariyātai is a relational product, something people produce when they give and receive. Since people give and receive everything from food to ash and words to gestures, mariyātai is, practically speaking, a potential effect of all transactions—indeed, all social actions.

My neighbor Parvathi was renowned for being one of the more rank-conscious residents of the village, particularly in matters of caste rankings. Her consciousness of rank made her an expert in making social distinctions, in making mariyātai. Parvathi had charge over two houses on the Brahman street, the Agraharam. Like many of the older houses in the Agraharam, both of these houses were relatively large two-story houses. They were airy, with high ceilings and rough-tile or polished-cement floors that were cool to the touch even on hot days and nights. The house in which she lived she inherited from her mother. The other house, two doors down, belonged to her "older brother" (here her parallel cousin, her father's brother's son). Since this cousin-brother lived 1,000 miles north in Allahabad, his empty house served conveniently as Parvathi's grain storage. She also used the well and pump in the back courtyard of his house to draw water when her own pump broke down. When I say "she used," I mean that she directed others to use. Parvathi herself, being somewhat elderly as well as tiny and bent from a congenital disability, would not often venture outside her own house. The men who, as a favor to her, took care of her field and grain and the young woman who worked for her as a servant often had occasion to ask Parvathi for the key to the second house when they were working on her behalf.

One day I was sitting and talking with Parvathi on her "inner veranda" (*uḷ tiṇṇai*), a porch room enclosed on three sides but open on the fourth side to the street. Vertical cage-like bars blocked easy access from the street for anything but raucous sparrows and the gazes of passersby. Pandi, the eldest son of the Thevar family who tended her field, came by to get the key in order to move some of the grain stored in the second house. He was a young man, just recently married. We watched through the veranda bars as he walked down the sun-drenched street toward her house. As he turned and approached the "outer veranda" (*veḷi tiṇṇai,* or *teru tiṇṇai*), really just a narrow stoop outside the house abutting the street, he lowered his hiked-up veṣti to its full floor length. Parvathi called him in. He climbed the three steps up into the shady veranda and asked politely for the key. She stood and handed him the key.

Later that day Balamma, the young unmarried woman of the vegetarian Pillaimar jāti who worked as Parvathi's servant, came to get the key in order to fetch water for Parvathi. She too came down the same sun-drenched street. When she came to the outer veranda, she ventured no further inside and from there asked for the key, which Parvathi found and then threw out the door. It clattered down the few steps to the cement stoop outside. Balamma stooped to pick it up.

Many of the acts that took place in these everyday and apparently simple interactions make mariyātai: Pandi lowered his veṣti and waited to be called inside; he deferred verbally to Parvathi using honorific pronoun and verb forms and he called her by a fictive kin term, "mother-in-law"/"father's sister" (attai); Balamma stayed outside on the stoop and bent to pick up the key, referring to Parvathi all the while with honorifics. In these ways, Pandi and Balamma both gave Parvathi mariyātai. Their manners of approaching Parvathi and receiving the key made social distinctions: they distinguished Parvathi as a person of high rank. Parvathi, for her part, gave mariyātai back to Pandi by calling him inside and standing up to hand him the key directly. She later explained to me how it was important to give Pandi's family mariyātai because of how much they help her out. Parvathi gave no mariyātai to Balamma, her servant. She threw the key outside, where Balamma stooped to pick it up. Parvathi also *distinguished* Pandi from Balamma by giving mariyātai to him but not to her. It is important to note that Balamma is of a much higher jāti than Pandi, though her family is relatively impoverished compared to his, so these rankings are not presupposed by caste. As Viramma, a rural Tamil woman interviewed by the Racines (1997, 160) comments, "In this *kāḷiyugam,* money's the master and when you know how to earn it, you make yourself higher than you were the day before."

Many signs of distinction (mariyātai) are spatial: bend your knees to bow lower, cover your mouth and lower your eyes, stay outside, lower your veṣti, give with your right hand or with both hands (right cupped in left), step aside to let a person pass. For now, it is important to keep in mind that mariyātai is not so much about the thing given—mariyātai does not necessarily inhere in things—but is rather a product of how *some* thing (ash, temple distribution, word, gesture, look) is given (or said or done). Mariyātai may result from the manner in which an item is given to one person as opposed to another, as in the example above. It may result from the spatial-temporal order in which one person or set of persons receives an item of exchange relative to others. It may result, as in the example above, from where a transaction takes place—whether it takes place inside or outside. Or mariyātai may result from the simple fact that one person receives an item while others around them do not. In matters of mariyātai it is, to borrow Levi-Strauss's familiar phrase, the differences that make the difference.

I will analyze mariyātai in detail as both an everyday and political-ritual idiom of social differentiation. Understanding some of its codes and its subtleties helps disclose not only further meanings of the ash theft and its outcomes but also subtle acts of subversion and reversal I will discuss in later chapters, acts through which lower and excluded jātis in part redefine their place in the ūr, as in life. I focus on two aspects of this complex concept of mariyātai: (1) mariyātai as a "line" or "series" of transitive rank and (2) mariyātai as a kind of inclusion versus exclusion from a group. Beyond the public displays of mariyātai that tend to follow predictable flows of rank by jāti, age, and gender, we will also see that mariyātai is a subtle, shifting language of interpersonal relationship that often defies expected purity rankings and jāti exclusions and so defies any sense of "normativity" or "transitivity" in matters of interpersonal relations between persons of different purity, wealth, and political standing. After working through these two aspects of mariyātai, I will return to the ash theft. Mariyātai, it turns out, is partly a matter of watching your step and of getting your ash the proper way.

LINES OF MARIYĀTAI

In many formalized contexts such as life-crisis rituals and temple rituals, ordered transactions of certain items and substances (including words) sort participants into single-file mariyātai "lines" or "series" (*mariyātai varicai*). Sometimes these lines are visibly displayed as persons stand or sit in orders of precedence. Since this common practice of creating lines of mariyātai is such a public and visible expression of social ranking, several scholars of South Asia have provided detailed analyses of mariyātai as an abiding expression of and means for creating unilineal rankings—most commonly understood as rankings by jāti—in a variety of social contexts, ranging from household and lineage rituals (Beck 1972; Dumont 1986/1957) to community-temple distributions (Dumont 1986/1957; Appadurai and Breckenridge 1976; Dirks 1987) to political speeches (Bernard Bate, personal communication) to linguistic forms used pragmatically (Levinson 1982).

The most extensively analyzed contexts for studying lines of mariyātai are temple distributions. Beck reports, based on research conducted in the 1960s, on the "fixed order" for distributing temple prasad (such as ash and food) established in temples in a village in northern Tamilnadu (1972, 174). Dumont's ethnographic work in central Tamilnadu in the 1940s reports, similarly, that temple distributions called "honors" (which he translates from *mutalmai,* or precedence, literally "firstness") followed a "traditional hierarchical sequence" (1986/1957, 417). Dirks too, writing of a politically "hollow" little kingdom in central Tamilnadu in the 1970s, writes that all his "informants concurred that their own standing and prestige in society was more importantly determined by their position in the temple, signified by honors, than by anything else, including the amount of lands they held" (1987, 290).

The temple "honors" (mariyātai, also māṉam) that Dirks and others describe are constituted in part by objects[1] that persons have rights to receive, for which they compete with others. These rights were staunchly protected and often adjudicated precolonially by local big men or royalty and subsequently by colonial and then Indian courts of law (see, e.g., Appadurai 1981, 165–211; Presler 1987). The objects may be silk vestments of the deity, garlands taken from around the deity's neck, and even common substances such as ash and food leavings that are made "honorific" by virtue of the very order in which they are distributed. These orders of distribution tend to follow a relatively fixed pattern, established as a set of rights (urimai) which may be inscribed into temple walls, copper plates, or (more frequently these days) in books and on plaques. I say "relatively" fixed because, in fact, new "big men" and even "big women" are made every day, as communities, such as Yanaimangalam's Thevars, establish social dominance and as individuals move up in the rankings by sponsoring festivals and donating large sums of money to the temple. Indeed, as Viramma stated above, wealth (over embodied jāti qualities, for instance) is increasingly an important factor in determining mariyātai orderings. Ramayya Thevar complained to me similarly one day, stating that it's now money, not a person's qualities (kuṇam) or anything else, that causes people to give mariyātai (see also Lamb 2000, 34).[2]

Lines of mariyātai (mariyātai varicai) both denote and—this is important—*constitute* orders of rank and authority within temple communities. As Dirks writes,

> Thus the gifting activity which has created and sustained so many temples in Southern India has at its root the goal of entering the temple community, and then increasing one's rank within it and one's relative proximity to the deity. (Dirks 1987, 287)

We have previously seen how North Ūr Thevars attempted to enter the goddess-temple community, for example. In 1989, they paid their required share of the temple tax. However, they were denied shares in the temple distributions and hence were denied their place in the community. When in protest they refused to pay tax the following year, they sealed tight their exclusion. "If you don't pay tax to the village goddess, you can't be in this village," said Ramayya Thevar. To be excluded from the distribution of shares in the temple is to be excluded from the community itself. The S. C. of Middle Ūr, of course, had no shares to begin with, and in rank they came last, standing and waiting for the priest to make his way through all the other worshipers and toss them leftovers from above to their lowly station outside and below the raised temple grounds.

In Yanaimangalam, lines of mariyātai are most vividly articulated in temple distributions and in life-crisis rituals. For example, the leftover foods and other items that have been offered to gods during temple pūja are distributed as divine leftovers, or prasad, in an established, though often contested and certainly changeable, sequence (varicai). The sequence of mariyātai is articulated both temporally and spatially: highest-ranked persons receive their shares earlier than others and in a more proximal position to the god. When priests distribute ash and other items of prasad, they move down rows of receivers, with the first few persons in the row receiving what are termed "first distinction" (*mutal mariyātai*), then second, third, and so on. Once the first few receive, the order becomes less definitely specified according to number, person, or family and more loosely defined by larger groupings such as jāti, gender, and age. Persons who are relatively high (ocanta) and pure (cuttam) among jātis, men among genders, and more generous among temple donors situate themselves closer to the head of the row while others make room for them to do so. Making room is also a way to confer mariyātai. During major rituals in the goddess temple, for example, Brahmans occupy the positions closest to the gods, the headmen and other big men of the ūrmakkaḷ jātis cluster themselves next, women defer to men by crowding together in the rear of the temple, while S. C. wait outside. Needless to say, in the dense and packed crowds at some festivals, there is much jostling as people claim places closer to the front, and at times the priests must pause to find the person they know has rightful precedence. In life-crisis rituals, ranked distinctions are articulated through the order in which *givers* are called to give. This is most clearly evident in the sequences in which adult relatives and guests give gifts and smear ash onto the bodies of subjects undergoing the rituals, especially weddings and girls' puberty rituals, sequences that generally follow age, closeness in kinship, and gender.

The lines of mariyātai described here so far all occur publicly in political-ritual displays where unilineal orders of precedence are laid out in a clear spatial-temporal order for all to see. In everyday life, however, rankings are more subtle and must be inferred from a discontinuous set of activities. Such inferred rankings are familiar to students of South Asia who have read about rankings that are inferred based on food-sharing, on degrees of access to certain restricted spaces, and on the reported use of honorific pronouns. Single orderings of such discontinuous data can be made by participants or observers only by presuming an implicit rule of transitivity (Levinson 1982), where if A ranks higher than B and B ranks higher than C, then A ranks higher than C. A rule of symmetry, what Levinson calls "alliance," may also apply, where if two persons symmetrically exchange foods or pronouns or other acts, they are considered to be of equal rank in that context.[3]

In the next section, I present an example of such inferred rankings by following two god-dancers as they go in their Firepot Procession through the village streets, giving out ash to everyone they pass. While we have seen that ash distributions constitute lines of mariyātai at temples and at life-crisis rituals, there are other ways in which ash smearings imply ranked distinctions. In particular, the manner in which ash is distributed, and by whom and to whom, matters a great deal.

Inferring Rank

At temple festivals, ash transactions are dense: outstretched hands surround and follow priests and god-dancers, who push through the crowds hastily flouring palms and foreheads. Fathers and mothers smear their children, older siblings smear younger ones, and during temple processions up and down the village's streets, people wait lined along their house stoops for the god-dancers to bring them not only darśan, the sight of the god or goddess possessing them, but also any smidgeon of cooling ash. I remember one old toothless woman who emerged out of shadows as I followed the 1990 procession through the village at 2 A.M.: her mouth and cheeks and chin were covered with white ash that she consumed eagerly, purifying herself inside and out.

During the 1989 goddess festival, I watched, compared, and then asked about the way that Turairaja, the Thevarmar firepot dancer, and Arunacalam Pillai, the Pillaimar firepot dancer, distributed ash as they flamed their way down the jāti-integrated "Brahman street." From the manner in which they each distributed ash it was possible to discern a difference in rank between them as well as among the devotees lining the streets. These ranked distinctions generally conformed to village residents' normative assessment of village jāti rankings based on idioms of relative purity (cuttam) and orderliness (oḻuṅku): the peaceful, cool, vegetarian Pillaimar man would be thought to rank higher than what many village residents would consider a violence-prone, hot, meat-eating, goat-sacrificing Thevarmar man.

The two dancers made their ways separately down the street in the middle of the night, closer to dawn than dusk. Turairaja Thevar followed Arunacalam Pillai by about half an hour. Before they reached the Agraharam, each had already walked first from the river to the goddess temple at the end of Muppanar Street. It is there that the firepots are fueled and handed over to the dancers. From there they had walked up and down all the other streets and bylanes of the Big Village. The Agraharam was the final street on their route.

They started from the west end of the Agraharam, near the red-and-white-striped Krishna temple, then started down the street, moving east toward the Siva temple, beyond which dawn would soon fracture the night from the dry summer fields. *Mēlam* drums and the boisterous *nataswāram*[4] accompanied the dancers and roused all the sleepers up and out onto their stoops to watch and wait for the firepot dancers to dance past. As they came down the street, the dancers distributed ash from cups held by assistants to all those waiting on their outer verandas—standing, sitting, and squatting under their corrugated-tin or stiff palmyra-frond awnings. In return, families fed the dancers' firepots with oil and poured small bottles of cooling rosewater over their heads. The dancers were drenched with fragrance: rosewater, layers of white jasmine and rose garlands, the sweat of summer and fire and hours of dancing. Long strands of braided jasmine blossoms hung from wilting jasmine caps and streamed over their shoulders and down their bare backs (Figure 2.5). This "shower of flowers" (*pūccōri*) twisted in the air and reflected the firelight as they turned and danced. Ash flew everywhere.

The first to come down the street was Arunacalam Pillai (Figure 2.5). Creaky, kind, and blind from cataracts, he did more than merely hand ash to people. He smeared ash directly onto their foreheads. He smeared almost everyone except certain older men and Brahmans—male and female, adult and child—to whom he instead handed ash, dropping it into the cupped hands they stretched out to him. When he and his entourage came to me, I was uncertain just what to do, and so he and I did our own dance. His hand went to smear my forehead just as I, unknowingly with arrogance, stretched my cupped hands out to receive his ash. No sooner had he lowered his pinch of ash to hand-level, matching my movements, when I suddenly caught on. I raised my right hand up to cover my mouth and nose in the deference (mariyātai) gesture I had observed others make. I bent my knees slightly, and craned my forehead toward him. He again raised his hand. He smeared my forehead decisively. Ash dusted my eyelashes. He moved on down the street.

When I dragged myself out of my cot half an hour later at five A.M. to watch the much-younger and more-vigorous Turairaja Thevar dance down the street, I expected a similar scene but was surprised to find him smearing very few people directly. Instead, he handed out ash to almost everyone. Those he smeared directly were for the most part Thevars, and even among Thevars only children, women, and men younger than himself. When he came to me, he placed ash into my outstretched palm. I smeared myself. (After finishing his rounds, he came again to give me a jasmine garland, bedraggled from bottle after bottle of rosewater, from the heat of the dance and air, from sweat and yet still sweet-smelling. This was mariyātai, my assistant Hari told me, for it was valuable prasad from the goddess who inhabits the god-dancer and his firepot, and I was the one to whom he gave it.)

Later, when I asked the reason for the different ash-distribution techniques (asked why, that is, Turairaja Thevar handed it out while Arunacalam Pillai smeared most people directly), I received the same simple answer from several different people: "That's mariyātai," they explained.

Here, as in the example of Parvathi's key, mariyātai is made in bodily and spatial acts. When Arunacalam Pillai gave ash into the cupped hands of my Brahman neighbors, including the youngest girl, who was 12 years old, he was giving her and her family mariyātai because, as Parvathi (herself a Brahman) told me, they are Brahmans. But when he smeared people directly, it was they who gave mariyātai to him: bending at the knees, covering their nose and mouth, saying "You smear me!" (*nīṅka pūcaṅka*) using deferential pronouns and verb forms. By comparing the different ways the dancers smeared different people, it is possible to infer (1) that Arunacalam Pillai ranks higher than Turairaja Thevar (for the former smears almost all but the Brahmans, while the latter smears no one but younger or female members of his own jāti) and (2) that Arunacalam Pillai ranks higher than all the other jātis on the street except Brahmans, while Turairaja Thevar ranks among the lowest on the street (for the former smears Pillaimar, Nayakkar, Muppanar, and Thevarmar, while the latter smears only Thevarmar). In each one of these myriad acts of smearing over the course of their entire five-hour route, the givers and receivers not only conform to acknowledged rankings, they remake and reinforce those rankings publicly. Any change in method could, in fact, challenge or subvert those rankings as well.

These two ash-smearing techniques do not, however, exhaust the god-dancers' repertoire. A third technique brings home the point that ash smearings mark as well as make distinctions, make mariyātai. A few weeks after the "ash theft," I watched a procession from S. C. Middle Ūr make its way from Middle Ūr to their own Panaiyatiyan ("He at the Base of the Palmyra Tree") temple, which was located at some distance down the road leading out of the village.

To get to their temple from Middle Ūr, the community had in previous years walked directly over the fields (which are empty and dry during the summer festival season). This year, however, they changed their route and walked in procession through the main village. Before entering the Big Ūr, their procession worked its way around and up and down all the lanes of Middle Ūr, where the several god-dancers stopped at households—all of them S. C. Pallar households—to smear and hand out ash. During this portion of the procession, the S. C. god-dancers used the same two methods described above. Generally speaking, men older than the god-dancers received ash in the hand while all others—younger men, all women, and all children—were smeared directly on their forehead. Among the god-dancers for Middle Ūr was one woman (the only female god-dancer in Yanaimangalam). She handed ash to all men, smearing only other women and children directly. In other words, mariyātai distinctions for the most part followed distinctions of relative age and gender—jāti here being moot, since they were all of one jāti.

The procession then moved out of Middle Ūr, down the narrow lane that curves through the rice fields, and about a quarter-mile later turned up onto Muppanar Street. As usual, all the residents of houses on the procession route came out onto their stoops, watched, and waited for ash. What I saw surprised me. As the S. C. god-dancers came along the street in procession, they bent at the knees and waist, looked down to the ground, and stretched out their arms to offer up their ash cups to the ūrmakkaḷ. Residents of Muppanar Street pinched their own ash from the cups. They smeared themselves and their families.

INTRANSITIVITY AND MARIYĀTAI

While the lines of mariyātai I have described so far follow presupposed rankings among jātis in Yanaimangalam, the fact is that the jāti rankings themselves do not make mariyātai. People do the making through their actions. In highly visible ritual settings where the village displays itself to itself *as if* it had a frozen structure, villagers do tend to remake ranks that conform to expectations based on previous jāti rankings. But in less-public everyday contexts, people commonly make or give mariyātai in ways that subvert or surprise such presupposed rankings, as the examples below show.

Levinson states that intransitive relations among castes (for example, a case where A ranks higher than B, B higher than C, and C higher than A) is tantamount to "chaos" and "simply couldn't happen" (1982, 126). Yet, as Beck has noted (1972, 155), everyday jāti interactions may not follow the same "formalized" lines of rank that are instantiated in temple distributions and life-crisis rituals. In other words, in everyday life, mariyātai transactions often contradict simple transitivity rules such as those presumed by Levinson, where mariyātai is given from lower to higher along a single dimension of rank and where, therefore, ranks can be inferred along that line. Ranking in everyday life opens up a space for rethinking rank through multiple variables and opens up the space for thinking of oneself and acting in a manner other than that displayed in the relatively fixed ranks of temple ritual. And indeed, as I will argue later, even within the context of temple ritual it is exactly the "chaos" of alternative rankings that calls into question dominant, would-be hegemonic, rank orders.

Turairaja Thevar, who dances the firepot during the goddess festival, also dances for the goddess out at another temple to Cutalaimatan ("Fierce God of the Cremation Ground"). One night during Cutalaimatan's big festival in 1990, Turairaja Thevar (a center of attention at this festival) singled out a man by going out of his way to walk over to him, stretch out his arm, and offer him some ash. Aruna watched me make note of this transaction and offered, "That's mariyātai." I asked her to explain. This man was from her own neighborhood, South Street, and like her was of a distinctively low-ranking jāti, Illuttuppillai. She elaborated that Turairaja Thevar's act of actually walking over to the man and handing him some ash (rather than waiting to be approached and then smearing him directly) was mariyātai. Why did he do it? Because her neighbor dances the firepot for the goddess in his hamlet for his jāti's goddess temple, she said, he is the "same" as or "equal" to (camam) Turairaja Thevar. By approaching him, Turairaja Thevar publicly acknowledged this sameness and so gave the man mariyātai. Turairaja Thevar purposefully distinguished this man who was of lower jāti, who was not part of the temple community in question, who labored in fields not his own, who was not wealthy, and who was of a low jāti residing outside Big Yanaimangalam.

Another example: one day, I was walking home along the road from the highway because the bus that goes all the way into Yanaimangalam was experiencing what village residents referred to in English as "breakdown." I caught up with Aruna and Mira, the Brahman schoolmaster's 19-year-old daughter, who had been walking on the road ahead of me. We all walked together. As we approached the fields that belonged to Yanaimangalam, we saw that an old Thevar man, head of his lineage, happened to be at the roadside shrine of his family deity, the goddess Issakkiyamman. He was the priest of that temple and was doing pūja there. We stopped to pray to the goddess. She is a fierce goddess, and we were crossing her path—for that reason alone, a prayer was definitely in order. After we prayed (it takes only a moment, the smallest of gestures), the priest proffered his cup of ash to us. Mira, a Brahman teenager, took a generous pinch. Aruna declined to take any directly from the cup, so Mira cupped and stretched out her hands to offer Aruna some of the ash that she had taken. Aruna took some of the vipūti Mira proffered and smeared herself. I asked the priest to please give some to me (*nīṅka koṭuṅka*) and stretched out my hands to accept it. He dropped a pinch into my cupped hands. I smeared myself.

These three acts were not preplanned, not unilineal, not transitive, and they certainly did not follow neatly any kind of presupposed jāti ranking. Neither did they conform to presupposed rankings of gender or relative age. Indeed, what Levinson might characterize as impossibly chaotic intransitivity pervades this example. Each of us had our own reasons for transacting the way we did. Mira, as a Brahman and the schoolmaster's daughter, had grown up in a family to which others tended to defer and was at ease accepting the mariyātai the Thevar priest offered her. When he proffered the cup she took her pinch of ash without hesitation, easily asserting her own higher and closer position to the goddess as well as her rank above this old man. Aruna later told me that she would never even consider taking ash directly from the priest's cup for fear (*payam*) that such an act would anger the goddess. Aruna deferred to the priest (by shying from his deference to her) and instead took her ash from her young teenage companion. Mira offered Aruna the ash in a manner that also gave Aruna mariyātai: she offered Aruna her ash-filled palm rather than giving her a pinch of ash from her hand. Worried about offending any person or goddess, I played it safe by giving the priest mariyātai, asking him politely to give me some ash into my outstretched hand.

The priest (an old man and a Thevar) tried to defer to everyone (probably due the presence of Mira, a Brahman, and myself, a white foreigner), but he succeeded in deferring only to the higher-caste rank of Mira, the youngest among us—still a girl really, and not even married yet. Mira deferred to the seniority of Aruna (whose jāti, Illuttuppillai, is considered low-ranking, as noted). Aruna, by refusing to accept the priest's deference to her, deferred to him (her refusal was accompanied by other modest bodily positionings that make mariyātai along different channels). Chaotic? The point of course is that none of the persons taking part in this brief event acted simply according to their caste components along a one-dimensional ranking. Rather, they acted as complex persons from many uniquely situated points of view constituted by past experiences, feelings, and ideas about the world. They made and remade their relationships with others, and their sense of self, with even the most habitual of everyday gestures.

Levinson's work on mariyātai, which focuses on the use of honorific pronouns, typifies an approach that emphasizes presupposed structures and contexts and downplays pragmatic creative use. That is, he analyzes actions *according to their context* and tends to see *use* as reflecting structure (like *parole* reflects *langue* in Saussurian linguistics or like behavior reflects cognition in cognitive psychology). Levinson, that is, encloses his analysis of pronoun use within an encompassing structure of rank and lets a priori orderings take over as the causal factors or agents in pronoun use, such that the enunciation of a pronoun merely reflects or at most "ratifies" extant structures (1982, 110–111, 154–155). Any deviation from expected orders are "secondary," "special," or even "ephemeral" (ibid., 110–111). His prior insistence on a single order makes this simple example of three actors exchanging ash into one of incomprehensibly complicated disorder. Yet such everyday complexity is as common as the village bus breaking down. Indeed, it is during such everyday and ephemeral interactions that actors open up a space for alternative reckonings of social life and social order as they also remake their own capacity for creating their own life among others. Mariyātai does indeed pervade most aspects of life in Yanaimangalam, but how people make it varies. The creative manipulations of mariyātai do much more than reconstitute public jāti rankings. Mariyātai provides a language, a tool, that people use to subvert social orders and to assert alternative orders of social relations in Yanaimangalam.

MARIYĀTAI AS INCLUSION

Mariyātai is not just patterned as a "line" of rank from higher to lower. Mariyātai may also be expressed as a form of inclusion versus exclusion from a community of receivers or givers. In sequences or lines of mariyātai, even the last person to receive mariyātai can claim membership in a community from which others are excluded. Just being included can constitute mariyātai.

On almost any given day, it seemed, someone or another would wend their way through the various streets and lanes of the village, going door to door to present invitations to weddings or puberty rituals or to give curuḷ, a small gift of fruit, sugar, and betel that marks the closure of temple festivals, recent weddings, puberty rituals, pregnancies, and births. On other happy occasions such as passing an exam, having a birthday, and getting a degree, a new job, or a promotion, village residents handed out store-bought pre-packaged sweets such as toffees from door to door. Givers of such tokens would not stop at every door on every street, however. They would pick and choose.

One day I asked Parvathi if giving these small gifts counted as "giving mariyātai." She immediately said "No, girl! These are not mariyātai" (*Illē mā! Atu mariyātai illē*). But after a moment or two, she amended her answer to explain that while the gift itself is not mariyātai, the fact that one person receives it and another does not does indeed constitute mariyātai. If I receive betel, sugar, and fruit after a birth in someone's family while my immediate neighbor does not, the giver is making mariyātai in that she or he is *distinguishing* me from my neighbor.

This example illustrates why I substitute the standard translation of mariyātai as "honor" with the term "distinction." "Honor" connotes a positive objective status, the kind that can be carried in badges and in objects such as gifts. "Distinction" better fits the logic of inclusion described in this example. Mariyātai is not essentially about *what* objects (or gestures or words) you are given. It is about the fact that you are given something while someone else is not or that you are given something in a particular mariyātai-making manner (with lowered veṣti, bowed head, deference pronouns, etc.) or order (first versus last) *relative to someone else*. In Tamil, the first-person plural pronoun functions as an honorific in exactly this way. The inclusive "we" (*nām*) makes mariyātai by including the speaker and the spoken to in one set, while the exclusive pronoun (*nāṅkaḷ*) distinguishes a set of included individuals from a set of excluded individuals and thus is not considered honorific. Again, it's the differences that make the difference, that make mariyātai.

Like publicly displayed sequences of mariyātai, inclusion sets also are sometimes spatially objectified. Those who are excluded are located outside or on the peripheries of an activity, while included persons are located, in network terms, within the "reach" of a specific giver.[5] Take the processions around the village and their accompanying ash transactions during the goddess festival. The god-dancers come around to all the Big Ūr streets and lanes. They stop at each and any house where people wait (to refuse to stop would be a great insult). But where do they not go? They do not go to the S. C. or Illuttuppillai hamlets. In 1990, unlike 1989, they did not go to the North Ūr's Thevar Street. While the drums and nataswāram and dancers and crowd make their way boisterously through the Big Ūr, these hamlets lie quiet across the fields in the ūr's kāṭu. If any residents of those excluded hamlets wish to receive ash from the god-dancers, it is they who must come into the ūr, stand on the edges of the procession route, and so follow the usual pattern of kuṭimai transactions, where it is the receivers who come to collect while the givers remain in central places. Coming to get ash is a way of conferring mariyātai on the giver.

Other exclusions occur as a matter of course. During temple festivals, when certain people receive shares in the distribution of certain leftover substances, others, present and hovering on the edges (not even allowed into the central part of the temple where the distributions take place), are not apportioned a share at all. When government officials come to call, they rarely visit the hamlets. When the government constructed a clean water system in the village, they neglected to put in a pump in the South Ūr, the S. C. Palaiyar hamlet. The residents of South Ūr still had to walk a quarter of a mile for clean water. Many ūrmakkaḷ had never ventured out to the kuṭimakkaḷ hamlets (when I returned from visiting the hamlets, ūrmakkaḷ would ask me questions: What were the houses like on the inside? What were they eating?). This asymmetry may ironically give some power to those on the periphery, a power of knowledge, for while the ūrmakkaḷ know little of the life of the kuṭimakkaḷ, the kuṭimakkaḷ were quite familiar with the big village and all its goings-on.

The inclusion of mariyātai is binary: either one is in the receiving group or one is out. Indeed, it is this contrast of in versus out that confers mariyātai. Any relation of rank among receivers is in this context irrelevant. The important relation that confers mariyātai is parity; that is, sameness in relation to a giver of certain kinds of auspicious gifts.

Kuṭimai, Mariyātai, and Affection

Kuṭimai can also be seen as a kind of inclusion, albeit of a very different kind. The inclusions of kuṭimai are not about mariyātai being conferred on receivers by a giver. Quite the reverse; the inclusions of kuṭimai are all about subordination within a structure of dominance. That is, kuṭimakkaḷ are related to ūrmakkaḷ through a kind of subordinate inclusion in an idiom of hereditary service attachment as "sons" and "daughters" to the ūrmakkaḷ families they serve. It is interesting that such a familial idiom often leads village residents from all walks of life to speak about kuṭimakkaḷ in terms of endearment: a landlord should have affection (*aṉpu*) for his kuṭimakkaḷ. And so the ūrmakkaḷ include "their" kuṭimakkaḷ in an idiom of affection, protection, and even possession. When the ūrmakkaḷ give cutantiram to their kuṭimakkaḷ, they often describe their givings as "gifts of affection" (*aṉpaḷippu*).

Where does mariyātai fold into this relation? In return for affection and protection which flows down and out from the ūrmakkaḷ, the kuṭimakkaḷ give mariyātai up and in. The inclusions of kuṭimai, that is, entail a return flow of mariyātai from the lower ranking and spatially peripheralized kuṭimakkaḷ up to the centrally positioned ūrmakkaḷ. The kuṭimakkaḷ give mariyātai to their ūrmakkaḷ, but they do not often receive it. What they receive is patronage and "affection."

Affection brings a person under the umbrella of patronage. Umbrellas are common metonyms of "the landlord," who at harvest time surveys his workers from under the umbrella's shade. Affection protects and provides as it also subordinates. It is not surprising that among the terms used to describe relations of permanent laborers to their landlord are the encompassing and patronizing (literally) terms "child of the family" (kuṭimakaṉ) and "one's own" (contam) (cf. Inden and Nicholas 1977, 17). To have affection for others is thus to encompass them protectively. This is the strategy of contemporary politicians, some (but not all) development programs, village headmen, family heads, and, as people imagine them, deities.

While rank in an idiom of affection connotes closeness, reciprocal mariyātai between persons in many contexts connotes not so much a "mutual respect" but rather a cold distance. This fact might seem counterintuitive to most Americans, for whom relations of mutual respect feel closer than those of hierarchy and for whom the idea of parents "respecting" their children is not at all a strange concept. But in Tamilnadu, rank differences may indeed entail affection of a kind. For example, I once hurt the feelings of my 20-year-old neighbor, Vijaya, when I used the respectful second-person pronoun (nīṅkaḷ) to address her. She addressed me in this manner, and I thought that by reciprocating this pronoun I could recognize her as a person of equal adult status and thereby make her feel good and full of self-esteem. Instead, I hurt her feelings. She felt I had no affection for her. Aruna explained it all to me. It was more appropriate for me to call her by nonhonorific pronouns because I was a bit older and I had an M.A. In ash-smearing, as in other more everyday contexts such as pronoun use with a young person, inappropriate distancing through reciprocal mariyātai communicates a lack of care and affection. Indeed, the use of one pronoun or another creates the contexts of cold distance or warm affection. Politicians deploy this hierarchical idiom to gain constituencies, as they are able to create a message of affectionate care for their constituencies through powerful patronage. As I note in the next chapter, this aspect of Tamil democracy has deep roots in precolonial kingship strategies that are by no means separate from the temple politics I discuss in this book.

Some kuṭimakkaḷ use their capacity for subordination through giving mariyātai as a life strategy. They defer to survive, and they may do so not without some feelings of closeness and real attachment to their ūrmakkaḷ families. Other kuṭimakkaḷ, however, resent their encompassment and refuse its terms. We have seen already how the Carpenters stopped collecting Poṅkal paṭi, a "gift of affection" (aṉpaḷippu) because they didn't like going from door to door like beggars, as the Carpenter's wife put it. Even those who still receive these "gifts of affection" do not usually use that term but stick to the idea that receiving these prestations is a "right," using the Tamil word "urimai" or "cutantiram," something they command in return for services rendered. So what the ūrmakkaḷ may see as hierarchical affection, the kuṭimakkaḷ may conceive of as "reciprocal" mutual transactions. As

Nicholas Thomas writes, "subversion can proceed through the assertion of reciprocity in the face of dominance" (1991, 7).

MARIYĀTAI AND SPATIAL DISTINCTIONS

In everyday interactions, people make mariyātai in fluid, unfixed, and intransitive ways, while in more formalized public events, mariyātai-makings appear to follow relatively fixed consensual orders of jāti, gender, and age rankings. (Ultimately, these orders are not fixed either; they do change more slowly, however.) One everyday context for making, displaying, and objectifying mariyātai rankings and inclusions is also relatively "fixed": the context of architectural space. Houses, villages, temples, and other constructed and inhabited places are ordered into relative interiors and exteriors, into ūrs and kāṭus, into places for cooking and places for shitting. Along with these spatial distinctions go mariyātai in both its ranking and including aspects.

For example, village residents map a metaphoric human body onto their houses and fields. They speak of the "heads" and "feet" of their houses and fields and refer to the yield of a field's crop as its "body." Just as different parts of the human body are thought to have different qualities, so too with houses and fields. The head is the most pure part of the human body and the feet are quite impure, so much so that touching something or someone with your feet, or even pointing your feet at someone unintentionally as you stretch your feet out to relax or cross your legs, is taken as an insult and requires a very deferential apology. The metaphoric head of a house or field (the portions that point to the south or west) also rank higher than their metaphoric feet (which point to the north or east). In matters of inheritance, when the person who heads the household dies, his house and fields are (if possible) split among his sons. The inheritance follows the body metaphor, with the oldest, higher-ranking son receiving the favored "head" portions of the house and field and the youngest receiving the "feet."

One of the most ubiquitous spatial distinctions Tamils make in a variety of contexts is that between interior and exterior, uḷḷe (uḷ-) and veḷiyē (veḷi-), or in more literary parlance, *akam* (*aka-*) and *puṟam* (*puṟa-*). The distinction between the interior ūr and exterior kāṭu follows this pattern, but the distinction pervades Tamil cultural constructions running the gamut from bodies (the inside palm—*uḷ kai*—versus back of the hand—*veḷi kai*) to houses (the house—akam, in some dialects—versus the yard outside—the *puṟakkaṭai*) to epistemological formulations (interiorized, or what Daniel [1984, 235] glosses as "synthetic" thought—*akapporuḷaṟivu*—versus exteriorized or "analytic" thought, called *puṟapporuḷaṟivu*) to the theater stage in popular-performance genres (Seizer 2000). The earliest known manifestation of this distinction is in 2,000-year-old Tamil Sangam poetry, which is divided into two genres: poetry of the interior (akam), which concerns love, emotion, and landscape, and poetry of the exterior (puṟam), which concerns places, kings, battles, and heroes (Ramanujan 1967, 1985). Ramanujan further shows the analytic power of akam and puṟam for distinguishing contemporary folklore genres (1986). Interiors connote intimacy and emotion. Exteriors connote objectified orders, public arenas, social complexities, and disorders. The concepts do not correspond to a sharp distinction between public and private, however, for here interior and exterior may be relative and interpenetrating aspects of experience (see also Dickey 2000).

Concepts of interior and exterior are foundational aspects of houses and temples. The architecture of both houses and temples (whether they are permanent or temporary structures) helps give orderings of mariyātai their linear and inclusionary forms. Most houses in Yanaimangalam have several thresholds marking human movement from relative exteriors to relative interiors. Along with greater interiority goes greater intimacy, greater sharing. Mariyātai is made when some outsiders are allowed farther into the interior spaces of a house than others and, conversely, when outsiders "respect" the boundaries of interior and exterior and stay outside unless invited up and inside (see also Parish [1996], who reports similar spatial/caste distinctions at work in Nepal). Earlier in the chapter we saw one example of this when we saw how mariyātai was made in the key transaction. One of the channels of mariyātai-making was positional: Pandi, the Thevar young man, was called up onto the inner veranda (uḷ tiṇṇai), a move explicitly reckoned to give him mariyātai, while Balamma stood outside on the outer veranda (veḷi tiṇṇai) and stooped to the ground to pick up the key that Parvathi had tossed out the door.

Another event where the mariyātai of relative interiority became apparent to me occurred shortly after the death of the Brahman schoolmaster's elderly mother. On this day, the family of Ramayya Thevar came to the house and walked into the main room of the schoolmaster's house (no one knocks in Yanaimangalam: if they feel it's appropriate, they walk right into your house; if they wish to give mariyātai, they call in from outside). They had come to "hear the sorrow" (*kaṣṭattaik kēṭka*), a common practice by neighbors and friends soon after a death. In this case, the visit proved controversial. The schoolmaster's family was somewhat upset because, as Parvathi put it, the "Thevars" (referring to them by jāti and not by family name) just walked right in when previously they would have given mariyātai to the Brahmans by staying outside. From Ramayya Thevar's point of view, however, they were all neighbors living together on one street now and they spoke in a kind, friendly manner on a daily basis, so it would have been a slight (a lack of mariyātai) *not* to go and hear the sorrow. Politically, of course, Ramayya Thevar's family was more powerful than the schoolmaster's. Even simple visitations carry a complex load of meaning.

The mariyātai of both linear rank and relative interiority can also be viewed in front of the TV. By the time I left the field in 1990, five houses had televisions, all of them small portable black-and-white TVs that cost an exorbitant 2,500 rupees (at that time about 150 dollars). (By 2001, televisions were much more common.) Most people kept their TVs in the same room where they kept their gods, the main room that sits between the kitchen—the most intimate and "interior" space—and the inner veranda (uḷ tiṇṇai), which is for most people the usual site of socializing. Indeed, the seating arrangements for TV viewing at Parvathi's house resembled nothing so much as a temple line of mariyātai: relative proximity to the TV constituted relative mariyātai among the viewers. Closest sat Parvathi and around her other Brahman women and girls. They all sat in the main room with the TV. The rest of the audience, mostly women and girls and young boys (because Parvathi was a single woman, she kept most men out of her house most of the time) sat in the inner veranda and craned necks to see the TV through the doorway or the barred window that was there to allow night breezes into the main house when the doors were shut at night. Sometimes Parvathi came out to rearrange the seating on the veranda in order to give those to whom more mariyātai was due better seats on one of the two benches she set out, for these were nearest the window and doorway that opened into the TV room. Others sat on the floor (unless the benches were unoccupied). Finally, a few urchins who she would not let inside at all (or who she chased out for one reason or another) hung hopefully on the vertical bars separating the interior veranda from the exterior or street veranda to see as best they could. Old Arunacalam Pillai (otherwise known in this chapter as the ancient Pillaimar firepot god-dancer who smears foreheads with ash) sometimes came over, sat sternly, and "watched," though he was too blind to see more than flickering lights and shadows. Whenever he arrived on the scene, Parvathi bustled out and officiously repositioned the audience to afford him the best seat in that part of the house. (If the audience became either unusually silent or unusually vocal, he would ask "What? What's happening?" A child would quickly fill him in.) In other houses, the situation was similar. Previous orders of distinction were ratified in front of the TV, and some people were excluded from some of the houses altogether. One household actually started charging a fee to some for watching, a somewhat scandalous fact that was discussed frequently on Parvathi's veranda. Commodification seemed to confer an utter lack of mariyātai, an alienation of the sociality that ranks as it also binds people together in an asymmetrical community.

Table 4.1. Aspects of Dominance in Yanaimangalam, 1990

Overlapping Aspects of Interjāti Relations in Yanaimangalam

Kuṭimai			**Mariyātai**	
Mutuality	**Exteriority**		**Lines**	**Inclusions**
	Separations	**Patronage**		
Kuṭimakkaḷ exchange their service and labor for ūrmakkaḷ grain and wages.	Kuṭimakkaḷ take on the negatively valued substances of ūrmakkaḷ and take them "out" of the village.	Urmakkal include kuṭimakkaḷ under an umbrella of patronage.	Higher persons come first in line and lower persons come last.	Persons are included within a community from which others are excluded.
Stresses reciprocity	Constitutes distinctions between inside and outside, center and periphery, ūr and kāṭu	Asymmetrical kinship established through "gifts of affection"	Higher persons are positioned closer to important figures (gods, TVs, ritual subjects) and lower persons are positioned further away.	Stresses social distinctions between insiders and outsiders, self and other, ūr and kāṭu
	Stresses biological-moral and spatial distinctions	Stresses kuṭimakkaḷ subordination and ūrmakkaḷ generosity	Stresses ranked orders	

FIVE ASPECTS OF JĀTI RELATIONS

Before explicating the multiple contraventions of dominance implicated in the man getting his own ash, it will be useful to recapitulate in brief form all the different aspects and meanings of interjāti relations covered in the previous chapters. Table 4.1 summarizes five aspects of interjāti relations under two headings: kuṭimai (attached rights and obligations of servitude) and mariyātai (distinction, honor, respect). Some of these aspects correspond quite closely with the three aspects of interjāti relations that Raheja (1988) teased out of her data in Pahansu, a village in the North Indian state of Uttar Pradesh. What Raheja terms "mutuality" (following Wiser), "centrality," and "hierarchy" appear here as aspects of kuṭimai in the first two cases and as "lines of mariyātai" in the third case of "hierarchy." The correspondence is not exact, however. I have made further distinctions to flesh out what residents of Yanaimangalam appear to recognize as key aspects of relations among jātis in agricultural and ritual practices. Interested readers may wish to further compare Raheja's material with my own. These five points are not separate "types" but rather, as Raheja also argued in her analysis, coexisting "aspects"; that is, interpenetrating and co-occurring modes of relating. Any one aspect may be pragmatically foregrounded in a given context, but all five are available modes or accents for enacting and interpreting interpersonal realities.

At no place or time do these aspects of interjāti relations appear to coalesce so completely as they do at the yearly goddess-temple festival. It is this very coalescence that has made Indian goddess-temple festivals so available for functionalist analyses: these festivals are in part metasocial events (see also Sax 1991; Parish 1996). That is, they are social events that, while ostensibly about worshiping the goddess to ensure a healthy new year of production for a village or region, are at the same time also about the social organization of village or regional life. They are events and places where villagers display to themselves their own social order. In Yanaimangalam, while participants consciously hope to reproduce the well-being of fields and family, the festival participants ("the whole village") are in fact also reproducing the social organization of caste *as it should be* according to those who have the power to design and maintain the festival—that is, according to the ūrmakkaḷ. Even though this ideal is contested over and again—and any given festival is also a pragmatic event where social rankings and inclusions are argued and reconstituted—the goddess festival is also a venue where villagers create, contest, display, and publicly enact their own social organization. Caste relations are multiply replicated and reproduced in the goddess temple. Examining these processes in greater detail will help us understand both the import of a man taking a pinch of ash and the import of a temple boycott.

FIVE

Habit, History, and Thevar Dominance

Seeing a man walk from the temple, a flash of ash on his forehead, would in most cases signify almost nothing. A more common sight, a white stripe of ash on a forehead in the vicinity of the goddess temple in the morning, could hardly be imagined and would usually at most occasion a merely phatic greeting from passersby: "Have you been to the temple?" But in this case, the coexistence of three signs—ash on a forehead, the forehead being that of a Pallar man, and the correctly inferred absence of the priest from the temple signified by his presence elsewhere (walking with some ūrmakkaḷ toward the temple while the Pallar man was walking away)—confounded expectations. A routine act here appeared as an incongruity, a happening worth retelling to others. When the men who spied the ash on the forehead reported their morning sighting to the Thevar headman, the latter responded with an action of his own. He reported the incident to the police stationed in a neighboring town, and in the course of his reporting, a pinch of ash became an attempted theft of a bell.

Given the multiple aspects of interjāti relations, as summarized in Table 4.1, it can be said that the S. C. man *multiply* contravened dominance relations with his walk up into and through the temple to retrieve his ash at the goddess's lotus feet. And in discussions about the incident, village residents did respond differently according to their own various positions, or "accents," on the issue of caste at the time. Most ūrmakkaḷ simply stated that as an S. C. man, he should simply stay out of the temple or, more specifically, that his entering the temple went against muṟai, proper order. Even those who did not approve of the trumped-up theft charge the Thevar headman used to lure the police to Middle Ūr could not quite bring themselves to accept the man's act as anything but violation. So even after the priest Subramaniyam had stated publicly that the man had pinched nothing more than ash, villagers maintained "He shouldn't have." Even Aruna, who is critical of exclusionary practices based on caste, objected to his act. She objected not because he had entered the temple but because he had taken the ash directly from the cup, which to her was *tappu,* a moral mistake that showed a lack of humility and mariyātai toward the goddess. Ariraman of Middle Hamlet disagreed with these interpretations, stating that the man's act was purely devotional, a desire (and a rightful one, he argued) for a mutual relation with the goddess, a relation which, moreover, he claimed to be his community's right as the goddess's original "slaves" (*aṭimai*).[1]

Why did villagers, and Thevars in particular, care so much about this small act? At the time of my research, and even as I first wrote this account, I assumed that the answer lay in the way in which the goddess temple is the venue, like no other in Yanaimangalam, where structures of local dominance are most efficiently represented to and valorized for the residents of Yanaimangalam. Under that circumstance, pinching ash—whatever the man's intent—did in fact critically comment upon and implicate the entire structure of ūrmakkaḷ dominance. But as I later read accounts throughout the 1990s of increasing regional violence between Thevars and Pallars, I realized that this smudge of ash incited such passion not only because of its subversion of local dominance relations inscribed in temple spaces but also because of the way it brought home to Yanaimangalam a regional dispute between Thevars and Pallars. The goddess temple was not just a venue for asserting dominance in Yanaimangalam; it was an arena for localizing this broader conflict as well.

I will first consider the "ash theft" in terms of the multiple aspects of social relations, in the idiom of caste dominance in which the ash "theft" as well as the subsequent boycott can be interpreted. I will then take a closer look at what was at stake for the Thevars in the dispute. This inquiry will lead to a discussion of how a single pinch of ash refracted wider regional histories and politics.

ŪR DOMINANCE AND ŪR TRANSGRESSION AT THE GODDESS TEMPLE

All kuṭimakkaḷ, especially S. C. laborers, are confronted with a contradiction each time they visit the goddess temple, especially during formally structured festivals. The goddess is responsible for the well-being of all village residents. She ensures both human and agricultural productivity. She is "mother" to every nonatheist in this overwhelmingly Hindu village. Yet to go to the temple means to abide by the forms of domination that structure the ūr, for those same relations structure the goddess temple as well.

By worshiping at the temple and participating in the festival, kuṭimakkaḷ are able to reproduce their own well-being and productive capacity. Yet in order to do so, they must also reproduce their subordination in relation to ūrmakkaḷ. In fact, at the goddess temple it would seem that the one (the well-being of the person) depended on the other (the subordination of the kuṭimakkaḷ). This holds true especially for the S. C., as even standing in the places they are allowed publicly reconfirms their subordination through exclusion from the dominant ūr.

Activities that occur at the yearly goddess-temple festival not only replicate and reproduce, even as they may contest, the shape of ūrmakkaḷ dominance, as detailed in Chapter 2; they also replicate the ideal structure of caste interrelations along all the dimensions outlined in Table 4.1. Briefly, the koṭai reproduces kuṭimai by (1) invoking service relations of kuṭimai in the production of the festival—Barbers sweep the grounds, Dhobis provide cloth for the rituals, Carpenters bring wooden ladles for cooking, Potters make pots, and so forth—and (2) the ūrmakkaḷ are seen as the patrons of the goddess, the temple, and all temple servants (kuṭimakkaḷ). As patrons, it is the ūrmakkaḷ who receive the benefits from the koṭai, which then trickle down to others only by virtue of ūrmakkaḷ productivity and largesse. This trickle-down patronage is publicly displayed when ūrmakkaḷ distribute temple-worship products to kuṭimakkaḷ who wait on the edges of the temple grounds.

The temple koṭai reproduces as it also serves as a battleground for establishing relations of mariyātai in two aspects: (1) rank from high to low as village residents receive prasad in order of jāti rank and (2) inclusion in the temple association, and by extension in the ūr, and the consequent exclusion of all those who are not allowed to receive temple shares directly. Some kuṭimakkaḷ may have rights to certain temple shares, but again only as mediated by the ūrmakkaḷ who gain further distinction and greatness by having the authority to distribute shares to others. S. C. are generally excluded from even these secondary distributions of shares.

Mutuality, that aspect of kuṭimai relations that emphasizes simple reciprocity without the burden of social asymmetry, is the only relation in the temple that can be construed as nonreplicating of dominance. Mutuality is expressed in the individual relation of devotion that all worshipers bring to the temple as they interact and transact with the goddess. Yet for the S. C. who participate even this relation is curtailed because they are not allowed close enough to the temple doors to see the goddess at the height of the festival.

These relations of dominance are not just enacted during the yearly koṭai; they come to be reified in the very structure of the temple. First, the goddess temple is, like the ūr itself, an interior central place of order (muṟai) and relative purity (cuttam). From such a place, chaotic substances need to be removed, not introduced. A man who partakes of the nature of the kāṭu entering into the center of the ūr (read: temple) needs, like evils, ghosts, and diseases, to be removed and passed out to a periphery. Indeed, banishing the man and his fellow jāti members from the interior temple effects such a removal and reconfirms the centrality and dominance of the Thevar as ūrmakkaḷ proper. The S. C. man's entry into the temple could be taken as an incursion of chaos into the ordered center of the ūr and the Thevars' response as an appropriate removal upholding the order or dharma of the ūr.

Second, social distinctions of mariyātai are inscribed in the temple structure. In Yanaimangalam, the goddess temple, like Brahmanical temples, was constructed according to textual (*agamic*) rules of temple architecture, which includes, among other things, a structure of ranked spaces that are graded on the basis of relative interiority. The most interior space is that where the deity resides, the purest place of the temple. This room is called the *garbagraha,* literally "the womb room." It is here where the image of the goddess resides. Only the priests enter this room, its purity (cuttam) thereby protected. Immediately outside and in front of the garbagraha comes a second small chamber, in which a few other gods rest on a raised cement block. This room is reserved for Brahman worshippers. Only they may enter this room unless no Brahmans are present, in which case other big people sometimes enter this space as well, making it then the room of distinction for the most highly ranked persons present. Anyone invited up into this room is being given mariyātai, for they receive positions closer than others to the goddess. The next, and final, enclosed room of this temple is the largest of the three. It is in this most "exterior" room of the temple that most worshippers enter and jam together in sweltering proximity during festivals.

The S. C. are excluded from this room. They (are supposed to) remain outside the temple altogether. In regular daily life, they may approach the temple and climb the outside stops to peer into the temple and see the goddess from outside. But during the festival, even this line of sight is cut off. The whole temple is located on a plot of land that has been raised up higher than the surrounding fields (Figure 2.1). During the festival, ūrmakkaḷ transform this entire raised compound into still another interior by erecting a large *pantal* all around the temple. (A pantal is a temporary awning-type structure fashioned of woven coconut-frond walls and roof, all supported by bamboo poles.) S. C. participants must remain outside of even this expanded pantal-covered area. They remain out in the fields, below the temple's ground level and lower than other worshippers and out of direct visual contact with the goddess.

Architectural distinctions become social ones as groups lay claim to relative interiority, relative nearness to the pure and powerful temple interior. During the goddess festival, these spatial distinctions of interior and exterior map onto social distinctions in a double sense, giving visible form to two aspects of interjāti relations: the social power of exclusionary orders and the rank of pure to impure. First, members of the central and powerful ūrmakkaḷ jātis line up *inside* and those excluded from direct rights to shares and membership in the community are left to mingle *outside,* where they may later receive valued food leftovers only via their ūrmakkaḷ patrons. Second, the "high" (ocanta) jātis position themselves at the head of the row of mariyātai and the low (*kīḻ,* taḻnta) jātis mingle at the end of the line. Because social distinctions of dominance and subordination are spatially reified in the temple, concretized in brick and mortar, the movements of persons through, into, and out of those places even on ordinary days can always potentially be interpreted as statements about social relations.

It was just such a statement for which the Middle Ūr man was made culpable when he walked into the goddess temple and took a pinch of ash. With his walk into and then up to the front of the temple, he contravened in an instant the dominant spatial objectification of the temple as a place of privileged access. First, when the Middle Ūr man entered the temple on his own accord to take his own pinch of ash, he was stepping over a boundary separating the interior orderly ūr of ūrmakkaḷ domination (free from evils and faults) from the exterior chaotic kāṭu (the place of sin and fault). His transgression, then, was moral as well as social. Some villagers believed that his entering the orderly pure interior of the temple was wrong because of his own disorderly impure nature. Others perhaps cared not so much about moral order or impurities but did care about their own position within a caste-oriented structure of domination: the man was uppity.

Second, as he walked against a flow of rank where he "should be" positioned last, he contravened relations of rank, "lines" of mariyātai. He walked from the temple courtyard into the temple, from the outer hall up into the inner chamber reserved usually for Brahmans and other pure, orderly, and honored guests or patrons; and from this inner chamber his impure and disordered body reached into the garbagraha, the abode of the goddess, where he found the priest's cup of ash. He crossed several thresholds between exteriors and interiors, asserting for himself an inclusion in the temple and thus in the ūr from which he was formally excluded, again through practices of domination. In other words, his pinch of ash asserted a kind of parity with other village people: like them, he too could receive his pinch of ash directly from the goddess. His action, though Ariraman claimed it was intended as a humble daily act of devotion (*bhakti*), a search for a pinch of ash, was indeed also a challenge, a sign of insubordination to ūrmakkaḷ dominance. His walk into the temple crossed the very boundaries of exclusion that the circular processions discussed earlier create and so became part of a motile discourse about social relations, about rank, inclusion, and control over space.

Whatever his intent, the result was clear. Important Thevars, members of the newest jāti among the ūrmakkaḷ, took the entry as a transgression of the structure of domination and used their power—and influence with the local police—to publicly and, for many, properly push the S. C. back to the periphery: they openly banned them from the temple with the threat of force and stated that any S. C. participation in the festival must remain, as always, below and outside the temple interior.

Declaring Independence

As Fuller (1992, 139) and Dirks (1991, 228) report, temple boycotts have become a common S. C. protest strategy all over South India. When the residents of Middle Ūr decided to boycott future goddess festivals, they were refusing to participate not only in the festival but in all the social and moral relations that the festival reproduced. It may be that their utter exclusion from temple processes made this step easy.

Through their boycott Middle Ūr residents would step out of a process that publicly reproduced their kuṭimai, their subordination and dependence on the ūrmakkaḷ, and thereby challenge the harmonious "whole" of the ūr. The boycott would separate the S. C. off with their own goddess and so mark a refusal to participate in the reproduction of their own place in kuṭimai relations. When Ariraman said "From now on we'll be happy with our own goddess," he was declaring a radical separation, a desired alienation where even labor would be strictly commodified into "salary" (cambaḷam) or "wages" (*kuli*) instead of the obligations and "rights" of subordination called kuṭimai.

The S. C. were, in short, declaring that second kind of cutantiram defined earlier: independence. More important than even the actual boycott was how Ariraman's declaration signaled a different accent in local discourse about interjāti relations. He did not use terms of kuṭimai or even S. C. Rather, he drew on a familiar nationalist phrase—Ati Dravida, Original Dravidian—and from there constructed an alternative history of village caste relations. He asserted primacy for his own community in the village and therefore with the goddess. And taking the concept of Original Dravidian quite literally as a historical fact, he reframed kuṭimai. No longer a given structure of nature, an essentialized subordination, he refigured kuṭimai as an historical outcome of domination. He shifted the ground of discourse from one of embodied and emplaced qualities of difference to one of historical injustice and oppression.

The declaration of boycott was also a declaration of parity, a kind of equality. Parity occurs socially when people are all equivalent in relation to something or someone else. The boycott declared a parity of all villagers in relation to the goddess and was achieved by exploiting the meanings of mutuality and separation: we'll be satisfied with our own temple. It is significant that Ariraman also said that they would be satisfied with the goddess temple "in our own ūr," not "kuṭi." Again, this word choice connotes parity by declaring a separation and a structural equivalence: we have an ūr and goddess, the same as they do. The S. C.'s own goddess temple, a manifestation of the very same power (cakti) that inhabits the ūrmakkaḷ temple, would provide Middle Ūr residents with the direct, unmediated devotional practice they claim as their right. In this way, Middle Ūr's devotion, or bhakti, corresponds precisely to the way that bhakti is sometimes potentially revolutionary or, as Ramanujan writes, "counter-structural" (1973, 33–35). Devotional movements and acts may run counter to social propriety in their claim that the only thing that really matters is mutual care between deity and devotee. More politically, Ariraman's claim to be the rightful and first worshipers of this village goddess was certainly an inversion of ūrmakkaḷ claims to preeminence in power as in ritual. But the boycott itself? What would it accomplish?

By boycotting the goddess festival, Middle Ūr S. C. would refuse to participate in the public construction of their own exteriority, their kuṭimai: *they would not be there* to hover outside the temple grounds and in that way publicly confirm their place outside the ūr and inside the exterior kāṭu. Middle Ūr residents *would not be there* to receive, second-hand, shares of the temple distributions from their ūrmakkaḷ patrons. Middle Ūr residents *would not be there* to be last in line for receiving prasad from the goddess via the priest who anyway would only come to the edge of the raised temple grounds and fling ash and water over the crowd, not even bothering to place it directly into the palms of their outstretched hands. And *they would not be there* to be openly excluded from distributions of special items such as the feast. In short, by declaring independence, they also refused to participate in the production of their own subordination. The declaration also opened up a space for pursuing more immediate and public action later.

"THE FRIENDSHIP OF A MARAVAR IS AS GOOD AS THE SHADE OF THE PALMYRA TREE"

Clearly, at stake for Middle Ūr S. C. in their temple politics was a hope for a dignified life in an egalitarian world. But what was at stake for the Thevars in this dispute? Why not just ignore that smudge of ash? Reducing any dispute to a bidimensional struggle of the oppressed against the dominators distorts the likely multiplexity of conflict. Thevars are not mere ciphers of domination. They too, like most people, are struggling to make and remake a world for themselves. What world was thrown to them? And from materials available in the world they inhabit, what world are they trying to make? The powerful Thevars in the ūr were working to assure their own social and political place in the world. What was at stake was not simply their power in Yanaimangalam but also a whole vision of the world, of how power works, of how order is maintained, and of how the Tamil world is sustained.

Not just the headman but many Thevar men and women in Yanaimangalam enact a fearsome tough persona in everyday life. Some of them capitalize on this tough reputation to enact their will over others. But village residents also depend to an extent on Thevar toughness. For example, Thevars hold the right to serve as village guardians, as the *talaiyāris* who protect fields from thieves and stray animals and who accompany the tax collector (the appointed village officer, who lives in a neighboring village) on his rounds. And when it came time for the ūrmakkaḷ to collect the goddess-temple tax the years I lived there, they called on Ramayya Thevar's brother, Venkala Thevar. One day, as we sat at the Pillaiyar (Ganesh) temple waiting for the bus, Ramayya Thevar explained to me why he could never collect taxes but his little brother could: unlike him, his brother was so fierce and tough and coercive that no one would dare not pay. And when the Thevar headman engineered S. C. banishment from the goddess temple, many ūrmakkaḷ saw that act as ultimately a dharmic one; that is, an act in accordance with the proper order of things.

If you ask residents of Yanaimangalam why the Thevar headman and others use such forceful tactics and display such fierce personae, the most likely first answer would include some reference to the concept of *paḻakkam*. Most succinctly translated as "habit," paḻakkam means more elaborately habituated and embodied practice. To understand Thevar actions in the here and now, one must understand both the concept of paḻakkam and the changing place of Thevars in regional history, particularly their political history as warriors, little kings, colonized "criminals," and, more recently, as a powerful ethnicized constituency in Tamil democracy.

PAḺAKKAM: A TAMIL CONCEPT OF PRACTICE

For most village residents, Thevar threats, violence, and rough-and-ready expressions were seen as predicable actions based on embodied natural qualities characterizing the biological-moral makeup of the jāti itself. This view is tersely expressed in a proverb Aruna once told me in the context of a story concerning a specific Thevar man's dishonesty: "The friendship of a Maravar [the Thevar subcaste in Yanaimangalam] is as good as the shade of the palmyra tree" (*maravariṉ naṉpaṉ cari, paṉaimarattiṉ niḻal cari*). How good is that? Not very. The palmyra tree is a desert tree, tall and skinny with a small stiff tuft of pointed fronds on top. It bends in the wind. Its shade offers little if any protection or shelter. As the Thevars—who, like most village residents, practice regional caste endogamy with some preference for marrying classificatory cross-cousins—also tend to be tall and skinny, this proverb works not through mere simile but as homology.

While such a perspective may first appear as a kind of "ethno-essentialism," it is in fact more aptly understood within a wider pragmatic understanding of the person as a fluid karmic product of embodied and emplaced action. In Yanaimangalam, as in other parts of Tamilnadu and South Asia, residents understand their own personal qualities and characters (kuṇam) to be affected by the places they inhabit and by the people with whom they interact on a regular basis. E. Valentine Daniel's ethnography of Tamil concepts of person illustrates the relation between persons and the places they inhabit: the persons who inhabit an ūr are thought by Tamils to "share in the substance of the soil of that ūr" (1984, 63) through such practices as eating the soil's products and even simply inhabiting the soil (ibid., 84–85). Through continuous sharings, places and persons become mutually habituated (paḻakkam) to one another and, in a sense, become aspects of one another. Thus, the qualities of both a place and a person may change to more closely match one another. Further, persons who interact frequently, and who thereby become paḻakkam to one another, also come to share the same qualities (kuṇam) (Trawick 1991, 98–99).

The workings of "repeated practice" (paḻakkam) are confirmed by residents of Yanaimangalam. During my fieldwork I was often cautioned against Thevars and even once or twice admonished for venturing too often into their neighborhood for visits and interviews. My Pillaimar landlord also spoke this way and was especially concerned that I refrain from eating their food and thereby imbibing their qualities. I think he was so concerned in part because as owner of the house where I lived, he worried about my imparting Thevar-like, meat-eating qualities to the house itself, thereby altering its appropriateness for his own vegetarian family's subsequent occupation and grain storage. Parvathi sometimes opined that if I wanted to talk to Thevars, I should call them to me. Dumbfounded by the image of my employing such an imperious anthropological technique, I ignored their advice. During a particularly intense period of mapping and interviewing on Thevarmar Street, my 12-year-old Pillaimar neighbor Kuru, no doubt echoing the sentiments and overheard conversations of the adults around her, suggested that I should no longer go there because the Thevars are "no good." I challenged Kuru: "But what about Ramayya Thevar? Isn't he a good man? He's Thevar, no?"

Ramayya Thevar and his family lived on the Agraharam and had done so for several years. Not only did I visit them frequently (sometimes being fed delicious mutton curry) but they also visited Parvathi almost daily for both gossip and business: it was Ramayya Thevar and his sons who looked after Parvathi's fields for her and it was Ramayya Thevar's oldest son to whom Parvathi gave her house key with relative mariyātai. To watch Ramayya Thevar, a tall lean gray-haired man, walk slowly up the road after coming from the goddess temple did not exactly inspire fear. Granted, his bearing was regal, but the flowers he had gingerly tucked behind his ears—flowers received as prasad from the goddess—completely destroyed any semblance of ferocity.

Kuru, Parvathi, my landlord (less enthusiastically), and a few other neighbors concurred: Ramayya Thevar's family, and even some of the other Thevars who had moved from Thevar Street onto the Agraharam, had a relatively good quality/nature (*nalla kuṇam*). But, I learned, their good nature was no counterargument to Thevar nature in general. Rather, their good nature was seen as a pragmatic outcome of their own altered emplaced life practices. By living for some time now on the Agraharam, previously a purely Brahman neighborhood, these Thevars had become "habituated" (*pa<u>l</u>akiyāccu*) into a better quality. Living daily life in the place itself as well as among these higher-caste people had altered their character by altering their habits (pa<u>l</u>akkam). Here certain Thevars had become pa<u>l</u>akkam with Brahmans by sharing their place and by sharing their daily lives, interactions, transactions, conversations, and foods.

Relations were particularly dense up on the west end of the Agraharam street, as Thevar and Brahman neighbors had become quite close companions. Rumors were flying that the Brahmans up on that end of the Agraharam were sharing even more than food, friendship, and conversation: two Brahman women were having affairs (one widow openly, one married woman in secret) with Thevar men who were their neighbors. These new habits of place and relation had altered the qualities of Thevar bodies and consciousness, and it had altered their capacities for forming certain kinds of relationships. All things are relative, though, and still the Brahman schoolmaster had been somewhat upset when Ramayya Thevar's family entered his house to "hear/ask the sorrows" upon the death of his mother. And furthermore, since the changing qualities worked both ways, many Brahmans on the east end of the street would no longer so eagerly take food from those Thevar-habituated west Agraharam Brahmans.

This Tamil understanding of habitual practice is a pragmatic theory of action that overlaps substantially with some contemporary theories of activity and practice. In brief, the Tamil concept of habituation points to a dynamic and dialectic view of the self or person that resembles in some ways existential, karmic,[2] activity-theory, and semeiotic understandings of the person or self as always emerging potentially anew in a process of growth that occurs through action or through "being-in-the-world," where "being" is understood as a verb, as a kind of "becoming" through engagement with others and with the world at large (May 1958, 12).

In these approaches to human being and experience, a person is composed not of static substances, essences, or mechanisms. Rather, persons are understood to have a capacity to grow and change through their actions with others in the world, as the world and those others too may be changed in the process. Persons are never frozen forms or functions. Rather, the world and our selves are perpetuated, instantiated, and potentially altered through our activity. That is to say, we are "thrown" into an existent world beyond our making, but through our activities in that world—activities that are constrained and conditioned by the forms of engagement possible in our given social and physical environments—we bring that world into being, bring ourselves into existence, and potentially alter self, other, society, and even our physical environment as we do so. The person is, in other words, a sign. It is a meaningful entity always coming into being and growing through practice and use.

Colapietro notes that this self is no isolated subject but is a fully social being that carries—we can also say collocates—community structures and history as much as personal experience: "We are bearers of the past: History speaks through us in ways we just barely comprehend" (1989, 41). This notion, that the self carries the past into the present through actions, also accords with the Tamil concept of pa̱lakkam. People can pass their habits, formed in society, on to their descendants, just as the outcomes of an ancestor's past social actions—formed in relation to the community in which they act—are understood to be carried fully into the biological and social lives of descendants. In this Tamil view of action, actions are what Peirce would call "real agencies." They have a real effect on a person's capacity for further action in the world, for further self-, other-, and world-making. Like karma, which means "act" as well as the results of acts, human action brings about results not only in the outer world, but also in the actors themselves.

Margaret Trawick, for example, explains how

> the idea of pa̱lakkam was in some ways like the idea of karma (*vi̱nai, pāvam-pu̱ṉniyam*). It was, and was created by, action; it was embedded in the person and it was hard to get rid of; it was carried from birth to birth and could be passed on from generation to generation. (1991, 99)

And as I have written elsewhere, Tamil concepts of action include the notion that one's acts "stick" to the person, altering their own capacities for future action (Mines 1997b). Furthermore, these acts that stick to the person pass down from generation to generation, such that in one case I recorded, grandchildren suffer the consequences of a murder their grandfather committed. The grandson contracted polio, and the granddaughter lost an eye to infection. Her family interprets these losses of capacity as direct consequences of the negative substances passed down from their grandfather's evil (pāvam).

Here too, then, as persons act, whether by habit or invention or accident, they bring into existence (into present real activity in the world) their past, family, history, and community structures, instantiating these over and again each time they speak, give mariyātai, issue a threat, smear ash, or use any sign whatsoever. Tamils are not ahistorical essentialists, and though the trope of historical discourse may not be the most common mode of causal explanation among Yanaimangalam's less-western-educated residents, the concept of habit and repeated practice is in fact consistent with some historical approaches to human activity. Through paḻakkam, history conceived as "ancestral acts" speaks through present actors, who bring the past into the present.

In this way, Thevars in Yanaimangalam enact and perpetuate a fierce reputation and a project of domination that is not merely embodied but also embedded in regional history, in their own ancestral acts performed in a social field. Thevar dominance in Yanaimangalam can be read in the context of several centuries of regional history, from precolonial royal practices through colonial actions and concepts—including the British designation of Thevars (among others) as "criminal castes"—and into postcolonial electoral politics. In the following sections, I show how the Thevars in Yanaimangalam, when they push S. C. out of the ūr using strong-arm tactics, are enacting a paḻakkam built up through a complex past of historical action. They are bringing community structures and history into the present realities of Yanaimangalam.

Bearing the Past

Colonialism and Caste

Caste as it now plays out in India is in many ways the "product of previous activity, the work of other lives" (Jackson 1998, 27), and not all of those other lives are Indian. As Bernard Cohn (1987) and more recently Nicolas Dirks (2001) have argued, caste as it operates in India today bears a heavy British legacy. The British, influenced by their own cultural categories and understandings of class, attempted to identify and fix caste orders to create rational social categories that they could count, characterize, and create policy about. They effectively turned fluid and locally disparate jātis into fixed universal categories and, by implementing policies and practices such as the census and ethnographic description, reified caste identities. This solidification of jāti as identity has subsequently had a profound impact on Tamil and on Indian democracy.

Thevars in Yanaimangalam, as an example, are among those jātis whose reputation and treatment were vividly influenced by colonial practice. In 1911, British colonial administrators in the southern Madras Presidency designated them criminal castes. As it turns out, it was the British, not the Tamils, who exhibited ahistorical causal reasoning. Unlike the pragmatic Tamil theory of action and habit that would predict a relatively mutable character based on an accretion of past actions and habits in context, the British essentialized Thevar character as inherently criminal. As Rachel Tolen demonstrates, criminal castes such as Thevars (at that time referred to by subjāti names such as Maravar) were thought to be by nature predisposed to manifest what the British conceived as their inward basic criminality (1991, 111). Tolen argues, furthermore, that the British compulsion to identify some Indians as criminal *by caste,* as opposed to relying on evidence of actual individual crimes committed, was in part an outcome of British cultural preconceptions that they brought with them from home and mapped onto the Indian social world. (In Britain at the time, it was common to identify certain social *classes* as more prone to criminality than others.)

While the British conception of Thevars' "criminality" as inherent and fixed was surely erroneous, it may not have been entirely without basis, for many Thevars, drawing on their precolonial role as protectors of the realm in a royal idiom whether as "village guardians" (*kāvalkāraṅkaḷ*), as forces in royal militias, or (in some areas) as "little kings," were most definitely among those who resisted colonial domination. What the British defined as essential criminality was likely in some part actions that some Thevars undertook as part of a forthright resistance to colonialism, for many of the most notorious thorns in the side of British rule in southern Tamilnadu were Thevars. As Guha (1999/1983) has demonstrated, all over India the British defined as "criminal" any acts of anticolonial insurgency. Tolen too points out that some communities may have indeed taken on the mantle of criminality in direct response to power asymmetries extant not only in colonial social orders but in indigenous ones as well (1991, 109). Thevars today continue to identify strongly with this aspect of their colonial legacy, symbolized nowhere more profoundly than in the person of Muthuramalinga Thevar, who gained his fame in the 1930s as a "freedom fighter"—that is, a resister to British colonial rule. Hailing from Ramnad District, which abuts Tirunelveli District to the east, Muthuramalinga Thevar derived his popularity in part from membership in a lineage of long-standing little kings of Ramnad District and consolidated it through the use of the symbols and strategies of precolonial royalty, symbols that continue to operate in Tamil politics today. Muthuramalinga Thevar remains a figure of identity formation for Thevars all over southern Tamilnadu, as statues to him are erected and celebrated—and defaced by political rivals—in public places over which Thevars assert some political power.

In summary, contemporary discourse about Thevar pa<u>l</u>akkam (tough, untrustworthy, powerful thieves) is likely to be in part a legacy of colonialism. Perhaps even Aruna's proverb, cited above, was not in any sense a "traditional" piece of wise lore but rather a more recently popularized proverb plucked out of context by a colonial scholar, for as Raheja (1996) shows, even folkloristic studies under colonialism worked to further colonial agendas because they could be used to prove the truth of British judgments concerning the inherent criminality of certain castes. Furthermore, Thevar pa<u>l</u>akkam, which includes tough and sometimes even "criminal" acts, such as lying to the local police about the theft of a bell from the goddess temple or violently attacking other communities, may in part be a habit picked up from their anticolonial actions and so still attributable in part to their colonial legacy internalized now by ordinary Tamil citizens. An even more powerful legacy of the colonial practice of fixing caste that bears on contemporary democratic practice is what Pamela Price (1993, 1996a) calls the "ethnicization" of the Tamil electoral process. All over Tamilnadu, political parties gain their major support from supercaste groups. Such groups form statewide political "caste" associations that operate as constituencies for the major political parties. In local news analyses about electoral process, Tirunelveli District is often referred to as the "Thevar belt," signaling the district's support, these days, for the AIADMK. We will return to this legacy below.

Precolonial Antecedents

Thevar pa<u>l</u>akkam is, to borrow from Saurabh Dube (1998), surely inextricably "entangled" with its colonial past. It is also entangled with its precolonial past. Price (1993, 1996a) has argued that much of contemporary Tamil politics, both statewide electoral politics and village politics, retain forms and practices consistent with what she calls its precolonial antecedents, particularly with the forms of kingship and local power that characterized Tamil polities from about 1500 to 1800 A.D.

During that period, Tamil kingship was not highly centralized but was rather highly segmented. That is, there was no single monarch whose authority extended throughout the Tamil country. Rather, power was highly localized, with "little kings," clan chiefs, and local big men vying for local control (Price 1993, 496; Stein 1980). These local rulers were able to assert control over their own territories and were more or less left alone as long as they paid tribute to regional monarchs and, if they were able to, supplied military support and other labor as needed. While there were variations in the structure of local communities during this period (see, for example, Ludden 1985), the form of local dominance was generally modeled upon the political structure of powerful royal centers, such as the Pandya kingdom, which flourished over a wide territory (including Tirunelveli) from ca. 800 to ca. 1300 A.D. By the end of the precolonial period, even in villages, local big men produced and exerted their power in a royal idiom in which political dominance was inextricably linked to, indeed constituted through, temple control.[3]

What was this royal idiom? It was akin to what we see operating in Yanaimangalam, where big men, including leaders of the ūrmakkaḷ jātis, exert their power through control, protection, and patronage of temples which are, recall, the centers of dharma or order in a realm. Big men display and establish their power by receiving first distinction or "honors" (mariyātai) in temple distributions and through largesse (*vaḷḷaṉmai*) not only to the temple but to the community at large as they redistribute honors (food and other items) from temple worship. In Yanaimangalam, one sees this process at work throughout the summer festival season. For example, in 1990, Muttaiah Thevar, a rich moneylender from a neighboring village, attended a temple festival in the neighborhood of those indebted to him. He came to Yanaimangalam's North Ūr Cutalaimatan festival and gifted dozens of men's and women's clothing sets to the temple. After the gods received the clothing, he received them back as prasad and, sanctioned by the gods themselves, commenced to distribute them out to his clients. Through his largesse, he enhanced his status as a good man and reestablished in a royal idiom his power over those in his debt. The usurious nature of his business was thus overshadowed by his moment of generosity.

When South Indian precolonial economic systems and the political power of kings collapsed under colonial economy and rule, the large temples that served as sites for reproducing royal power were taken over by the government (through the Hindu Religious and Charitable Foundations Board, discussed in more detail later). But because of the segmentary structure of power in the region, the method of gaining political power through local temples not worth the colonial state's bother did not collapse. Rather, as Price writes, "smaller village temples and shrines assumed major importance in transmitting political values" (1993, 498). Price argues further that villages, already relatively autonomous in the Tamil segmentary polity, became even more politically autonomous in matters of local dominance and political control, and the competition for power through temple patronage became more insular. The "village" in this respect became an even more important unit for the production of a person's or local group's power than it was previously.

Thevars in Tirunelveli District have most definitely been heirs to royal strategies of temple control. While Thevar dominance came later to Yanaimangalam, Thevars in surrounding regions (Maravars in particular) did exert power both as local big men and as little kings. As they moved into new regions, they competed with other castes for dominance and worked to assert that dominance in part through temple control. Ludden, for example, reports on a struggle between Thevars and "Shanars" (now referred to as Nadars) in the mid- to late nineteenth century in eastern Tirunelveli District (1985, 190–196). At that time, low, virtually outcaste Shanars were gaining economic power in the area, seeking to improve their position in society. Their quest was bolstered in part by increasing conversions to a nominally egalitarian Christianity; missionaries in the area promoted conversion as one route to Shanar "uplift." Thevars, seeing their own dominant position in the towns and villages of the region threatened by the real economic gains made by the numerically strong Shanars, resisted Shanar attempts to assert their rights and met those assertions with temple exclusions and finally with violence (ibid., 191–196). Similar violence characterized political disputes between these two caste factions in neighboring Ramnad District as well (Irschick 1986, 200–201).

In Yanaimangalam, the sight of the Thevar headman sitting in front of the goddess temple, as he does most days, conveys the importance placed by all on the goddess temple as the seat and symbol of sociopolitical dominance in Yanaimangalam.

Electoral Politics and Egalitarianism

Just because political control of many aspects of social life is local does not mean that it is not also caught up in wider regional political movements today. Just as Price notes that villages became important centers for the transmission of political values during and after colonialism, it is also true that Tamil formations of democratic process have also contributed, if ironically, to the continuation of power differences in a caste idiom. In some respects, Thevar dominance is also a localization of postcolonial Tamil democratic process.

Beth Roy's (1994) study of a village conflict between Hindus and Muslims in Bangladesh is instructive here. In that study, Roy writes about a local dispute that arose when one man's cow ate from another's field. This seemingly quotidian bovine act led to what authorities described as a "riot" between Hindus and Muslims, followed by a revision of political relations in the village that marginalized Hindu power and promoted Muslim control over local affairs. The dispute took place soon after Partition and, as Roy argues, crystallized locally a change that had already occurred nationally: Muslims now formed the state government, and for Muslims marginalized in Hindu-dominated villages, this change prompted a change in their own thinking about their place in the power hierarchy. Local Muslim residents were now ready to wrest control locally, just as their heroes had wrested it nationally. Village social hierarchies were changing to "get in line with" the changing polity of the new Muslim nation of Bangladesh.

In parallel, the rise of Thevar dominance in Yanaimangalam is coincident with their ascent to influence within statewide electoral politics. Thevar prominence in the village began around the same time that the DMK (Dravidian Progress Association) rose to state power, due in part to its allure for relatively impoverished and low-ranking Thevars. Thevars today are among those in Yanaimangalam who most forcefully uphold caste divisions and especially the exclusion of Untouchables in a royal idiom of dominance, a fact which appears ironic given that their rise to power was built in part upon an explicitly anticaste rhetoric of self-respect and egalitarianism (*camattuvam*) in the name of Dravidian autonomy. The DMK used a rhetoric of egalitarianism and anti-Brahmanism to convince Tamil voters to reject the Congress Party, then constructed as the newest form of North Indian hegemony. As we have seen, decades later Ariraman of Middle Ūr used the very same language to reject Thevar hegemony in Yanaimangalam. That is, the very same slogans that DMK-inspired Thevar youths once used to protest northern Indian hegemony were now the slogans S. C. used to protest and declare their independence from Thevar dominance.

The DMK developed as an offshoot of an earlier anticolonial political movement founded by E. V. Ramaswami Naicker (EVR). Through his Justice Party, later renamed the Dravidian Association (DK), EVR propagated an atheistic and anti-Brahmanical platform, seeing northern Brahmanical cultural influence as detrimental to the future of the Dravidian South. In the 1920s, he founded the Self-Respect (cuya-mariyātai) Movement, which was intended to do away with distinctions based on caste and replace them with a universal concern for one's *own* honor (mānam, or mariyātai, what I have been translating also as distinction). One's own honor was to be achieved precisely by acting just as honorably toward one's self as toward other humans, regardless of caste.

Price (1993, 1996a) illustrates in detail how this platform of egalitarianism was undermined by the structure of the party itself once the DMK gained power in 1967. At the same time that it preached egalitarianism, the party structured itself hierarchically, drawing on precolonial forms of power in the idiom of royalty. Religious values and symbolism, particularly those construed as belonging to the glorious ancient Tamil past of autonomous kingship, were associated with the glory of the Dravidian past, which needed now to be reclaimed by Tamils. Within the party, hierarchical distinctions were and continue to be most clearly seen as relative proximity, but to the party leaders rather than to gods, and the leaders themselves are made popular and larger than life through religious symbolism that actually conflates these leaders with the gods. As Bernard Bate (2002) has demonstrated, Jeyalalitha, who was in power in the mid-1990s (as she is again now in 2004), appears in local newspaper ads taken out by her devoted constituents as the divine power of the Tamil people. These ads draw vividly on religious iconography and from precolonial poetry familiar to Tamils from devotional songs commonly sung in temples, both urban and rural. Political activists further a hierarchy of political devotion by subsuming themselves and the Tamil people under Jeyalalitha's bounteous and divine umbrella.

Today, Thevars form one of the largest caste constituencies that supports Jeyalalitha's party, the AIADMK, a rival offshoot of the DMK. Their power as a constituency is in part an outgrowth of their ethnicization as a solidary caste, a process that, as we have seen, started under colonialism but continues apace today. As Price puts it,

> Ambitious politicians, hoping to capture electoral advantages and possibly the state government, encourage the emergence of marked ethnic identities in an attempt to develop their own ethnic constituency as their base of electoral power. (1993, 501; see also Vincentnathan 1996)

Thevar today is a supercaste. The name is applied to what in other contexts, and most particularly in previous contexts, were considered to be different jātis, which, in the past and to a lesser extent in the present, would not intermarry because of the qualitative differences between them. Thevar now most particularly refers to Kallar, Agamudaiyar, and Maravar, the latter being those who inhabit Yanaimangalam. Even among Maravars subgroups existed that previously did not see themselves sufficiently alike to marry. But now, as a political constituency, they emphasize their similarities built in part upon their past common identification as criminal castes as well as their precolonial reputation as guardians (kāvalkāraṅkaḷ), warriors, and even kings. Among Maravars in Yanaimangalam, for example, two separate endogamous subdivisions existed, "Big Tali Maravar," and "Little Tali Maravar" ("tāli" refers to the marriage badge worn by women). In 1989, when I first learned of this division, people talked about it openly but claimed that it really wasn't that relevant anymore because the two groups had recently started to intermarry. In 2003, when I asked about it again, I was told abruptly that it was an ethical mistake (tappu) to even ask about these old divisions. Now they are all mixed (*kalantatu*) as one jāti.

During my first period of research, from 1988 to 1990, the S. C. of Yanaimangalam mostly voted for the Congress Party in both general and local elections because they saw Congress as the party that historically represented a chance for equality in the nation. The DMK and the AIADMK, parties supported by ūrmakkaḷ, were understood by S. C. to support local structures of domination. By 2003, the proliferation of political parties in Tamilnadu was amazing, and many people said that they simply didn't bother with any party anymore. Every jāti (defined now in terms of ethnic identity) had its own party, they said, and they were all essentially the same. None seemed to voice an interest in structural change, only in their own position within the extant structure of caste-association interests. And within this system, when I interviewed the AIADMK woman who was president of the panchayat board for this and another nearby village, if I brought up any caste designation, she promptly and honorably said that we were not allowed to speak in those terms, as if silence on the matter of jāti could somehow make up for the highly caste-oriented politics of the village, party, region, and state.

Thevar dominance in Yanaimangalam collocates several strands of historical action, from precolonial royal process to colonial criminalization and revolt to postcolonial democracy. Thevars in Yanaimangalam may not be aware of their historical legacies in the same terms as I have discussed them here, but they are nonetheless enacting a complex set of historical movements in their contemporary habit (paḻakkam) of fierce competitive dominance. In this sense, Thevar paḻakkam, or habit, can also be viewed as the outgrowth of ancestral acts or historical process. If it is their "habit" to be fierce and frightening, it is a habit built from centuries of interaction in a social and political domain. Their habits today are furthering the form of electoral politics in Tamilnadu by continuing to valorize idioms of honor and dominance. Temples remain the local route to establishing and displaying that dominance, a dominance that is truly local but which also at every moment signals Thevar connection to statewide dominance even on the body itself, as Yanaimangalam's political actors wear veṣtis into which the party colors are woven.

For Thevars, control over temple access (who could go in and, if so, how far, etc.) and distributions of substances such as ash were among the most visible means of publicly asserting their newly achieved prominence. Asserting dominance depends, of course, on one's capacity to subordinate someone else. As the newest members of the ūrmakkaḷ group—and as a group themselves looked down upon by other, higher-ranking ūrmakkaḷ jātis—the Thevars had the most to gain by putting the S. C. "in their place." At stake for many Thevars was not just a sense of self and community (as tough, strong, and capable people) but also their growing dominance in the village (as in the region). Their fearsome reputation for violence was one means through which that desired dominance would be upheld and continue to grow. When the S. C. man ventured into the heart of the temple to retrieve his pinch of ash, he effectively called into play the whole set of meanings and relations that define dominance in Yanaimangalam.

The banishment of Pallars from the goddess temple refracts all of these histories and sheds light on what for Middle Ūr Pallars is a searing contradiction between the rhetoric of the state political parties and the actual structure of dominance and oppression that persists in their lives. That is, while the political parties continue to promote equality and a casteless society, local power (achieved in part by participation in electoral politics built around egalitarian rhetoric) continues to produce caste inequities and precolonial idioms of dominance through temple control.

By 2003, S. C. in Yanaimangalam no longer raised the orange, white, and green flag of the Congress Party, and they certainly had no truck with the red and black of the DMK or the red, black, and white of the AIADMK. Most older residents I spoke with eschewed any flag at all, but one day, several young men from Middle Ūr led my husband to a spot where they lined up and asked him to take their picture. He did so, then later showed me the result. There the young men were, standing under their own flag, the red and green of a new political party called the Pudhiya Thamizhagam, "The New Tamil State." This is the party of Tamilnadu's Pallars.

Alternative Powers

Among the greatest of social powers is the power to define the prevailing meaning of an act, symbol, or any other sign—that is, to have one's own accent dominate over others. Conversely, among the greatest disenfranchisements is to have the meaning you ascribe to a sign validated nowhere and misconstrued everywhere. As Peirce writes, "my language is the sum total of myself" (EW 1992 vol. 1, 54), meaning that through our outreaching signs, words, actions, and expressions (themselves products of our pasts, our social realities and structures), we bring ourselves into relation with the world and so into being. When persons cannot communicate their meanings and intentions, when they are radically silenced, they are also powerless to bring themselves into being in a world of their own making, a world over which they exert some control, some "say." To lose one's language is to lose oneself (cf. Jackson 1998, 200).

When the local police, in collusion with the Thevar headman, banished Middle Ūr from the goddess temple, Ariraman's angry response was vocal yet hidden in the hamlet where he lived separated from the Big Ūr. The Thevar headman had defined the meaning of the act as a "theft" for the police and as a transgression of ūrmakkaḷ-defined order for the village. Ariraman insisted it was devotion and mythologized it moreover as a right his community held as the original inhabitants of the land.

The S. C. residents of Middle Ūr proved to be reluctant subjects of Thevar domination. The direct pressure of Thevar domination operated almost schismogenically to create a greater resentment and a greater will to resist among Middle Ūr residents. To paraphrase Guha (1999/1983, 11), Middle Ūr residents were well aware of the world they lived in, and they had the will to change it. Not only had they the will, they had a language built up over the twentieth century, a language of egalitarianism and justice, of S. C. inclusion and uplift. They had heroes to look toward and they had their own gods.

A few weeks after the ash incident, Middle Ūr responded again. But this time they did not hide their words in the safety of their own hamlet. Rather, they responded loudly and openly. They exerted control over a world of their own making, and they did so smack in the middle of the only road leading into the Big Ūr. How they did so brings us back to temples again, for as it turns out, the goddess is not the only powerful deity in the village, nor is she the only kind of powerful deity. By drawing on their own gods and temples, S. C. and other kuṭimakkaḷ jāti members are able to voice alternative political claims, alternative orders of rank, and even alternative visions of the social world.

Guha (1999/1983, 18–19) suggests that worshipping gods in fact merely reproduces dominance, for by supplicating gods, humans merely echo the gestures and rankings that condition social life and thereby religiously (mystifyingly) justify distinctions of power and dominance. Yet this argument fails to take into account an important aspect of the gods' powers. The power of a god is not transcendent. It is immanent. That is, a god's power is not only construed as a power *over* but is also often construed as a power *within*. A god's power can be a dynamo for human power and capacity. In Yanaimangalam, it was through their gods that the S. C. were able to transform their anger into outrage—that is, into public political action that critiqued ūrmakkaḷ dominance and asserted an alternative future of justice and egalitarianism.

Within the domain of Tamilnadu village politics, as in state and national politics, temples remain a key resource for competitive claims to rights of inclusion and distinction. Temples are powerful places for political discourse not *in spite of* being "religious" but rather precisely *because* they are places where humans can enhance their social power as a group with the power of the gods. Activities involving fierce gods, in particular, serve up critical commentaries on specific relations of and even forms of dominance in Tamilnadu.

Part II

REMAKING THE VILLAGE

SIX

Gods of Yanaimangalam

Residents of Yanaimangalam distinguish among three kinds of gods, what I will gloss here as Brahmanical gods (pirāmaṅka tēvarkaḷ), village goddesses (ūr ammaṉkaḷ), and fierce gods (māṭaṉ, or pēy; lit. "ghost"). Residents compare these gods along several dimensions of contrast—high to low, pure to impure, vegetarian to meat-eating. But the dimension of contrast they stress the most is that of soft to fierce, words which depict the relative stability versus instability of the gods as actors, as real influences in human affairs. For example, when I asked Ramayya Thevar why the village goddess went on procession through the village streets while the fierce god Cutalaimatan ("Fierce God of the Cremation Ground") did not, he spoke not of relative rank or purity but of relative benevolence. The goddess is mother (*tāy*), he said. She protects people and the village. Fierce gods such as Cutalaimatan, he said, are dangerous to people in the village. Similarly, one summer day when I was hiking across the blistering, dry fields from the fierce Cutalaimatan's temple accompanied by two young Brahman priests,[1] Subramaniyam and Venki, I asked these young men why the Brahmanical god Murukan, son of Parvathi and Siva and brother of elephant-headed Ganesh, lived in the village's central residential area, nestled among houses and freely gazing down residential streets, while Cutalaimatan lived so far out across the fields in the wastelands around the cremation ground. They replied that Murukan, like the rest of his "type" (using the English word and meaning Brahmanical gods such as Siva, Krishna, and Ganesh), are soft (*metuvāna*) while fierce gods such as Cutalaimatan are cruel or fearsome (*payaṅkaramāṉatu*).

From one end of the spectrum to the other, soft gods (of which the Brahmanical are the softest) are those who are generally calm, stable, and beneficent. Fierce gods, on the other hand, are wild, unstable, and unpredictable. The fierce gods may prove protective and beneficent at one time, then cruel at another. They may unpredictably attack a person if they feel the slightest insult or if they simply feel overheated by, for example, seeing a beautiful young woman walking by. The village goddess belongs in between, as befits her well-known dual or "ambivalent" nature (Doniger 1980; Ramanujan 1986, 55–61; Kinsley 1986), in that sometimes she is identified with the Brahmanical and benign cool goddess Parvathi, devout wife of Siva, while at other times she is identified with the fearsome Durga or Kali, unmarried forms of the goddess who wield weapons, ride lions, crack skulls, and drink blood to match their hot nature.

I will introduce some of the gods of Yanaimangalam by briefly describing some of the stories and histories of temples and gods in the village. I then turn to consideration of the pragmatic reality of gods in the village; that is, how gods and persons connect in socially productive ways. The relations between humans and gods are not limited reflective mirrorings. Rather, I argue that in order to fully understand the place of gods in human life, the actual events that link human groups to specific gods is key.

BRAHMANICAL TEMPLES

On the day of my first visit to Yanaimangalam in 1988, about two months before I was able to move into my house in the village, I was invited to "see" the gods in the Siva temple at the end of the Agraharam street, the Brahman neighborhood. Officious elders sent a boy to fetch the temple's priest. The priest arrived. He was blue-eyed and blind with cataracts, a bit plump, and he wore his white hair in the manner of Brahman priests, shaved in front and with the long hairs in back tied behind his head in a thick knot. I followed him down the street and a dozen or more children followed behind me like an eager wagging tail. At the end of the street sat the temple—the largest structure in the village. Weeds grew from fissures in the weathered stone walls, long ago painted in red and white vertical stripes. In front of the temple, a square tank choked with lotuses gave way to the flooded rice fields beyond. The priest unlocked the thick, castle-like wooden doors with a prodigious skeleton key. They creaked open and we, along with the sun's light, entered the temple's dank interior. The light startled temple bats, and as we ducked through the ever lower doorways that led farther into the temple toward the interior "womb-rooms" (garbhagraha) that housed the images of gods, hundreds of bats shot past us out of those same doorways. The blind priest walked smoothly through their parting rapids and I, at least intellectually aware that bats with their precision radar can avoid even moving objects, tried to follow smoothly in his wake. My failure in this endeavor to "look cool" worked much to the amusement the giggly tail of children who squirmed so close behind me. Once we had all traded places with the bats and approached the shrines (there were several in the many-halled temple to different forms of Siva and to his consort goddess Parvathi), the priest lit camphor to show us the deities one by one. A bronze image of Nataraja, the "Dancing Siva," was clothed in cotton with a leopard-skin print and draped in wilting flowers from the morning's pūja. The camphor flame sparkled off his chiseled features and the bronze frame that surrounded him. As the priest circled the camphor flame, we looked at the god, obtaining darśan, that visual exchange so central to Hindu worship in which god and devotee mingle or even "touch" one another through eyesight (Eck 1981; Fuller 1992, 59–60). Then the priest passed a tray of purifying ash (vipūti) out to the few worshipers present. I placed two rupees on the tray as an offering, took a pinch of ash to smear my forehead, and then headed outside, shielding my eyes from the open sunlight.

After visiting the Siva temple, I was beckoned down a wide earthen path leading away from the village, through the rice fields, and toward the river that flowed on the north side of the village. At the riverbank stood another temple, this one to Visnu. Another priest who specialized in serving the various forms of Visnu conducted me through the large temple. There I received not ash (ash is Siva's special substance) but some red powder (kumkumam) to dot my forehead and some leaves from Visnu's favorite plant, *tulsi.* This temple, I later learned, was 600 years old, much older than the 300-year-old Siva temple. This village, I eventually realized, had a long history.

The stone walls of both the Siva and Visnu temples carry chiseled inscriptions that bear witness to regional and village history, though recent renovations have covered some of them in new concrete. The inscriptions are chiseled in several languages, including Telugu, Malayalam, and Tamil interspersed with old Granta script, mostly unreadable to average modern Tamil readers. The inscriptions are, however, clear indications of the kingly past of temple and village patronage. The inscriptions tell of the founding of the temples, name the kings who founded them, and record important transactions, gifts, patrons, and hereditary servants of the temples. Smaller village temples to Krishna and Ganesh also bear such inscriptions.

Yanaimangalam's red-and-white-striped temples to Siva, Visnu, Krishna, and Ganesh put Yanaimangalam on the map of history. They link the village both to the administrative present and to official histories, Sanskrit myth, high art and architecture, and literary languages. These are temples that link Yanaimangalam to the "great" tradition of Indian civilization, a tradition that Ramanujan (1973) describes as Classical, Sanskritic, Male, and Universal. They also provide historical data for scholars, recorded in stone and then recorded again in colonial and Indian government documents that detail the bronze sculptured images, the dates the temples were constructed, the kings that commissioned them. All of this information is based on the inscriptions etched into temple walls, translated into English, the language of the great bureaucratic tradition, in epigraphical records that may be found in libraries at the University of Chicago, Harvard, and Berkeley. When I lived in the village, government officials would come to Yanaimangalam in their jeeps to record another inscription or to show a new district collector the glory of the region's past inscribed in the paṭṭikkāṭus (the "rustic," "hick" villages) of the region. Village residents are aware of the historical interest outsiders have in these temples and are eager to show them off to visiting officials and, it seems, anthropologists. Today these old Brahmanical temples are administered centrally from Ambasamuttiram, a large temple town about twenty-five kilometers distant, where the nearest office of the HRCE, the Hindu Religious and Charitable Endowment Department, is located. In Tamilnadu, Brahmanical temples as well as more wealthy temples to other gods are administered centrally by the Tamilnadu government through this board. The board controls income and supports the temple by funding basic requirements for sustained ritual activity. This includes hiring priests. For more wealthy temples, the board also manages the temple income. The board was first established in 1926 by the British administration and then reinvigorated in 1951. As Franklin Presler (1987) has detailed, temple administration has from the nineteenth century on been a way for the modern state to control Tamil temples, and not just as cultural and economic resources; many temples control much wealth, including land. Temple control also echoes precolonial religious-political idioms of power, in which control over temples went hand in hand with political rights over territories. When the anti-Brahman movement in Tamilnadu became a platform for Dravidian political parties in the 1920s, Dravidian control over Brahmanical temples became one way to publicly reassert the primacy of Dravidians over northern Brahmanical influences. Many Brahmans consider the HRCE, which is run by state parties that maintain the anti-Brahman policies of their predecessors, to be uninterested in really maintaining the glory of these temples. Brahmans in Yanaimangalam today see these administrators as stingy and unwilling to maintain the temples or priests as they should.

In 1990, these temples were in bad shape, faded and dilapidated structures with plants growing in fissures that spread along the old walls and towers. By 2001, the Visnu temple had been restored, the expenses paid by a Brahman patron now living in Chennai but hailing from Yanaimangalam. By 2003, the same man had financed a partial restoration of the Siva temple's exterior walls and towers. For some Hindus today—especially urban, nationally conscious middle-class Hindus—these old temples provide a sense of a past, promoted by some as a lost past to be mourned and yet restored through religious nationalism and financial patronage. Temple restoration has becomes a sign of the resurgence of a "lost Hindu nation" that never really was. The new patrons, like the old kings whose names the renovations have covered in cement, get their names inscribed in the temple, perhaps on a plaque rather than in stone.

VILLAGE GODDESSES

Despite the historical, artistic, and more recent Hindu nationalist significance of the village's Brahmanical temples, very few village residents spend much of their time or many of their economic resources worshipping in these temples. Occasionally a Brahman family from Bombay or Delhi, Chennai or Tirunelveli Town, or, in one case during my stay, from Monterey, California—strangers to Yanaimangalam's current population—would come to visit one of these gods whom they claimed as their lineage (*kula*) god. Usually it was Visnu by the riverbank they came to visit and reclaim as their own. But as we know, it is the village goddess whom "everyone" in the village worships. To her is attributed the power of fertility—fertility of soil, humans, and animals. There is no one in the village unaffected by her power (cakti) to assure good crops of rice and to help the living bear healthy children.

But the ūrmakkaḷ's goddess temple is only one among several in the village. Ten more goddess temples and shrines are planted there. To begin with, each of the five residential areas that Yanaimangalam comprises has its own goddess temple. In addition, several lineages sponsor their own temple or shrine to the village goddess. Though the goddesses have different names (Yanaiyamman, Uccimakakkali, Muppatatiyamman, and Mariyamman, among others) as well as independent temples on different sites, all eleven are said to be the same power (*orē cakti*). As the Tamil saying goes, "The life is one, the forms are two [many]" (*uyir oṉṟu, uruvam irantu*). A few other goddesses, such as the "fierce goddess" named Issakkiyamman, are said to be a "different power" (*vēru cakti*).

Puzzling one day over the many forms of the one life that is the village goddess, I asked a respected older man in the village, Virapandi Muppanar, to relate the "birth story" (*piranta katai*) of the goddess named Muppatatiyamman, who lives in a small alcove built into the wall of a house compound in the Muppanar neighborhood. I noticed her one day as I was passing by. He denied any knowledge of her "birth story" and suggested I ask someone else. Obviously I had asked the wrong question, so I rephrased it. This time I asked how it was that the same goddess could be in so many places at once. He then started to tell me the story I had been hoping for. It wasn't the story of her birth (which I later figured out meant a Sanskritic myth, a *purāna*), but the story of how she came to be in Yanaimangalam, in this place and that.

He started out by relating a little about how in the old days, long before there were people in the village, the goddess had come down "from the north" and passed through the area, wandering about, pausing to rest here and there. As she walked, small traces of her powerful substance, her cakti, were left behind in the places she traversed. In the places where she paused or stopped to rest, her cakti soaked into the soil, and there it remains to this day. Sometimes her presence in the earth is discovered by people. Other times her image might appear on its own, as they say about the main village goddess, Yanaiyamman. Virapandi Muppanar continued by telling me in a tape-recorded interview how her presence in the alcove was discovered. In his translated words:

> It was a long time ago, about five generations ago, about the time of the white man, and about the time of the Vikkayamarattin Kottai story. There was an unmarried boy, about eighteen years old, one of four children in his family. The goddess was always possessing him. She would possess him and he would dance from village to village. His family picked a fight with him over this strange behavior, so he ran away. But a few days later he came back. He said to his mother: "I'll show you the truth!" He took a clay pot full of burning rags and danced with it all night around the village. Many people figured he was just pretending to be possessed, and they spoke disparagingly about him. He went all around the village and early the next morning he came back. He went straight into the shed under the tamarind tree in his family courtyard, and there he put down the burning firepot, came out, and locked the door behind him. A few days later, he returned. It was a Tuesday. He took up the pot again and went around the village. Even though several days had passed, the pot was still aflame! It was still burning, just like that! Seeing this, the people changed their minds and thought that there must be a goddess in that place [in the earth under the shed by the wall].

As far as the human residents of Yanaimangalam are concerned, goddesses have always-already been in the village. Long before humans settled the village, the goddess wandered, and as she wandered, she marked the earth with her substance, her cakti, thus establishing her real presence in places. She is rooted in the soil, and her image might spring up anywhere, like a tree's root might throw up shoots far from its trunk. Her power is a quality that shapes the village's topography: it creates zones of greater and lesser energy (cakti), and discovering those places links human beings to that power.

FIERCE GODS

In Yanaimangalam, there are at least sixteen temples and shrines to fierce gods and goddesses. Most of these gods live on the margins of the village territory, outside the residential areas, out in the fields or beyond in the wasteland (kāṭu). Even those that live within the residential village are nonetheless talked about as living outside. Outside is, after all, a relative term: outside the house in the courtyard (Figure 6.1) or outside the courtyard on the street. Unlike the village goddesses and unlike Brahmanical deities, fierce gods are not paraded through the streets in processions, nor are they generally brought inside the house for worship. If a fierce god residing in a house courtyard proves too violent or touchy for peaceful daily life, families have been known to remove them as they brought them—in a handful of earth—taking them out into the wasteland, farther away from settled areas. In myth and ritual, these gods are often subordinated to the village goddesses as guardians who live near but outside her temple, much like the humans who live outside the central village residential area are thought to be subordinate and unruly as well.

As unpredictable and unstable as anger itself, these gods may protect or attack. Residents of Yanaimangalam give them wide berth in many daily contexts, choosing their paths of movement to avoid directly passing by or standing in front of the hot disordering gaze of a fierce god. Stories abound of the dangers of the gaze of such gods. One old man (called "Shaky Grampa" for his Parkinson's-like tremors) told me of a fierce god his family discovered not only near his new government-subsidized house but, unfortunately, staring directly at it. Unable to relocate, his family adopted the god as their own and sacrificed a chicken to him now and then in order to placate him and so reduce the potential anger of his gaze. Aruna told me another story of a woman who became dangerously possessed by the god Vellalakantan (see Chapter 8) after having engaged in some shouting and mud-slinging with another woman right in front of his shrine and right in his line of vision out in the rice fields. The power of eyesight flowing from a god—and even from persons—is not to be underestimated. As Suzanne Hanchett shows, the eyesight of some deities has the power to kill (1988, 159; see also Scott 1994).

While the eyesight of gods is more powerful than that of humans, still all eyes carry qualities from what is seen to the seer and from the seer out to what is seen. "Seeing is a kind of touching," as Eck writes (1981, 3; see also Babb 1981, 390–391). This holds true for both gods and humans. Sight is perhaps less a *kind* of touching than it is a sense which, like all the senses, including touching, may be understood to transfer qualities: there are cer-

Figure 6.1. Preparing food for a "backyard fierce god," Kollaimatan.

tain things that are best not seen (touched, heard, tasted, or even smelled) and certain people who had best not look (or touch or speak . . .). One simple example bears out this claim about vision. One day I was sitting on the stoop of my house writing my field notes. The day was hot, the streets were quiet in the afternoon, and the only person in sight was a man carrying a load of hay on his head coming down the street toward me from my left. The hayload covered his whole head and I could not see his face. Gazing about, I turned and looked down the road to my right. I saw two women from Pillaimar Street walking toward me from that direction. But no sooner had I noticed them then they abruptly dashed and ducked into a doorway a few houses down. After a few seconds, one of them peeked out of the doorway and peered up the street. I turned my head up the street to follow her gaze and caught sight of the man carrying hay just as he turned off the street onto a side path and disappeared out of sight. The two women came out from their hiding place and continued up the road. When they were passing me, we greeted one another and I asked them why they had ducked into the doorway like that. One of them answered me as if this were certainly one of my more stupid questions, "Well, we didn't want to see the hay, did we!" I inquired further. She explained that they were going to see a newborn baby. I stared blankly. She spelled it out. They couldn't very well go look at a newborn after looking at the hay, could they? It might harm the baby. The upshot of this anecdote is this: people are affected by what they see and they carry that affect with them and can pass it on. Such is the logic of the ill-translated "evil eye" in South India. The eye is not so much "evil" as it is merely powerful. It can carry inauspiciousness (hay is dead plant life and hence as inauspicious as any corpse), envy, and other negative qualities. But as Margaret Trawick shows, eyesight can also carry too much power of any emotion, even the love of a mother for an infant: "Anni said that a mother should never gaze lovingly into her child's face, especially while the child was sleeping, because the loving gaze itself could cause harm to the child" (1990, 93).

If the strong love of a mother for her baby can be so dangerous, think of the danger of the eyesight of a fierce god, so jealous and full of anger and so uncontrollable. Mostly the gazes of these gods guard the peripheries of the village, intimidating passersby. Or they gaze out away from houses toward the open fields, threatening possible intruders. The Brahmanical god Krishna, on the other hand, looks straight down the Agraharam, bathing the whole community in his beneficent gaze.

While kings and, more recently, the Tamilnadu state and wealthy upper-caste patrons established and patronized Brahmanical temples, and while the goddess traveled to what is now Yanaimangalam independently of humans, leaving powerful traces in the places where she moved and rested (hence "self-appearing"), village residents see fierce gods as having come to Yanaimangalam in two different ways. More rarely, fierce gods are created in the village itself as gods or goddesses born from men or women who have met violent deaths. All over Tamilnadu, fierce gods are born this way, in violence and injustice (Reynolds 1980; Blackburn 1988; Trawick 1991). Sometimes these violent origins may be linked to Brahmanical purānas in which fierce gods are the offspring of anger, intrigue, and violence or injustice among those gods thought to be more benign (Knipe 1989; Hiltebeitel 1989). Either way, the violence of their origins and their vengeful natures are often reflected in their murderous depictions as sword-wielding mustachioed heroes ready to fight (Figure 6.2) or as fanged terrifying women who look ready to bite.

More often, fierce gods come into Yanaimangalam from elsewhere, often through the agency of village residents who, usually unwittingly, transfer these gods to the village. They bring gods bodily and they bring them in substances, such as trees and, commonly, in "handfuls of earth" (piṭimaṉ) (see also Inglis 1985), as the following story, summarized from the stories told to me by several village residents, illustrates.

> Many years ago, a group of men from Yanaimangalam went up into the forest near Sabarimalai [a nearby mountain that rises in Tamilnadu and peaks in Kerala] to cut a tree for the flagpole in front of the Siva temple. In the tree-cutting party was a

Figure 6.2.
Vellalakantan shrine.

Carpenter to do the cutting, a Thevarmar man, and two Pillaimar men. They ascended the mountain and searched the forest for a tall tree. They found it. They cut it down. They brought it back to the village and set it up in front of the Siva temple. Then, all at once, the four men were struck violently ill. A specialist determined that ghosts and other fierce beings inhabited the tree they had brought down from the mountain. Being deprived of their home, these fierce beings had grabbed hold of (*piṭiccatu*) the culprits; that is, possessed them. One remedy was available. The families of each of the men were instructed to go back to the place where they found the tree, take a handful of earth from that spot, and bring it back to the village. There they should deposit the earth near their houses and on those spots build permanent shrines to these fierce beings, adopting those gods into their lineage as lineage gods (*kulatēvaṅkaḷ*). This way the gods would be satisfied and leave the men be. And that is how the temples for Kalamatan, Talavaymatan, Cappanimatan, and Cutalaimatan-by-the-Carpenter's-House were established.

A similar story, first told to me by a woman from the Thevar neighborhood and retold here, reveals how the god Sivalaperi Cutalaimatan—who, like all Cutalaimatans, was brought into Brahmanical tradition as a manifestation of Siva—came to Yanaimangalam.

> One day, a Thevarmar man went all the way to a village called Sivalaperi about 30 miles from Yanaimangalam in order to swear an oath to the god Cutalaimatan who lived in that village. The man had been accused of theft in the village, and the accuser agreed that if the suspect swore his innocence in front of this fearsome god, he would let the matter drop. So the accused went to Sivalaperi and swore his oath. But he was afraid and so this is how he did it: he took a handful of earth from right in front of the god's image and moved that earth a little distance from the temple. That's where he swore his oath. Apparently he was worried to tell a lie straight in the face of the god. Well, despite his precautions, dire consequences proved imminent. A black goat followed the man all the way home from the temple. Once home, the man tried to kill the goat (for curry), but the goat grew huge and attacked both him and his kinsmen with disastrous and deadly consequences—a pregnant woman in the family was killed. To quell the god's righteous anger, only one recourse was available: the accused not only had to admit his guilt but also had to establish a shrine to the god in his backyard near the shed. He did this by returning to Sivalaperi with surviving family members. From there he took a handful of earth from the temple floor and brought it back to Yanaimangalam, where he "planted" it, and thereby the god's power, in the courtyard outside his house.

The woman continued by saying that because the power of this god was so great, the family did not keep him in their courtyard but rather moved him again—with a handful of earth from the courtyard this time—out to the cremation ground, far away from any human habitation.This is how East Cutalaimatan temple was established. This temple, which began as a lineage shrine, soon became a temple for the entire Thevar jāti in Yanaimangalam, perhaps in part as a way for them to partake in the fame of West Cutalaimatan temple right next door, in which they had no rights.

Just as the goddess's cakti resides in the soil, so too does the power of fierce gods. Even the images of these gods are often formed from earth (Figure 6.3), whether as simple, temporary mounds of earth formed by devotees for worship, which then erode back into earth with wind and rain only to be reformed for the next pūja, or as more shapely terra-cotta forms sculpted by Potters (see Inglis 1985).

SASTA

In addition to the "village goddesses" described above, there is one more deity, Sasta, who can perhaps best be described as a village god, for like the goddess, he too is associated primarily with the ūr, though unlike the goddess he is less associated with the soil and more associated with families

Figure 6.3. Earthern images at the Panaiyatiyan temple.

who originate in the ūr. Like Aiyanar in northern Tamilnadu, Sasta is also considered a guardian deity (hence resembling the fierce gods in some ways). And he is also associated with a Brahmanical myth. Like the goddess, then, Sasta appears to be polysemically associated with all three "types" I am distinguishing here. In the south, every village has a Sasta and every person in the region has a Sasta temple which they consider their own, through their patrilineage. It is interesting that the Sasta temples with which Yanaimangalam's residents associate are, with only a few exceptions, located in villages other than Yanaimangalam. Similarly, most of those who worship Sasta in Yanaimangalam are strangers to the village. Since people worship the Sasta located in what they reckon as their lineage's original ūr (their patrilineal *conta ūr*), the movement of people across the territory to worship distant Sastas indicates the fact *and consciousness* of the movement of families over territory through time. It is clear to all that the village as it is now constituted is not the village as it always was.

TEMPLE ASSOCIATIONS IN YANAIMANGALAM

In Yanaimangalam, there are thirty-five temples to the three kinds of gods described above. Most days, the temples are quiet places. Priests go there daily, or maybe only twice a week in some cases, to feed and bathe and care for the gods. Passersby may drop in for darśan, to offer a prayer, or make a request. On their way home from morning baths in the river, many drop by the conveniently located Visnu temple or the goddess temple to see the gods and obtain some red powder or white ash to smear on their clean foreheads, a final cleansing ritual to begin the day. For most of these temples, there are also occasional festivals—in some cases there are several festivals a year; others are annual, and some are even less frequent. Some festivals are relatively small, limited to just one lineage in the village. Others are multilineage and multijāti affairs in which most village residents participate.

The festivals for the Brahman temples are, in Yanaimangalam, curtailed celebrations known usually as *tirunāḷ* ("holy day"). These are funded not by a united association of taxpayers (defined by ūr, jāti, or lineage), but rather somewhat haphazardly by donations collected door to door as well as by individual and voluntary sponsors who may particularly like these gods, consider them their *iṣṭatēvaṅkaḷ,* or "favorite gods." The HRCE also allocates some limited funds for maintaining the ritual life of these temples.

The goddess temples and fierce-god temples, on the other hand, are patronized and funded by various combinations of village residents who compose what I call "temple associations" that together fund and produce temple festivals called koṭais (gifts). These associations have different criteria for formation along the lines outlined above: by ūr, jāti, and/or lineage.

Temple associations form around most of the eleven ūr goddesses. In most cases these associations correspond to residential clusters. That is, North Ūr, South Ūr, Middle Ūr, South Street, and the main ūr each form separate associations for the goddess temple attached to their own residential areas. In these cases, each koṭai festival is funded by a compulsory tax levied on the members of that particular ūr, or hamlet. The remaining goddess shrines are funded through smaller jāti or lineage associations. All but the excluded S. C. goddess associations connect their celebrations directly to the festival of Yanaiyamman, like satellites included within the purview of her festival. In these cases, lineages and their goddesses participate in the main goddess koṭais, forming stops on the procession routes.

Temple associations form for fierce gods similarly, sometimes on the basis of location (such as around Middle Ūr's god Panaiyatiyan in Chapter 9), sometimes on the basis of jāti identification, but most often the fierce gods are linked to lineages of humans. Often lineages of different jātis and ūrs are thrown together into somewhat idiosyncratic combinations because of the history of the temple and the gods' relations to humans, as I detail below.

Figure 6.4 summarizes all the temples for which koṭai festivals are organized, lists fierce gods and ūr goddesses, and indicates the association membership.

GODS AND HUMANS: METAPHORS AND METONYMS (OR SYMBOLS AND INDEXES)[2]

As noted, residents of Yanaimangalam commonly compare both human jātis and gods along similar dimensions of contrast. They describe both gods and jātis as relatively high (ocanta) versus relatively low (taḻnta), as big (periya) versus little (ciṉṉa), as "neat" or ordered (*muṟaiyāka*) versus messy and disordered (*mōcam*), as pure (cuttam) versus impure (acuttam).

Given the parallel associations between humans on the one hand and gods on the other, it is certainly easy to see why many scholars have presented analyses where the pantheon of ranked gods "symbolizes" ranks among humans (e.g., Fuller 1987, 33; Dumont 1986/1957, 460; cf. D. Mines 1997a). I too find the metaphoric resemblances stark and convincing. Yet this symbolic parallel is of only limited value for understanding the relation of gods to humans. The relation between gods and social orderings among humans can be more fully comprehended by not just thinking about the metaphoric "reflection" of two separate sets of relations (gods there and humans here) but by analyzing the pragmatic relations that link humans to the gods. Humans and gods are linked by more than metaphor. They are linked together really and metonymically; that is, god and person are materially linked parts of one another.

The distinction here between metaphor and metonym—or between "symbolic" associations and "indexical" contiguities, to use the Peircian language of signs—hearkens back to Levi-Strauss's analysis of totemism, where he told us that animals are "good to think" and not just "good to eat" (1963, 62). Levi-Strauss theorized that human groups represent themselves with totems (kangaroos, wombats, etc.) not because of any positive or physically real relation of contiguity or metonymy between the group members and the species, as Durkheim (1965/1915, 216–217, 223) and Radcliffe-Brown (in his early analysis—1952/1929) had surmised. Rather, he argued, humans represent themselves with totems because of the compelling *metaphoric* relations between two systems of difference (Levi-Strauss 1963, 87). We may break this metaphoric or symbolic relation down into two aspects: icon and homology. Iconically, it is the *resemblances* among the differences that matter: the differences among animals in the animal system, on the one hand, and humans in the human system, on the other, are mapped as structural icons of one another. Homologically, it is the structure of thought itself that, projected onto both animal and human planes, creates the iconic resemblances among the differences (see, for example, Levi-Strauss 1963, 90–91).

Levi-Strauss argued, in other words, that thought, a symbolic system of structured oppositions, projects onto and determines the iconic resemblance

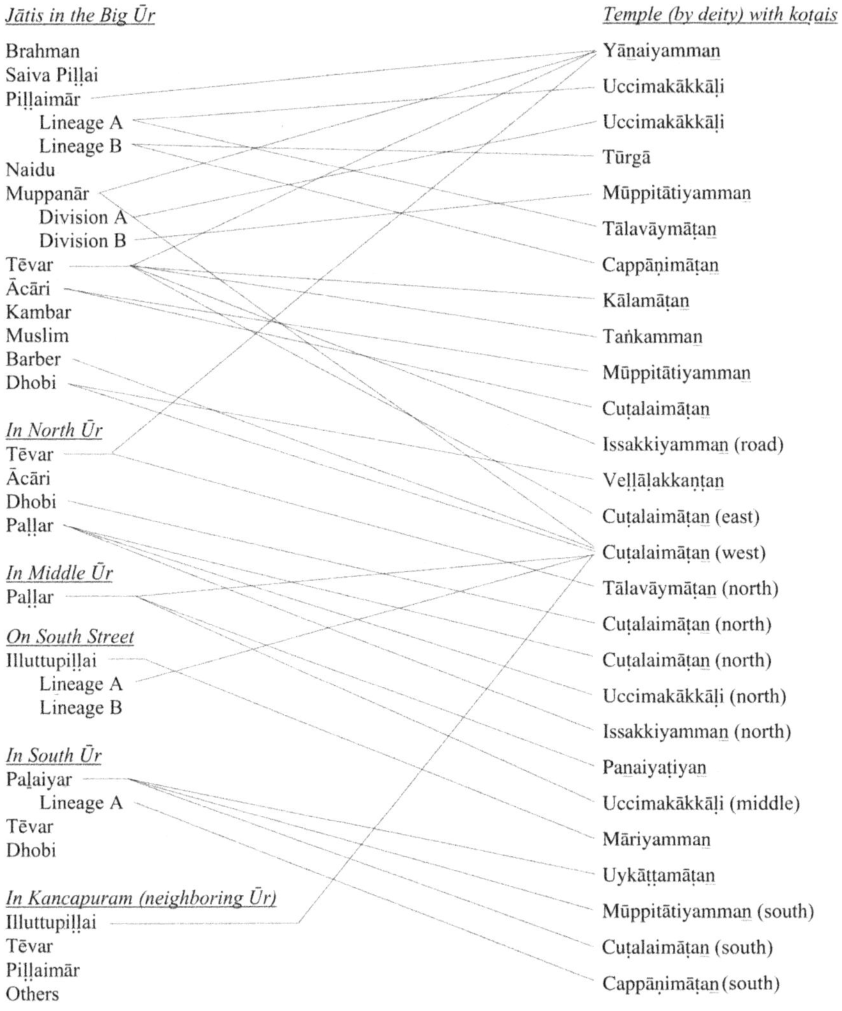

Figure 6.4. Temple associations in Yanaimangalam (designated by lines matching associated jātis, ūrs, and lineages with the temples, named by deity, that they sponsor), 1990.

between animal and human planes. In this model of totemism, Levi-Strauss purposefully sundered metonym from metaphor (or index from symbol, using Peirce's terms). The metonym (indexical trope), he said, belongs to the order of *event*; in contrast, the metaphor (symbolic trope) belongs to the order of *structure* (ibid., 27). Totemism made sense to Levi-Strauss primarily on the level of structure.

This very same separation of metonym and event from metaphor and structure characterizes symbolic analyses that have been used to map the Hindu village pantheon onto social orderings among castes in south Indian villages. Perhaps the most well known of these analyses is Louis Dumont's early ethnographic study of the Pramalai Kallar, a jāti group well known in western Tamilnadu and dominant in the regions west of the town of Madurai. Dumont's work here in many way forms the basis for his later structuralist thesis on caste, *Homo Hierarchicus* (1970). Based on fieldwork he conducted in the 1940s, Dumont argued that the rank order of the "Hindu pantheon" of gods from pure to impure (vegetarian to meat-eating) *mirrors* the hierarchy among castes. Presaging Levi-Strauss, Dumont formulated his argument on a principle of metaphoric homology by which an ideological principle (the opposition of pure and impure) is projected from an internal or purely mental system of ideas (the symbolic system) onto the outside material world of both castes and gods. In Dumont's words:

> It is impossible not to see that the [pantheon] *reflects* the opposition of the pure and the impure, that is to say the society of castes in its abstract elementary [mental] form. (Dumont 1986/1957, 460; my emphasis)

Fuller agrees in principle, saying,

> [W]ith Dumont, we can legitimately see the village deities as *symbols of* caste society, for their relational divinity *does reflect* the caste structure, wherein the high castes are *always* in a complementary hierarchical relationship with the low castes. (1987, 33; my emphasis)

These analyses, like Levi-Strauss's of totemism, limit their subject (and subjects!) to symbolic signs. They posit ideational systems of symbols (in the mind) that give structure to an external cosmology.

These symbols and metaphoric associations match in some respects Peirce's definition of a symbol as a sign that "signifies what it does only by virtue of its being understood to have that signification" (1931–1958, 2:304). In other words, symbols and metaphors signify by ideational convention. Any theory of meaning that focuses exclusively on this symbolic sign relation while it omits or sets aside the indexical also omits what is the "dynamo" (to borrow a metaphor from Sapir 1921, 14) of semeiotic, including symbolic, processes. It is the indexical relation that generates the *process* of semeiosis (sign-action) of which both index and symbol are related parts (Colapietro 1989, 17). In other words, it is precisely the contiguity—the indexical metonymic relation—between gods and humans that make gods into important, pragmatically real agents in social life. The relation between gods and social orderings among humans can be more fully comprehended by reintroducing the indexical metonymic relation into the equation.

CONTIGUITIES

Gods and devotees in Tamilnadu are indexically linked, and humans understand their relations to gods (lineage gods [kulatēvaṅkaḷ] in particular) in this way. The indexical relation between humans and gods can best be described as a metonymic relation, a substantial relation of part to whole.

This metonymic relation is neither a priori nor absolutely essential. Metonymic relations are made through action (event) and explained mythohistorically. The following narrative, for example, explains the relation between a lineage of a middle-ranking jāti (Muppanar)—one of Yanaimangalam's three politically and economically dominant ūrmakkaḷ jātis—and a low-ranking, blood-eating, fierce god named Muntacami who lives out beyond the edge of village fields at the cremation ground with his brother, the god Cutalaimatan. I retell a version of the story here.

> One day, about a hundred years ago, a Muppanar man was out working in his field by the riverbank. He saw something floating down the river toward him. He fished it out and found it was a banana-plant shoot. He planted it on the edge of his field.
>
> Now it just so happened that his field lay in the line of sight of Cutalaimatan at the cremation ground. To help gain the god's favor (instead of jealous wrath) the farmer made a vow. He promised Cutalaimatan that he would give him the first stalk of bananas his new tree produced in return for the god's protecting the plant and field.
>
> Well, a year passed and the banana plant flourished and produced a big stalk of bananas. The owner came out and cut the stalk and took it home, forgetting his vow to Cutalaimatan. He took one banana from the stalk, peeled it, and took a big bite. Immediately he choked, spat out the banana, and could eat nothing from then on.
>
> He realized that the fault was his for forgetting his vow and so this higher-caste man went to see a local man favored by Cutalaimatan, a lower-ranking Dhobi named Kantan, to enlist his aid and find a solution. He went to Kantan because Kantan and his entire lineage were the special devotees of Cutalaimatan. They took care of him and he took care of them. Kantan was the one whose connection to the god was closest: Cutalaimatan regularly possessed him and communicated his needs through this human host (cāmiyāṭi). The solution that the Dhobi and the god offered was that the Muppanar man and his whole lineage should adopt Muntacami, Cutalaimatan's younger brother, as their own special god. They should construct a shrine to Muntacami opposite Cutalaimatan's shrine and worship there from then on, side by side with the low-ranking Dhobis, *as equals.* So to this day the Muppanar and Dhobis are equals in that temple.

A chance event (a banana shoot floating down the river) led to a vow made and then a vow broken. A vow broken established a permanent relation between a low-ranking peripheral god and a relatively high-ranking central jāti. This relation between Muntacami and the Muppanar lineage is metonymic. It is understood as an enduring substantial bodily relation between the god and lineage members, and it cannot be attenuated at will. The Muppanar lineage (which corresponds roughly to the local Muppanar jāti grouping) is forever substantially connected (*cērntatu*) with their new lineage god, their new *kulatēvam.* The god inhabits their houses, bodies, and lives. The god eats what they eat, possesses them, fills them with energy, and can also cause them illness if he is weak or displeased.

The new relation of "equality" established between Muppanars and Dhobis in fact inverts the dominant rankings that are confirmed each year at the goddess festival, where the ūrmakkaḷ Muppanars serve as patrons and the Dhobis as servants and where Muppanars receive mariyātai relative to the Dhobis. This inverted relation takes on a social, publicly enacted reality in temple festivals that take place three times a year at the cremation-ground temple that houses both lineage gods. During these festivals at the Cutalaimatan temple, it is the Dhobis who receive first honors and the Muppanars who receive second honors (and others in order afterward). That is, the Dhobis receive their shares (paṅku) of the temple leftovers first and have authority over the distribution of remaining shares. Moreover, when devotees make their rounds, visiting the gods at the shrine, they pay homage first to Cutalaimatan and his Dhobi god-dancer and only second to the Muppanar's lineage god and god-dancer.

This reversal of rank does not always go smoothly, however, because it does not set well with all Muppanars. While I attended a minor cool-season festival at this temple in December 2001, a fight broke out over this very reversal. During one of the high points of the festival, half a dozen god-dancers were joined (cērkkai) with their gods and were dancing the gods' dance. After twenty minutes or so of dancing to loud drum and nataswāram music in front of the gods' shrines, the men paused in their dance to hand out oracular "words of grace" (*aruḷvākku*) to devotees who clustered around the god-dancers to ask the gods' advice on matters of urgency to them. Devotees received not only words but also cooling and auspicious ash from the god-dancers, who carried around copious supplies in small ornate brass cups (Figure 6.5). The dancing then resumed.

It was during this period of dancing punctuated by advice that the fight broke out. All of a sudden, the visual and aural cacophony of the scene—god-dancers moving through the temple from shrine to shrine, devotees following their favorite and hoping for a quick gift of ash or a brief word of graced advice—gave way to a focused roar. Loud voices

Figure 6.5. God-dancers at the Cutalaimatan temple, December 2001.
© Richard Rapfogel. Used by permission.

shouted. We looked and realized that the women in the crowd had moved away from a center of action and men were surging toward it, pushing, shouting, and shoving. In the midst of the throng, we saw cooler heads prevailing over hotter ones, keeping anyone from actually swinging punches or landing blows. And from the center of the throng slipped out an old man carrying a flaming torch. He disappeared into the shadows beyond where we stood.

The thin old man who slipped out and disappeared was none other than the god-dancer for the temple's chief god, Cutalaimatan. He was insulted. He had taken off for home and, someone said, refused to return to finish the festival. Silence descended on the crowd and a long period of waiting began. This pause gave me some time to get the full story of what was happening from Aruna, who now, as she had been ten years previously, was my extraordinary research companion. The fight had started when a young man from the Muppanar jāti in the village became enraged because the Dhobi god-dancer—indeed, the old man who had disappeared—had failed to show respect to a Muppanar god-dancer. In particular, the old god-dancer had not used honorific pronouns when speaking to this other god-dancer.

In this case, however, the young man proved wrong. The Thevar headman, who has no share in this temple but does in the neighboring temple that celebrates its festival simultaneously, took him aside and fined him 2,000 rupees (no small change) for starting the fight and putting the festival in jeopardy. A broken festival can prove disastrous. Many villagers believe that if the fierce Cutalaimatan becomes angry at the humans who worship him, he can wreak vengeance in many ways, including death. While the young man was receiving his fine, other elders from the temple community, including the Muppanar headman, took off on foot down the cart track to the village about half a mile away. Armed with honorifics of their own, they hoped to persuade the old god-dancer to return and finish the festival, which he eventually did.

The Dhobi god-dancer does not need to show mariyātai to the Muppanar in this temple. Rather, the Dhobi has precedence. Because he is connected to the older-brother god, the Dhobi is first among equals. It is the real, bodily connection between the gods and the men they possess that makes this inversion possible. Finally, even though this is the most renowned temple in the village—the one that draws the most attention in the region—the temple association does not include any ūrmakkaḷ except the Muppanars. Rather, the temple association consists of a Dhobi lineage, a Muppanar lineage, an Illuttuppillai lineage, a Barber lineage, and, finally, a lineage from S. C. Middle Ūr. All other ūrmakkaḷ are excluded from rights in this temple, though most village residents do attend the festival and many gather around to ask politely for advice and ash from these lower-ranking god-dancers.

While the ranking among gods may indeed be said to "symbolize" the value of rank because it also iconically reflects rankings among humans, this example suggests that such an analysis falls short of fully explicating the relation between gods in a pantheon and humans in ranked social orders. Gods are not merely symbols that stand for relations among humans, echoing frozen and unitary ideational structures whose origins are mysterious. In the preceding stories and events, as in other origin stories and festivals of fierce gods, the gods are real powers contiguous with humans, powers that make humans into powerful agents with the capacity to potentially restructure the system of conventional rankings that may exist at any given moment. In the present case, the symbolic value of rank from high to low (and if I were to carry the analysis farther, from center to periphery as well) is both reversed and then denied through the metonymic or indexical relation between gods and humans. The symbolic value of rank is reversed when a higher-ranking human lineage becomes substantially joined with a lower-ranking god and must socially enact their new subordination to the Dhobi lineage in temple ritual. Gods, as real, present, material beings, thus participate in the process of making social relations and contesting conventional understandings of social relations. Gods, who are indexically linked to humans, help make symbols grow.

The metonymic link between gods and humans can be further illustrated in cases where individuals and families in Yanaimangalam have attempted (unsuccessfully) to break or avoid the relationship between themselves and their kulatēvaṅkaḷ, or at least to weaken its intensity. Humans can choose their favorite gods (iṣṭatēvaṅkaḷ), but they cannot choose their lineage gods. The lineage gods are part of the family. Arunacalam Pillai, whom we met in Chapter 2, an old man (now deceased) who danced with the firepot for the village goddess, recalled to me how as a young man he had purposely avoided the goddess temple after his brother died. His brother had been the god-dancer for this goddess, a task for which the goddess chooses a man and his whole descending patrilineage. Arunacalam Pillai feared that after his older brother was dead, the goddess would call him to be her next god-dancer, a job he did not want. He claimed he did not even believe in the gods. That year, during her festival, he walked far upriver away from the temple to bathe in order to avoid passing by the temple. But after his bath, as he described it, his legs simply walked him—against his will—to the goddess temple. She activated him. Another example has parents locking their unmarried son in the house so that their fierce lineage god would be unable to walk him to their lineage temple. This god had no god-dancer yet and had possessed the youth once before. They felt that their son, because he was unmarried, was not yet pure (*tupparavu*) enough to survive repeated powerful possession by their lineage god. Yet, somehow—no one knew how, but they all credited the god—the youth ended up at the temple, dancing for the god.

That gods and their devotee lineages are contiguously linked is further illustrated by the case of a young woman named Pecciyamma who started cooking for her husband before the two were married. Her husband-to-be happened to be the god-dancer for his lineage god. On the very day that the couple was finally wed, that god possessed the bride violently and spoke, through her, his anger. He was angry that she had fed him (with food fed to her husband) without being of the lineage. Her lack of contiguity with the god made her an inappropriate feeder of the god. And her contiguity, established upon marriage—an act which substantially joined her to her husband's lineage—opened the channel for the god to possess her too.

In Yanaimangalam, as all over South India, humans have multiple indexically defined relations to gods. Humans are thus overlapping agents; they have many (and sometimes conflicting) sources of power. They participate in multiple "societies," multiple rankings, misrankings, and unrankings. They participate in multiple social realities. In Yanaimangalam, ranks of high to low—and even the ideology of rank itself—may be broken and made and even denied altogether in multilateral discourses among actors who are agents of local gods and who become agents of local gods not because of a priori symbolic associations but rather because of contingent past events and actions. As we shall see, residents of Yanaimangalam join with gods to argue out the social-cum-spatial contours of the village as they sometimes also draw on wider social and political discourses that provide alternative formulations of possible social worlds. First, however, I describe some aspects of the event called koṭai, gift, the festivals for which temple associations convene and during which these alternative villages and relations are refracted.

SEVEN

Making Good at Koṭai Festivals

Temple associations—whether they gather as a residential cluster for an "ūr" god or as a lineage for a lineage god (kulatēvam) or as a jāti for a jāti god or as some combination of all three, as at the Cutalaimatan temple at the cremation ground—convene only periodically, and they do so primarily to organize and celebrate the temple festivals known all around Tirunelveli and other surrounding districts as "gifts" (koṭai).[1] More-prosperous and more-popular temple associations produce major koṭais once a year as well as smaller but nonetheless fairly well-attended ritual events throughout a yearly cycle. Smaller or less-prosperous associations produce festivals only once every two or every five years or only irregularly. One temple festival I will discuss in some detail in Chapter 9 was held in 1990 for the first time in forty years.

Koṭais give their association members the gift of social power. As association members organize and enact the small and large gifts they give to the gods, they do more than fete their god or goddess. They also reproduce their family's ties to their lineage, jāti, and temple association. They display those connections to visitors—both kin and nonkin—who come to the village to attend the koṭai festivals. They build for themselves social reputations that extend beyond the ūr. Moreover, and this is critical to the argument of this book, it is the strength of the koṭai, built up through the funds, detailed acts, and ideas of its participants, that enables a temple community to display, dramatize, and effect political critiques of relations of dominance in the ūr. Because it is through the small acts of particular households and persons that the social and political power of a temple association is made, I devote considerable attention to description and analysis of these acts around a constellation of key values that participants say they produce in koṭai activities.

All koṭai festivals take place in the hot summer months, from mid-March to mid-June, when agricultural work is at a minimum and residents are relatively flush from the recent harvest of both rice and bananas. Koṭais stretch out over two weeks, usually from Tuesday to Tuesday, though most activity is concentrated in the three days spanning the first Monday evening to the second Wednesday morning of that two-week period. For the entire two-week period, however, certain restrictions and responsibilities apply to all persons defined as belonging to the temple association in question: none may leave the village overnight, all must whitewash their houses, and temple god-dancers as well as any persons giving special vows must fast, which for these occasions usually means eating rice only once a day in the evening after dark (some, including the god-dancers, will have started their fasts even before the two-week period commences). In addition, each household must organize funds to pay the temple tax (vari) required for funding the event. In all of these ways a temple association sets itself apart from other village residents during this period.

Koṭai taxes are head taxes levied on individuals at various rates predetermined by association headmen. Depending on the temple and year, this rate ranges widely from as little as ten rupees to as much as 350 rupees per head, with children, widows, and unmarried adult women usually counting as half a head. These figures are based on 1990 rates, at which time ten rupees was about seventy-five cents and 350 rupees was a whopping 23 dollars, at the time about the equivalent of a man's monthly salary at minimum-wage field labor. Many families struggle to come up with the temple taxes they owe each year. Tax collectors appointed by the association collect the tax only after the two-week period begins. Advance funds, as needed, are borrowed from wealthier association members or are taken from the collective bank accounts some communities have established.

While each koṭai differs in certain particulars, all follow more or less the same pattern and all are punctuated by certain required events. In what follows I will not delineate each event but rather focus on the general outcomes desired and generated by worshipers.

KOṬAI VALUES (OR THE VALUE OF "GIVINGS")

The outcomes that koṭai participants say they produce for themselves or their groups through their koṭai participation include general fruits (palaṉ) or benefits (literally "goodness," *naṉmai*) as well as specific outcomes such as getting loan money to build a house, getting good grades in school, landing a steady job, regaining good health, exorcizing an unwelcome spirit, achieving good marriage matches for their children, conceiving a child, and so forth. Koṭai participants speak enthusiastically of the ends they desire. They speak of increase, growth, and prosperity for the temple, for the temple association as a whole, and for each of its members. Residents of Yanaimangalam express this general value of increase in both general terms and very specific ones. For example, when Ramayya Thevar explained to me the meaning of using a forked branch as opposed to a straight one in part of an inaugural ritual for the Cutalaimatan koṭai called "planting the post," he stated that the forked branch used as the post signified the koṭai's potential for contributing to the "growth" (*vaḷarcci*) of the families in the temple association (because a forked branch indicates the potential for two branches to come from just one); when discussing a practice called *cūṟai,* a "whirlwind" (of cotton) which is thrown out into the crowd at the festival at a popular regional temple (Sankarankoyil), Aruna stated that this action is performed for everyone's *viḷaiccal* (lit. "yield," as a crop yields its grain), a word which also refers to future productive and reproductive potential more generally. Koṭais are directly linked to the successful productivity (viḷaiccal) of members' fields.[2]

I use the general term "increase" to refer to a cluster of interrelated concepts that village residents use when describing the outcomes of koṭais as of other productive actions and processes. These concepts include growth (viḷaiccal), production (viḷaivu), and expressions of excess or overflow that I describe below in the context of cooking poṅkal (a rice dish). The koṭai as a whole, as well as the particular activities that take place during the koṭai, are directed toward producing increase, whether that be understood as personal gain, family prowess, general prosperity for the temple association, or the reputation of the village to a wider audience. Increase is not the only general value of koṭai productions. A second, though not unrelated, value that koṭais produce translates literally as "bigness" or "greatness" (perumai). Bigness is generally considered to be a positive quality that can characterize persons, places, and things. Another appropriate gloss for perumai is, as we shall see, "reputation." Perumai produced in koṭais may attach to particular persons, to participating jātis, to the temple association, and to the village itself. Jātis may be described as "big" (periya jāti), as might people belonging to big jātis be described as "big jāti people" (*periyajātikkāraṅkaḷ*), a synonym for ūrmakkaḷ. Others belong to small jātis (ciṉṉa *jāti*), and these "small jāti people" (*ciṉṉajātikkāraṅkaḷ*) are the S. C. and other "low" and peripheralized jātis in Yanaimangalam also known as kuṭimakkaḷ. A person can be big (a "big man," *periya āḷ,* or *periyavar*), especially if they have a lot of wealth, many followers (Mines and Gourishankar 1990), or a reputation for largesse (*vaḷḷaṉmai*) (Price 1979, 1996).

As we have seen, what often makes persons big, and then bolsters the social power their bigness gives them, is their capacity to give things away. This is not just true locally, where village big men vie to display their own largesse; politicians in Tamilnadu today often use largesse as a campaign strategy as well. They gain perumai (bigness) and votes precisely through what some Tamil scholars calls "competitive populism" (MIDS 1988, 333, quoted in Price 1996a, 360); that is, a strategy of giving things away to the people as a sign of their concern with the material conditions of ordinary people. While I was in the village, there were numerous "free" giveaways of foodstuffs, clothing, holiday cash bonuses to workers, and other gifts. In one case, everyone in Tamilnadu who was considered below the poverty level (a fact entered on ration cards they use to procure cooking oils, rice, and kerosene at subsidized prices) was allotted a free portion of rice on Tai Poṅkal, a yearly holiday that, like the poṅkal described below, assures prosperity and growth for agriculture, ancestors, and one's own path in life. The face of the chief minister of Tamilnadu, at that time Karunanadhi of the DMK, adorned the bags used to package the rice, and people referred to the rice as a gift (*paricu*) from him.

The connection between worshipping a god and these two values of increase and bigness is nowhere more clearly represented than in the way in which the values come together in the very image of the gods being worshipped. Performing pūja to gods—the central act of koṭais as well as everyday worship—is said to make the images themselves grow or swell. This is true for gods in temples and for gods in houses. For a particular household goddess (the Tamil saint Auvayar[3]), for example, women often claimed that small earthen images of the goddess had over the years had grown significantly in size, a little more with each year's pūja.

The increase and bigness that come about for both the gods and the temple associations who sponsor them are both sources of and signs of the power of a god and community. The social power gained from a successful koṭai festival can produce competition among village residents in several ways. Families measure their strength by the numbers of kin that show up for a given festival, the ūrmakkaḷ can prove and reproduce their bigness (as shown in earlier chapters), and even "little," relatively powerless persons and communities can create for themselves a context in which they assert power and can publicly voice their own social accent on village affairs, perhaps gaining even some influence (*celvākku,* lit. a voice that runs [as opposed to being blocked] or is valid). Understanding how the koṭai contributes to a person or group gaining such power and influence is the primary aim of this chapter.

INCREASE AND THE KOṬAI

To illustrate in more detail how persons and communities produce increase and bigness through koṭais in Yanaimangalam, I present detailed descriptions of two koṭai events: cooking poṅkal and giving vows (*nērttik-*

kaṭaṉ) to a deity. These two processes best evoke the productive processes of other koṭai events and of the koṭai as a whole, processes that while seemingly about linking persons and families to a deity's beneficent power also build up into social power for the association and for the communities (jātis, lineages, ūrs) they include.

Poṅkal

The word "poṅkal" has several referents. A noun formed from the verb *poṅku,* it connotes these actions: "(of milk) boil; (of floods [and tears!]) rise; (of dough, etc.) swell; (of emotions) swell; cook (rice)" (*Cre-A's Dictionary of Contemporary Tamil,* 776). "Poṅkal" in its noun form denotes most commonly a special kind of cooked rice that results from a particular method of cooking. Poṅkal-cooking is an evocative metonym for reproduction and increase in general and for koṭais in particular. All cooking is a transitional act, turning the raw into the cooked. In cooking poṅkal, this transitional aspect is highlighted, as poṅkal comes to signify the production of production; that is, poṅkal signifies the ways that humans can turn inert and dead substances into productive and life-giving ones.

Women cook poṅkal on special days throughout the year, most notably at Tai Poṅkal, a first-fruits celebration that occurs on the winter solstice and emphasizes the important ritual activities of humans through which they produce their own lives, connections, and well-being. The cooking of poṅkal signifies the process of growth and creation that enable humans to live.

The most important kind of poṅkal women cook is called white poṅkal (*veṉpoṅkal*). Poṅkal is cooked in a different manner than everyday rice. Not only is it cooked in a different place with different fuels, but it is also made from "raw rice" (*paccarici*) that differs from most peoples' everyday rice, which is translated into English as "parboiled rice." The difference has to do with the way in which the husk is removed from the grain. The "parboiled rice" is husked through a cooking process: the paddy is heated so the rice expands and cracks the husk, then the paddy is dried again—you see people spreading it out on roads and streets all over Tamilnadu—and finally milled, if not by hand then in one of the many privately owned mills that punctuate streets the way laundromats do in the United States. The loosened husk falls away easily. Raw rice, on the other hand, is husked without any other cooking process. It has never been cooked in any manner whatsoever. The husk comes off less cleanly, leaving some of the inner husk as red traces lined on the white kernel. A second major difference in the way poṅkal is cooked is that while daily rice is generally rinsed well before cooking, poṅkal rice is not. Poṅkal is cooked in its own "milk" (*pāl*); that is, in the white liquid that results when water mixes with rice. This milk is metaphorically linked to mother's milk, another human-produced substance that nurtures growth and life. Third, the place of cooking is not in the kitchen but rather at liminal spaces, literally on the thresholds of the house, either on the inner veranda or on the street just abutting the doorway. Finally, the cooking fuel used is not one of the everyday cooking fuels—not kerosene and not gas and not wood and not cow-dung cakes. Rather, the favored fuel is dried palmyra palm leaves (other dried agricultural products may be used as well, such as paddy straw or even, I observed in some cases, dried banana leaves). And so the dead refuse of one crop fuels the generation of a new year's productivity, symbolizing the human capacity to convert death into life-sustaining growth with the help of gods and the ancestors, who are the first recipients of the cooked poṅkal. Cooks tend their fires carefully (the leaves burn quickly and hot) and watch the rice attentively to catch the very moment it boils over. As soon as the liquid breaches the pot's lip and starts to dribble down toward the flame, any women or girls there cooking or watching ululate (*kuravai pōṭu*). On Tai Poṅkal, all morning long, these high-pitched announcements issue down the street from one house after another. Once the poṅkal has boiled over, the cook scoops a ladle of liquid from the pot and circles it around the pot three times and then pours it out to the side of the hearth (destroying tiruṣṭi for the sake of the pot, perhaps). Then the poṅkal pot is removed from the fire and set down in front of the household pūja area as an offering to gods. Later, when it is time to eat, the poṅkal is offered first to god and second to the ancestors, who appear as crows and consume poṅkal from the roof of the house where kids toss it for them. Then the family eats poṅkal, now converted into prasad from the god, in front of the household shrine. Later, kuṭimakkaḷ may come to collect a portion of poṅkal from ūrmakkaḷ homes (though only the poorest do so) as they also collect their Poṅkal paṭi, a cutantiram prestation.

While domestic poṅkal-cooking on Tai Poṅkal promotes household and family growth by making and remaking productive ties to affines, ancestors, and the extended productive unit of contam that includes kuṭimakkaḷ, cooking poṅkal at temple festivals ties each household and each temple association into another crucial source of productivity; namely, the specific gods on whom village families and communities at large depend for their well-being.

The meaning of poṅkal-cooking at temple koṭai festivals is central to the koṭai's productive power. Poṅkal signifies and expands the productive capacity of the entire temple association—the unit that together sponsors a koṭai. It also brings particular gods and their places of worship into productive processes, making these gods central to the productive processes of its social units (be they lineages, jātis, ūrs, or some combination thereof). By communal poṅkal-cooking at koṭais, the smaller family units join together and connect themselves to these more powerful cosmic sources. In doing so, they reproduce not only their links to powerful gods but also their own social forms, their characteristic parities, exclusions, and rankings.

People vow and cook poṅkal at all koṭai festivals. Regular white poṅkal is cooked twice during a festival. It is cooked on the eighth day of the two-week period (the second day of the central three) and again—in a much less elaborate fashion—on the last day of the two-week period (the eighth day after the beginning of the central three days, which is why it is called the "eighth poṅkal"). The cooking procedure is the same as that outlined above for Tai Poṅkal. During the central night of the temple festival (the second night of the three-day core of the festival), each household that has vowed to cook poṅkal for the god brings its pot and rice and implements to the temple and along with everyone else sets up its poṅkal pot in a "row" (varicai) inside the temple grounds within the eye-flow of the god or goddess to whom they have vowed it. (Anyone who has vowed any vow at all must also cook poṅkal. So, for example, if a boy or girl carries a milkpot as a vow earlier in the day, their families also cook poṅkal at the temple that night.) The rows of poṅkal cookers is ordered, corresponding approximately to the orders of mariyātai varicai, rows of mariyātai, discussed in Chapter 4. I did not myself record the order of pots, but people reported to me that those higher in established rows of mariyātai tend to cook their poṅkal earlier and closer to the god or goddess in question. Thus, for example, Kantan, the Dhobi who dances the god for Cutalaimatan at the cremation-ground temple cooked his poṅkal (or, rather, his wife did) high in order of precedence at that temple, while at the goddess-temple festival, the "higher" (ocanta) and more central "village people" jātis cooked theirs closer to the goddess, the Thevarmar somewhat behind the Pillaimar, the Muppanar off in their separate temple, and the S. C. down in the field, outside of the pantal-covered area. The S. C. also, unlike the others, did not take their poṅkal inside the temple to set it in front of the goddess once it was cooked but left it under the shelter of some banana leaves leaning against the electrical utility pole that was within the goddess's line of sight, in the fields below the temple ground.

Koṭai poṅkals share many meanings with Tai Poṅkals. For example, the transitional themes indicated above—calendrical and spatial—are also aspects of poṅkal in the temple. Calendrically, many people in the village make a direct connection between the koṭais and the agricultural cycle, seeing the former as preparing the way for the latter, particularly with transforming the hot and dry festival season into the cooler wet planting season that commences in mid-June.[4] This is particularly true of the goddess temples, for cooling the goddess during the koṭai is thought to help usher in the rains and ready the soil for planting. Spatially, koṭai poṅkals are cooked under the temporary sheds (pantals) which are erected specially for the koṭais and become for the festival's duration an ambiguous area which some consider outside the temple and others consider inside (thus some do not remove their shoes in this area, while others do). Perhaps more significant, the temple itself is a medial location. As Inden (1985) points out, Hindus have not seen temples in what is now India to be mere symbols or metaphors of the social order. Temples and the gods they house are part of the social order, linking humans and gods together into a single social/divine world. Cooking poṅkal in the local temple thus connects the participants with the gods that link humans to a broader social realm that includes (versus simply models) the heavens (Figure 7.1).

At the village goddess temple, a special type of poṅkal called *matup-poṅkal,* or "nectar poṅkal," potently expresses the dual themes of productivity and power that combine in all temple koṭais. Nectar poṅkal is "cooked" during the third day of the goddess festival and is the festival's climax, when the eyes of all bystanders focus simultaneously on three polka-dotted poṅkal pots, white dots on earth-red pots. The preparation of nectar poṅkal differs strikingly from the cooking of white poṅkal. Nectar poṅkal is made at two spots during the Chariot Procession, when the goddess is brought around the village on her movable "chariot" (capparam). The first spot where nectar poṅkal is made is on the street-*vācal* (entrance threshold) of the Pillaiyar temple at the head of Muppanar Street. It was here, before the procession came around and while the ground for the poṅkal-cooking was being decorated with kōlams by a Thevarmar woman whose family had the right to do this work or service (*kaiṅkaryam*), that I spoke for a while to the Kambar woman whose right (urimai) it is to prepare this poṅkal, for which work she receives cutantiram. She told me some details.

The preparation of nectar poṅkal begins a few days earlier than its cooking does. On the first day of the two-week koṭai period (the day of the "flag-raising"), a small procession of ūrmakkaḷ bring the paddy from which the nectar poṅkal will be made to the kitchen shed behind the Muppanar temple. Each year this paddy is donated by the same Saiva Pillaimar household as a vow, and the procession begins from his house. The Kambar woman who makes the nectar poṅkal explained that either a man or a postmenopausal women such as herself may make this kind of poṅkal. When I spoke to her she had been fasting for eight days, since the paddy for nectar poṅkal had been brought to the temple kitchen.

After the paddy was brought to the temple kitchen that day, she and her son took it home to their own village, where she husked it and pounded it by hand to make rice flour. To the flour she added water and set the mixture to ferment until the time came for the Chariot Procession (see Chapter 2). The ūr, she said, provided all the materials. The Potters (who

Figure 7.1. Cooking poṅkal at the temple, 2003.
© Richard Rapfogel. Used by permission.

live a couple miles down the road in another village) were responsible for, and received cutantiram in return for making, the pots, which they decorated with white dots.

Ūrmakkaḷ men pulled the chariot slowly through the village on a squeaky platform with metal wheels, avoiding low-strung electrical lines with some difficulty. As they pulled it along on its journey, they stopped frequently for the temple-association members who come out of their houses to offer *arccaṉai* (individual offerings) of coconuts, flowers, bananas, and cooling rosewater. And as they trundled nearer the Pillaiyar temple, the Kambar woman set rapidly to work preparing the place at which she would pour the nectar.

She and her son first spread out several banana leaves, and as they did so a crowd began to gather and watch closely, squirming, jostling, and huddling tightly around the spot where they were working. She placed an overflowing paṭi measure of paddy onto the leaf and then spread more paddy out onto the leaves. She set three pots on this bed of paddy only after first holding them upside down over burning frankincense in order to fill them with the incense's cleansing smoke. Then she turned them right side up again, trapping the smoke inside with a lid made from half a coconut, which had been broken ahead of time as part of an initial pūja. Her son removed the coconut lids one by one and as he did so she quickly poured the nectar (*matu*) into the small pots (the middle one, the south one, and the north one, in that order). As each one immediately "boiled over" (poṅku), the crowd—men as well as women and most certainly the children—ululated as one, with great energy! Some of the young men began a "dance for fun" (*vēṭikkai āṭṭam*) behind the chariot as it continued on down the street. I hurried ahead to the goddess temple to await the chariot's arrival and the second pouring of matuppoṅkal.

When I arrived out there, the huge feast called *paṭaippu,* which had been cooked all the previous night by assigned members of the ūrmakkaḷ temple association, was already laid out in two huge piles inside the temple, both within the goddess's eye-flow (*pārvai*). A vegetarian paṭaippu crowded the room nearest the goddess (usually reserved for Brahmans) and the chicken paṭaippu cooked by the Thevars sat in a steaming and odoriferous heap in the middle of the temple's small main hall. The Kambar woman arrived ahead of the chariot (having also hurried ahead) and began to set up another receiving area.

From the edge of the pantal I watched the chariot come in. The goddess's image on the palanquin had been pushed and pulled through the streets on wheels, but to take it across the fields, dozens of ūrmakkaḷ men and youths heaved the palanquin onto their shoulders and ran with it in a weaving mass. A few big men from the community ran alongside, carrying their official big-man bags in one arm and waving the other as they shouted out sometimes conflicting directions (To the left! To the right! Straight! Turn! Slow! Hurry! Careful!!!). Her palanquin thus conducted once around the temple, the goddess was set down to the cheers and claps of the waiting crowd. The priests hurried up the steps from the fields onto the temple grounds and into the temple. The thick crowd parted to let them through, then closed together again in a dense circle around the sacrificial post (*pali pīṭam*) several feet in front of the temple doors. There the nectar poṅkal, ready to go, was without further ado poured out as before.

When the pots overflowed, the crowd erupted in ululations. The sound was astoundingly loud. It is said that if the nectar poṅkal fails to boil over, it bodes ill for the village; some difficulty (*kaṣṭam*) is augured. If it boils over in all directions, rushes smoothly over the entire lip of the pot, everything will go very well. After the nectar poṅkal "boiled," the goat and cock sacrifices began. When the *abhisekams* (bathings of the goddess with various substances, including turmeric water, ash, and milk, one after another) were over, portions of the matuppoṅkal were distributed to all the ūrmakkaḷ men in an established order of precedence. No shares were distributed to kuṭimakkaḷ.

The significance of temple poṅkal for production is the same as household poṅkal. In this case however, particularly in the case of nectar poṅkal, the pot, as a womb, contains not only the seed that bursts into new life but the goddess as well. She is the energy that leads to the growth inside the pot, and, as a communal pot, her container may be said to represent not any particular womb but the reproductive potential of the entire village (to whom the goddess is "mother," tāy), whether that reproductive potential be agricultural, animal, or human. Moreover, as the description illustrates, this poṅkal depends not just upon a single cook, but upon ūrmakkaḷ organization and kuṭimakkaḷ cooperation. The successful poṅkal validates the ūr's social organization by making that organization the key to productive success in the eyes of the goddess. Moreover, like poṅkal in general, this event highlights the power and potency humans have to effect their own future productivity through ritual practices.

BIGNESS: THE PRODUCTION OF SOCIAL VALUE IN THE KOṬAI

How does the increase that individual households and temple associations achieve through vows such as poṅkal translate into *social* outcomes among members of the temple association and for the temple association in general? The gods and goddesses are thought to aid human beings in their particular and general productive desires and goals, but what are the other social products of the koṭai? What I call the "density" of vows given during a temple festival effectively operates to convert personal, familial, and community increase into something socially productive. In short, through a density of vows over time, a temple association builds its reputation (perumai) and a place in the productive life of the village and region.

Density

Walk into almost any temple in Tamilnadu and you are likely to see a lot of *something.* In the village goddess temple, hundreds of glass bangles of all colors and sizes hang on long strings along one wall in front of the "womb room." These are signs of births that have taken place in village families. At the Issakkiyamman temple along the road into the village, dozens of small wooden cradles hang from the branches of the peepol tree that shades the shrine and arches over the road. These cradles are signs of difficult births survived and childhood diseases overcome. At a shrine on the main trunk road that intersects with the road to Yanaimangalam, old, broken, faded terra-cotta images of a goddess pile up in back of new, upright, and brightly painted ones. And during temple festivals, both gods and people become bodily centers of "density." Children and youths vowing pots of milk are smothered with cloth and garlands; god-dancers bury their ankles, arms, and necks with jewelry in silver and gold; and the gods are displayed wearing bright clothing, stacks of necklaces, and piles of flower garlands. It is the aggregate excess in places and on bodies that I call "density."

Density is not limited to the temple, though temple koṭais are certainly the most dense times and places in Yanaimangalam. At weddings and puberty rituals, the prestation called *moy,* a word which literally means to throng or swarm (Dictionary of Contemporary Tamil 1992, 875), consists of money that presenters line up to present to the person undergoing the ritual. The money piles up, crumpled bills overflowing in front of the recipient, a heap of cash. Each amount is entered in a notebook so that later, at a wedding or puberty ritual in the giver's house, it can be returned, usually with a small increment to connote growth and increase. Crops may also be dense. The "body" (*mēṉi*) of a crop may be multiple, the more the better, so that a two-mēṉi crop is one with a high yield (twice the norm), and a "half-mēṉi" crop is one of poor yield. Grains are said to pile up (*kuvi*) in huge heaps (*ampāram*) in the fields, and crops are said to be so thick that "there is no path for even a dog to walk" (from the Vellalakantan story, retold in its entirety in Chapter 8). And to describe a scene as "crowded," *kuttamāka,* is to extol the scene as something worthy of mention.

During the three central days of koṭais, the density of materials given, received, worn on bodies, and displayed is at its highest. Materials include food, precious metals, cloth, words, favors, and even promises for future gifts in return for assurances of some future benefit (naṉmai). These exchanges occur between persons and gods, between families and gods, and between the temple association as a whole (the tax-paying group) and the gods in their temple. In the case of the village goddess temple, as with ūr goddesses of hamlets, the exchange is said to occur between the "whole village" or the "whole hamlet" (in both cases, *ūr pūrāvum*) and the goddess.

"Milkpot" (*pālkuṭam*) is among the most popular of the many kinds of vows (nērttikkaṭaṉ, literally "straight-debt," or "reaching-debt") that take place over the course of any koṭai. The milkpot vow well illustrates how density is made and how density converts into social values such as bigness (perumai). This vow is usually made by parents and requires boys, girls (up to puberty), and unmarried youths to carry brass or shiny stainless steel pots of milk on their heads from the river, through their ūr, and finally to the temple in question, where the milk, a "cooling" substance, is poured over the deity in an abhisekam and then given back as prasad to all present.

Parents make these vows most often when the children are quite young. In one case from South Ūr, a family made the milkpot vow to the god Cutalaimatan—not in Yanaimangalam but in his place of origin, Sivalaperi

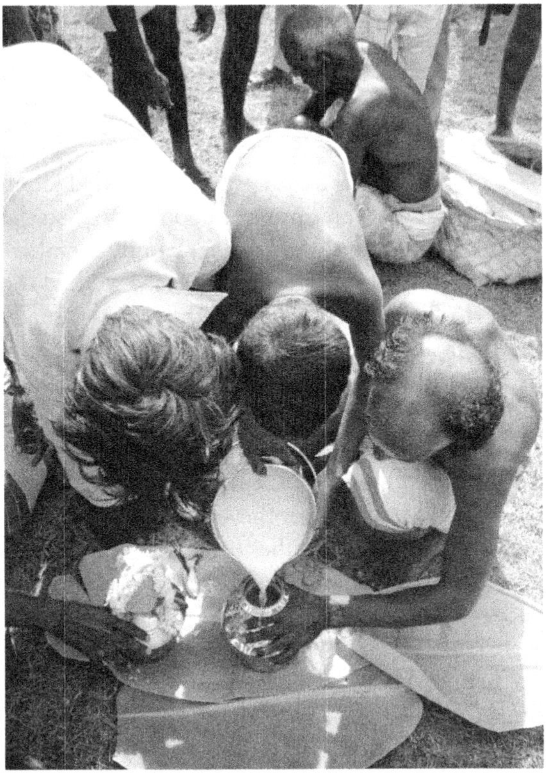

Figure 7.2. Filling Joti's milkpot, 1990.

town—in hopes that they would conceive and bear a healthy child. They did, and now their son, named Cutalaiyanti (devotee of Cutalai), carries a milkpot yearly for Cutalaimatan in Sivalaperi. Aruna's son Joti also carried a milkpot until he turned 19. He carried his to the Mariyamman temple on their street, South Street. Once, as a very small boy, Joti was quite sick. At that time, Aruna vowed to her ūr goddess Mariyamman that if he survived he would give her a milkpot at every other koṭai until he married or turned 19, whichever came first (Figure 7.2).

The milkpot proceedings for the village goddess koṭai in 1990 started, as usual, at the riverbank on the central Tuesday of the festival at around 9:00 A.M. The vow-givers, ranging in age from about 8 to 20, came with one or two adult male relatives, usually their father and their mother's brother. After the vow-givers bathed in the river, they lined up facing east in front of the row (varicai) of banana leaves that each family had set up on the riverbank. On these leaves, each family placed the ritual materials they brought with them: the new pot (usually a shiny stainless steel pot with a narrow neck), a new set of clothing (veṣtis and towels for the boys, "frocks" or skirts and tops for the girls), bananas, two coconuts, a small square of turmeric-stained cloth and piece of string, incense sticks, paddy, betel, a flower garland, frankincense, camphor, sandalwood paste, kumkumam, a one-rupee coin, and, in a separate container, milk in quantities varying from about half a liter to two liters depending on the size of the pot, which in turn depended on the size of the child. The preparation plodded along and was further delayed by the absence of an important god-dancer, so the musicians sat on the wall of the Visnu temple, gossiping. Family members and a few god-dancers milled around among the vow-givers, I studied the items on the leaves and felt the morning sun's heat, and the priests casually helped the vow-givers set up their supplies and ready their milkpots on the banana leaves. As with the nectar poṅkal described above, the pots were first cleaned with smoke. In no apparent order or rush, the vow-givers with the help of their relatives poured the milk into each of the new pots until they were full. They then placed a whole coconut to close the mouth of each pot. Displaced milk spilled and flowed over the sides of the pots. The vow-givers tied the turmeric-stained cloth with the turmeric-stained string over the coconut and around the lip of the pot to secure the coconut on the pot. They stuck the one-rupee coin onto the pot, using sandalwood paste as an adhesive.

All at once the pace quickened. The absent god-dancer had finally arrived. The vow-givers all lined up. The priests went down the line breaking coconuts and smearing ash. The musicians started beating and blowing their instruments. The god-dancers began shaking, jerking, and jumping as they connected with the goddess's power. And the relatives quickly adorned the vow-givers: they dressed them in the new cloth (which should have come from the "giving path" [*koṭukkum vaḻi*], that is from affines, ideally their mother's brothers), then smeared light-yellow sandalwood paste all over their chest and arms and daubed their bodies with red kumkumam.

One non-Brahman priest, a Garland Maker from a nearby village (a fellow who on most mornings can be seen careening down the village streets on his bicycle throwing packets of white and orange braided flowers onto the verandas of women with standing orders for flowers to adorn their gods, ancestors, daughters, and themselves), smeared ash on all the boys and girls down the row. The Brahman priest, having broken all the coconuts, went down the row (south to north) waving a lamp of burning camphor in one hand and ringing a bell with the other. As he did so, the musicians held their tones and rhythms in a sustained line, the signal of a climax, and a sign that the goddess (in this case) is connecting to the vow-giver and god-dancers. At this moment the relatives lifted the milkpots onto the boys' heads, leaving their own arms and hands there to balance the heavy pots. The vow-givers should now, ideally, be possessed by the goddess (though Aruna's son Joti, for one, said it has never happened to him, and his mother bemoans his lack of concentration). The procession then circled the pūja area three times and took off down the path towards the village. A kite (the bird) flew overhead, someone pointed, and a few people muttered "Krishna."

Only as the vow-givers moved out in single file toward the river path did I notice an S. C. family from North Ūr (father, mother, young son, and daughter) standing in a tight huddle off to the side of the pūja area. In her thin arms, the girl carried a large stainless steel plate on which sat a silk cloth, a gift vowed for the goddess. This family stood and watched as the procession moved out, funneling into single file as it reached the village path. They joined on at the very end of the line.

The procession beat a path past the goddess temple, which sits at some remove from the river path, and headed into and through the village, where by now the noontime summer sun soaked the earthen streets, sweltered the rooftops, glistened the white walls of houses lining the route, and beat down on the walkers as they walked. The S. C. family left the procession before it went into the Big Ūr. They veered off to the goddess temple straightaway and ducked secretly into the temporarily quiet, dim, and relatively cool temple at the priest's cautious signal.

As the Milkpot Procession snaked through the streets of the Big Ūr, it stopped at several points. When it stopped, the vow-givers lined up all in a row like soldiers at attention. Their milkpots wobbled on their heads. Their eyes focused straight ahead. They stopped and stood in the eye-flows of the gods whose temples they passed. They stopped also at certain intersections, in front of the houses of certain important people (particularly any god-dancers' houses), and near the houses or compounds of the participants' own close relatives. At each of these latter stops, relatives (affines in particular, many of whom had come in from other villages, towns, and cities for this purpose) came out from houses and tied more and more cloth, flower garlands, and garlands strung with rupee notes around the bodies of the vow-givers until many of them looked like swollen balls with stick legs.

The musicians signaled each of the procession's resumed movements with a change in rhythm and tempo. Just as the vow-givers thickened with cloth and flowers, so also did the procession itself, for as it wound through the village, more and more vow-givers, affinal gift-givers, and onlookers came out from their houses to join its march to the temple. Some bore gifts called "memory makers" (*ñāpakakkarttaṅkaḷ*), so called in part because they are labeled with the name of the donor and kept in the temple permanently. One of the Pillaimar big men came, for example, carrying a large brightly appliquéd umbrella for the goddess. The umbrella conveniently shaded him as he made his way with the procession down those sun-heated streets—an appropriate gift from a landlord! Others, particularly newly married women, joined carrying promised lengths of silk cloth for the goddess. These latter journeys start from pūjas on banana leaves that are not at the riverbank but are in front of the god and ancestor walls inside village houses.

Drums and the nataswārams played loudly the whole time, and the thickening procession wound through all the village streets and lanes. It took hours. When finally the procession made its way back to the head of the river path from whence it came, many people started to run, not walk, the rest of the way to the temple across the baked, clodded fields. Some of the vow-givers, now faint and heated by the goddess if not by the sun, were literally carried—and roughly too because footing is difficult on sun-dried dirt clods—across the fields to the temple by their relatives. A different relative grabbed each limb, one of them holding onto the pot and trying to keep it as close to the vow-giver's head as possible. As vow-givers arrived at the temple, they were variously carried, pushed, and cajoled once around the temple and then inside, where they deposited their pots of milk. There the priest smeared them with ash to cool them and halt the possession, after which they were quickly ushered back outside again to collapse in the cool shade of the neem trees that surround the temple. Relatives stripped them layer by layer of their garlands and cloth, fanned them, and revived them with sips of the cooling milk they had carried, which was now trans-valued as prasad from their goddess Yanaiyamman.

A short while later the priests performed a milk abhisekam. They poured pot after pot of the milk brought by the milkpot-givers over the black oiled image of the goddess. As milk streamed down the goddess inside the temple's inner sanctum, it started also to flow from inside the temple out to the temple grounds through special drains that run from the floor of the inner sanctum outside. Worshippers (especially children) crowded around the drain spouts to collect handfuls to slurp and small potsful to take home. The abhisekam finished. The pūja ended and the god-dancers danced. The priests emerged to hand and throw out ash. Then everyone went home to rest up for that night's all-night activity, which included poṅkal-cooking as described above and the Firepot Procession.

The Milkpot Procession to the goddess temple is a dense event. Its densities are displayed in the number of milkpots; the thickening of the procession as it winds along the streets; the quantities of cloth, flowers, money, and garlands that smother the vow-givers; and the crowd of worshippers gathered around temple drain spouts to catch drops of milk that have flowed from the body of their motherly goddess.

Density and Bigness (Perumai)

"Density" describes what Marriott (1976) might describe as the "maximizing" aspects of koṭai events.[5] Density shows up on the body of vow-givers: tight wads of cloth and garlands. It shows up on the bodies of god-dancers: silver bracelets stacked on their arms, gold medallions strung around their necks and tied tightly around their upper arms. Density shows up in the enormous quantities of food piled up in the temple, in the volumes of the ululations that signal poṅkal upon poṅkal overflowing the lips of pots. Such material excesses are integral to the production of value in the koṭai. Specifically, following a logic articulated elsewhere by Nancy Munn (1986, 3–9), I argue that density—a sign of increase—is converted by worshippers into a scale of value. That scale may be understood as relative "bigness" (perumai), and village residents display it and openly compare it (this is bigger than that, etc.).

Density is not an absolute quality. Rather, it describes relative quantity, specifically the quantity of people as well as reduplicated materials (e.g., many poṅkal pots, many bracelets, many goats, etc.) assembled in a particular place and time. The place and time could be a life-cycle ritual, a political speech, a function for the local literacy program, a demonstration at the district collector's office,[6] or, as Barney Bate shows, walls and newspapers of a city during a political campaign, where what he calls a "saturation" of posters and advertisements featuring images of political candidates contributes to a production of their greatness. It is not just anthropologists who note the pragmatic force of repeated images or objects. Rather, as Bate shows, this force is consistent with the Tamil trope *maṭakku,* which he describes as "the process of 'repetition' or 'folding' or 'refraction' that contributes to that density by saturating the visual field with repeated (or refracted) signs" (personal communication; see also Bate 2000, 268–274).

In koṭai festivals, density is produced directly by the number of participants and the scale of their participation (as vow-givers, for example). Each god gains a relative bigness (reputation) from the density of vows received—garlands, goats, jewelry, cloth, milkpots, etc. The density of vows, and especially of the god-dancer's durable ornaments which build up over time, signal the "bigness" of the event as a whole and convert into a name or reputation for the village via the perceived power of the gods who reside there. Density demonstrates the productive capacity of the god, the temple, the event, the place, and the community. People are more likely to make vows to gods who have gained a reputation for fulfilling the vows of others before them. That is, they make vows to gods who are thought to have enough power as well as beneficence to enhance the vow-givers' productive capacities by fulfilling their vows. Density signifies the productive capacity of gods because a god who does not effect positive transformations is less likely to receive vows and less likely to receive any kind of patronage or devotion, while a god who can effect such transformations, on the other hand, might attract many devotees from both near and far away.

For example, when I asked my neighbor Gurucami Pillai if he would attend his lineage temple's koṭai, he said that no, he would not. He paid his tax because he had to, but he would not go because that god had never done him any good. In North Hamlet's Cutalaimatan temple, on another occasion, a man was yelling angrily at a god-dancer, denouncing him for being no help at all. No matter how much good (naṉmai) the man did for the god (no matter how many vows he gave) the god returned only evil (*tīmai*). The man vowed to make no more vows to that god.

The productive capacity of human communities that worship gods is signified by the density of festivals as well, for a community that can gather together as one and produce a good koṭai will be able to connect to a god's power more then a community that is locked in dispute and unable to perform a unified festival. The history of dispute at the goddess temple outlined in Chapter 2 is one example of this. As Parvathi pointed out, such disputes were no good for the "honor" (māṉam) of the village, for people ridiculed their lack of unity. Ridicule deflates bigness. In Chapter 9, we will see how Middle Ūr residents worked hard to put on a very grand, dense festival for their god Panaiyatiyan in part because they were afraid that anything less would anger the god and turn him against them rather than convince him to work for them. We will also see how others ridiculed Middle Hamlet's efforts in an attempt to cut them down to size, a size appropriate for such a "small jāti."

Density is displayed, and the comments people make about relative densities (that temple has more people than that other, that god-dancer has more jewelry than that other, etc.) amount to evaluative statements about the relative value-producing capacity of different gods, god-dancers, or temple associations (and sometimes ūrs as wholes). Take, for example, the jewelry that god-dancers receive and wear. In the first place, this jewelry is a sign of the specific god's power (cakti), as well as a sign of the god-dancer's capacity to connect to and channel that power. Devotees come to the temples to talk to the gods through their god-dancers, to receive the "voice of grace" (aruḷvākku), or what in Yanaimangalam is more commonly called simply *kuṟi,* meaning sign or word. To the extent that the god is powerful, the god-dancer will be more densely adorned. The density of the god-dancer's adornment spills over to effect the god-dancer's reputation as a man, as a person of appropriate qualities to be a god-dancer. Successful god-dancers are accorded the respect of big men. People literally "give way," *vaḻi koṭu,* for them on the street and distinguish them with other signs of mariyātai. On the other hand, a god-dancer who collects no jewelry is said either to have a weak god or to be only pretending to speak for the god. People may ridicule such a god-dancer out loud and accuse him of being a false god-dancer, a "fake-god" (*poycāmi*). God-dancers who utter what people think are ungodlike commands or advice are sure to be ridiculed this way during the koṭai.

Perumai, or bigness, is a quality of persons and places, one that involves social and spatial extension. A big person (periya āḷ) is often someone at the center of relatively extensive transaction networks (a successful "maximal" transactor, as Marriott puts it [1976]). A village or a family too has perumai if they show themselves to be broadly connected to other places and people. Density plays a part in signaling as well as producing this kind of bigness. In particular, the display of density—plus the talk which the display generates—is one thing that makes perumai, for display of density is what begins the process of extension, and talk is what actually extends it: people see the productive outcomes of a person, a family, or a temple association, and they talk about it.

Take a life-cycle example for a moment, one in which I first heard about perumai in the way I analyze it here. At weddings, as at poṅkal, relatives bring gifts of the type called *cīr.* Rather than hide these gifts in a back room, the gifts are lined up and displayed—during puberty rituals they are even taken on procession—in a "row of cīr" (*cīr varicai*). During the wedding of a neighbor girl, I pointed out this row of gifts and asked Parvathi why people display their cīr so. She explained it to me using a counterexample: if the hosts put their cīr off in some side room where no one would see them, she explained, there would be no good in it. If it is all lined up in one place where people can see it, on the other hand, it is perumai for both the giver, the receiver, and the bride's family, who says with these objects "see how much we are sending off with our girl, how many resources we can muster from far and wide" (for cīr is collected from extended lineal relations and affines).

The milkpot vow also illustrates amply the way in which density, display, and bigness are bound together and simultaneously project their qualities along several social dimensions, from household to affinal relations to other wider kin relations within and beyond the village. The milkpot vow, to be maximally productive, requires inputs from affines, who must usually come in from other villages and towns to give gifts of cloth, money, and garlands to the vow-givers. The bulk of the cloth wrapped around the children and youths making the procession and the number of garlands and rupees that bury them are signs of their family's success in exchanges beyond their household with lineal kin and beyond their village with affines. But they are not just signs; not merely reflective signs, that is. They are signs that accomplish something. People whose relatives don't show up become angry and ashamed, while those whose children end up as round balls of cloth with money garlands of 10-rupee notes gain a reputation for having a family that does everything according to dharma (*muṟai*). At the same time, the generosity of their affines puts the receiving family in the position of planning for plenty of future reciprocating and, therefore, traveling to the villages or towns of their affines.

Take another example, this one from a funeral that took place in Aruna's hamlet, South Street. This ritual took place on the sixth day after a man's death, and among the many things that took place there was gift-giving by affines to the deceased's two sons. That is, the sons' wives' families (their fathers or brothers) were required to come and present the mourners with gifts of clothes, which the mourners were then supposed to wear. One set of affines brought gifts as they were supposed to do and presented them to the youngest son and his wife and their children. The affines of the older son, however, did not show up (they lived in Madurai, about 150 km north) and they did not send the clothes. This absence forced the older son to go buy his own clothes, which were few and meager because of his lack of money. This made him extremely angry and ashamed, particularly because his lack of affinal connection was displayed in front of all his relatives, who were all gossiping about it the whole night. Meanwhile, his younger brother and his family were all decked out in bright new clothes.

Like vision, speech too is outreaching and is one way in which one's reputation is made. It makes one's "name" (*peyar*). During the Cutalaimatan koṭai in 1990, for example, I arranged to videotape the entire festival. The video production required a crew: the director (Sam Sudanandha), two cameramen, two light men, an assistant, and a pal of one of the cameramen who boasted about being involved in the Chennai (Madras) film industry but who was in fact little more than overdressed. I was trying to figure out a way to feed them and host them without having to spend the entire festival on that task alone, so I arranged to have them eat at the temple along with the others who come there to work (the musicians, priests, etc.). But Turairaja Thevar, the god-dancer for the goddess who also dances with great density at the Cutalaimatan temple, had them eat in his home. I was worried that this would be an imposition but was told rather that it was good for the *ūr māṉam,* the honor or reputation of the ūr. He explained that these fellows—who were educated and urban—would be hosted well and then go back to Madurai and speak well of the village. Likewise, I often heard talk in the village about how good koṭai festivals were in other places and how I should go and see them. This positive speaking contrasts with what above I noted to be derision (*ikaḻcci pēccu*) and ridicule (*kēḷi paṇṇa*) which reduces bigness, perumai.

In all of these cases, promoting density by ensuring that the koṭai is well organized and as grand and dense as possible is part of the process of creating perumai for oneself and one's community. When the community cranks up the loudspeakers, blasting eardrums for miles around, they are even then locating the village, community, and person at the center of a broad and extending source of power.

CONCLUSION: THE DISORDERING POWER OF KOṬAI FESTIVALS

Through Yanaiyamman's large koṭai festival, associates of this spatially central temple produce dense aggregates of worshippers who are thought to maximize the general Tamil values of "bigness" and "growth" while also reproducing their own internal social organization and their spatial-cum-social definition of the ūr as the social unit they dominate. The koṭai festival, in other words, reproduces village dominance in form and lends it a divine validation: it is a large and dense festival in which the "whole village"—and their affines—participate. Do we then agree with the ūrmakkaḷ and many village residents, not to mention many anthropologists, who see rural South India goddess-temple festivals as central unifying rituals where "the whole village" is remade with gusto?

Perhaps, for a moment. But we have already seen how these unities are in fact not agreed upon by all. Middle Ūr promised a boycott. What about the other koṭai festivals in Yanaimangalam that are organized and celebrated by different associations of village residents? Do they reproduce the same unities that the village goddess festivals produce? Are other temple associations' actions similar to and harmonious with those occurring at the goddess temples? In particular, do the many other festivals produce similar densities, and do they reproduce the same specific parities, rankings, inclusions, and exclusions?

The answer to all of the above questions is no. In particular, festivals at the numerous fierce-god (māṭaṉ) temples of the territory sometimes convene large and dense aggregations, but memberships in these temples' associations and participation in their festival aggregations cut across memberships in the ūr's goddess-temple associations. The intersections of these sets of associations make for different combinations of jātis, residential units, and lineages. Their activities accordingly produce different orders of rank and mariyātai and different exclusions and inclusions. Their internal rows of distinction are rarely correlated with each other or with rows at the goddess temple: someone who ranks lower in one row may rank higher in another. By their differing exclusions, some associations peripheralize those who are otherwise central. Since such differences are argued through temple practices, the koṭais themselves may be seen as multilateral dialogues or discourses. Koṭai festivals are dialogically related to one another as well as to everyday social relations and in some ways may be seen to operate as metastatements about those relations. Participating in any one of them amounts to talking and acting and redefining and, most saliently, contesting the social relations that define the ūr as a social-spatial association.

From various dominating points of view, fierce gods are seen to be lower, more peripheral, and generally subordinate to other deities who are higher and more centered spatially and socially. Yet the impression that a "divine hierarchy" relegates these fierce gods to a position of subordination—an impression furthered by scholarship—misses telling the story from the point of view of the fierce and peripheral. The village that is so neatly—if contentiously—demarcated socially and spatially in the goddess festival is not the only village of Yanaimangalam. It has its moments of hegemony (as Pandi's self-erasing statement "all the village people" but "not us" illustrates), but like all hegemonies this one is hardly total.

Village residents participate in other village makings, alternative makings of village, self, and other, using the language of temple festivals, a language that includes not only the words of narrative and prophecy but also movement and mariyātai, time and space, as expressive creative communication. We begin remaking the village with the help of Vellalakantan, a fierce god who guards the other fierce gods at the Cutalaimatan temple out on the riverbank.

EIGHT

Waiting for Vellalakantan

Two temples dedicated to the god Cutalaimatan stand side by side at the cremation ground upriver, north and west of the residential areas. The temples are known as West Cutalaimatan Temple and East Sivalaperi Cutalaimatan Temple (referred to less formally as West Temple and East Temple, respectively). Between the temple grounds and the river lies Yanaimangalam's cremation ground on a narrow strip of cattle-chewed green grassy riverbank, which is interrupted here and there by a few spindly trees and, in the middle, the ashy cremation mound. While both temples are dedicated primarily to Cutalaimatan, a fierce, corpse-eating manifestation of Siva, both also contain an overlapping (almost identical) set of twenty other fierce gods and goddesses, a whole pantheon of fangs, or, as the colonial author of the 1917 district gazetteer describes using derogatory terms, "Sutalaimatan [*sic*] 'and his horrid crew'" (Pate 1917, 107).

Temples to Cutalaimatan are typically thought to be lonely, deserted, and ghostly places. Outside the residential areas of the village and beyond even the fields, they are located in the kāṭu, the "wasteland" or "wilderness." As one rides the bus through the dry countryside, these shrines show up on the outskirts of villages sometimes tucked among the thorn bushes that indicate wastelands. They usually overlook cremation grounds (the *cuṭalai* or *cuṭukkāṭu,* the "hot" or "burning wasteland") to which the recently departed cling, unwilling to leave the human world behind. Accordingly, these temples give most people the creeps and are largely deserted except for cultivators who labor in fields nearby, a non-Brahman priest from Pattamadai who does brief pūja for the gods twice a week, and the occasional devotee or funeral party.[1]

Yet three times a year the temple associations of the two temples gather to perform a large ritual for their gods. And once a year during the summer festival season, when crops are in and fields are dry, when cash is handy and work is minimal, the cremation ground swarms with people for three days and two nights. Children cram the cars of hand-cranked Ferris wheels; shops spring up to sell coffee, snacks, and meals; and visitors camp out for the duration of the three-day festival, the "densest" event of the year in Yanaimangalam.

West Temple is said to be much older than East Temple, and it is also the much more famous of the two. The West Temple koṭai draws in people from all over the region. The more people come, the more its reputation (perumai) grows. The place is thought to have a great deal of power, and people come there to be exorcized of unwelcome fierce gods and ghosts. A conversation I had one day with Andi Muppanar, the old man who god-danced for Cutalaimatan's younger brother Muntacami, highlights the power of the place. My conversation with Andi Muppanar followed up on my observations at the temple festival one night, when a woman known to no one in the village ran up to Andi Muppanar while he was speaking kuṟi—that is, acting as an oracle for the god Muntacami.

The woman came running from one end of the temple to the other, stopping in front of Andi Muppanar, who was positioned in front of Muntacami. She bore the signs of an inappropriate (or "unmatching," to borrow Marriott's term; see also Moreno 1985) possession—an unwelcome attack from a god—and Andi Muppanar (with Muntacami's power) began the task of ousting the invader. Among the procedures he used was feeding the woman divinely charged, pure, and cooling ash. Afterward I asked Andi Muppanar how it was that the ash had the power (cakti) to effect the exorcism, and he—both amused and appalled by my ignorance—shouted rather than spoke this exasperated reply:

> Cakti!? That's the god's cakti! It has nothing to do with my cakti.

The god-dancer then explained that his ash-feeding and -smearing could make the woman's possession stop because, as he put it,

> Between the god and me there is a . . . a kind of . . . a connection (cērkkai) [he claps his hands together to illustrate]. He thinks and it reaches me. It isn't because of what *I* do that it stops . . . it's because of the god's power *at this place.*

While the gods in the two cremation-ground temples are almost identical, the human associations that convene as patrons, the "taxpayers," of the temples differ significantly, and each has its own set of god-dancers. The larger and older of the two temples convenes an association comprised of five jātis: Dhobi (Washerman), Muppanar, Barber, one lineage of Illuttuppillai from South Street (Aruna's jāti), and the entire population of S. C. Middle Ūr. East Temple, the smaller and newer of the two temples, is common (potu) only to the Thevars residing in the Big Ūr, regardless of lineage or subjāti. (The Thevars residing in North Ūr own a separate fierce-god temple out on the riverbank near their ūr. Their fierce god is named Talavaymatan.)[2] Cutalaimatan at West Temple is said to be *cuyambu*—self-appearing—while Cutalaimatan at East Temple came from Sivalaperi in a handful of earth, piṭimaṇ, as recounted in Chapter 6.

Though these two temple associations convene different sets of village residents, they nevertheless cooperate with one another and celebrate their yearly festival together (albeit with some competition and contestation and frequent threats to separate the festivals). They share the same set of priests, who move back and forth to do pūja at both temples. The god-dancers, who are attached to each temple separately, visit and dance in the other temple at several points during the main three-day event. Spectators move freely back and forth between the two temples, following the action (and in some cases avoiding it). The timing of both festivals is regulated for the most part by the course of events in West Temple. Vellalakantan is one of the gods in this larger, older temple. It is he who times the climax of the festival in both temples.

MOVEMENT MAKES THE ŪR

It was past midnight during the Cutalaimatan festival in May 1990. Some of us had paid 50 paisa or so for a hot coffeeless concoction called "ginger coffee" to help keep us awake for this second consecutive night of the festival. Others had succumbed to sleep. Women jammed the corners and sides of the open-air temples, with their children squeezed among the folds of their saris and their babies swinging in cloth cradles hanging above them from the poles and beams of the temple's temporary pantal. A few people dozed on the cremation mound itself (certainly the most unlikely place for a nap any other night of the year!). Many men had vanished into the thick gardens downriver to drink arrack, illicit distilled liquor. The ten or twelve policemen deployed for the festival were hanging out in their undershirts and khaki pants in a tent they had pitched, their rifles leaning here against wooden cots and there against canvas walls. It was peaceful, but hardly quiet. Generators chugged. And bullhorn loudspeakers blared taped music from the temple out into the still night air, as if to announce to the surrounding countryside that there was a festival under way somewhere nearby.

Asleep or awake, we were all waiting around for the finale of the festival, when the gods would consume those huge steaming mounds of meals called paṭaippu and when the human god-dancers—gods in men—would eat blood from the dozens of goats, roosters, and pigs that were tied to every available tree, post, and oxcart wheel in and around the two temples, awaiting their sacrifice. The timing of this final event hinged not upon the conjunction of earth and moon, sun, or stars but on the return of a "double-agent" (Steedly 1994, 15) named Vellalakantan—a god and his human god-dancer—from a guard or watch (*kāval*) circuit around the village.

Vellalakantan (both man and god) is a Dhobi, a Washerman. Around midnight, just after the midnight abhishekam, a man had done what he had done several years previously and what he has done in years since. He took in the god's power, as he also took on the god's name, and set out from the village cremation ground for a lone procession "around the village." His simple accompaniment besides the sound of bells dangling from his spear and his jesterly hat, was a torch-bearer to light the path through the night fields. Vellalakantan walked a long and slow route along the periphery of the village. As he walked two hours, three hours, six hours passed, and even as dawn broke, the many hundreds of people gathered at the cremation ground to celebrate the festival of the fierce god Cutalaimatan waited. Until he returned, the festival could not come to its proper conclusion. But Vellalakantan's walk did more than enable the festival's conclusion. Vellalakantan's walk, the route he chose to take, and the actions he performed en route together articulated a discourse on village social and spatial relations.

It had been only four weeks since the dominant ūrmakkaḷ had made their procession around the ūr and defined an ūr that included themselves and excluded or peripheralized those living outside the Big Ūr. Among those excluded, remember (that is, among those who may not pay tax and whose houses are on the periphery of the ūr defined by processions and who are included only in subordinate positions as temple servants), were the Dhobis who live and work in Yanaimangalam.

The walk Vellalakantan walked from the cremation-ground temple and the talk he talked as he walked redefined the spatial dimensions of this dominant ūr. His walk included those who were in other contexts excluded, and his talk—as well as a story Dhobis and others tell about him—centered those who were in other contexts relegated to the outsides and peripheries of the dominant ūr's livable space.

Take first his walk. When Vellalakantan left from the cremation-ground festival after midnight, he started on a walk that pushed the ūr out to its widest perimeters. While the goddess-temple processions encircle the dominant residential area and at best assert a metonymic inclusion of those who live outside the ūr that the processions constitute, Vellalakantan's route took in everyone: every person and every fierce god on the road and in the fields. His walk made a space that encompassed all those within his purview and called that space the ūr. His walk was called *ūr kāval* (village watch), and it encircled the whole ūr.

Vellalakantan's capacity to constitute space through movement was predicated upon a triad of relations: (1) actors' substantial relations (embodied as habits, paḻakkams) with the places they occupy and frequent; (2) the similar relation of gods and places, indeed with god's power being located in the soil itself; and (3) the relations between persons and their gods, to whom the former connect through contiguous substantial connections. Taken together, this triad of relations—person bound to place, god bound to place, and god bound to person—makes god-connected Tamil actors into agents of the very place they occupy, of the ūr itself. Persons, gods, and land are linked inextricably, such that an act by one involves the others, and human actors may be seen as always in part agents of an emplaced divinity. As they walk "around the village" in powerful processions led by possessed god-dancers, humans reaffirm and recreate their identification with one another and with the territory, the land itself. Any one procession may alter, extend, contract, intersect, or bisect other paths and other walks by other agents. This is the village: a set of overlapping alternative spaces made in actions, including processions. Borrowing from Bakhtin, we might call this the dialogic ūr or, even better, the heterologic ūr, where through what Volosinov (1986, 23) refers to as the "multi-accentuality" of social life, a society multiply enacts its material social distinctions through their discourse, through their use of signs. While Volosinov speaks of language, of words as signs that literally take on the accents of discordant class interests, here the discourse is one of movement through space. (I point to the *Oxford English Dictionary*'s felicitous etymology of discourse: "to run, move, or travel over a space, region, etc. . . . to extend.") The different processional routes are outward signs of different social positions and different histories. Hence village residents (walkers and talkers) keep the ūr itself a living heterologic discursive practice, a sign of ideological and embodied competition, not a set of hegemonic habits "fossilized" as structure. Vellalakantan's walk was such a discourse.

Vellalakantan not only extended the ūr spatially to *include* literally "everyone" in it; he also inverted some social positions within that ūr. He moved from the peripheralized zone of Dhobis to the central point of transactions with people from all jātis in the village. As Vellalakantan made his long round of guard duty, he stopped at crossroads and at other temples that marked his route. People awaited him at these places. The bells that weighed his hat and lined his spear cut through the dark and signaled his approach. When Vellalakantan came, he stopped and gave prophecy; that is, he "gave signs" (*kuṟi koṭuttār,* otherwise called "the voice of grace," aruḷvākku). The man who god-danced Vellalakantan in 1990 gave kuṟi in a soft, barely audible voice which seemed to mark the silence of the dark night (the music drifts softly from the distant cremation ground). People awaited him as he walked along his route. As he walked his way around the village that his walk also defined, these village people came and circled around him to receive his kuṟi and to give him coins. They gave him mariyātai: they made room (space) for him and they deferred to his words and received the ash he smeared directly on their foreheads. Take the scene at the goddess temple on the night of Vellalakantan's guard round, where his social and spatial position relative to other ūrmakkaḷ contrasted most sharply with the position Dhobis take during the goddess-temple festival. There, at the goddess festival, Dhobis sit and wait on the periphery of the crowd, watch events from afar, wait for the last portion of paṭaippu. Down and out (though not so far or low as S. C.). At life cycle rituals too, Dhobis act as servants and occupy peripheries (outside the temple, outside the house), where they give mariyātai but do not receive it. But on this night, Vellalakantan arrived and moved to the steps of the goddess temple (which is locked for the night), his back to the goddess.[3] He stands closest to the goddess, with his back to her, and in her eye-flow. He is the center of attention, the center of transaction. He gives out powerful words and substances. The ūrmakkaḷ and other village residents or visitors gathered around and below him take what words and prasad—generally ash—he gives them and then they go home.

In an essay on the Ramayana, Ramanujan reminds us that a single story may generate hundreds of tellings. He writes, "[T]he story may be the same in [any] two tellings, but the discourse may be vastly different. Even the structure and sequence of events may be the same, but the style, details, tone, and texture—and therefore the import—may be vastly different" (1991, 25). So, for example, the story of Rama—his life, the sequence of events in his life—may be repeated 300 times, yet each telling may be discursively different: one telling of the story may be told in such a way or context as to comment on gender relations while another telling of the same story may be a discourse on Indian politics or on religious difference (Richman 1991).

Like two tellings of a story, two walkings of the village may be said to be discursively related. Vellalakantan's walk refuted the ūr constituted by the ūrmakkaḷ processions: he included those previously excluded, and he centered himself, and his community, in places where he and they might otherwise occupy a periphery.

By the time he worked his way all around his route, walking as far as the outskirts of the neighboring villages—even to a village across the river—where other devotees awaited him, many hours had passed and he was weighed down by a bulging sack of coins collected from devotees. He was ultimately unable to stand. His S. C. devotees from Middle Ūr carried him —as they must every year—to cool off in the river. He returned to the Vellalakantan shrine on the edge of West Temple. Music started, drums and nataswāram. In both temples the crowds which had been waiting—whether sleeping or staying awake drinking ginger coffee or arrack—woke up, sobered up, stood up, and crowded densely together to watch for the culmination of the festival: the temple big men laying out the paṭaippu in front of the gods; the appointed Thevars enacting the numerous animal sacrifices that filled the place with the hot smell of violent death; the double-agent god-dancers gorging on the raw blood of the animals they straddled, one animal after another and another; the final flurry of music, dance, and prophecy. The timing of all of this depended on Vellalakantan's successful return. If he did not return, nothing would happen, the festival would not finish.

Perhaps the most surprising aspect of Vellalakantan's journey, however, is not the route he takes, the inclusive space he makes or the center he becomes, but rather the fact that he makes the journey at all. His walk is specifically a guard circuit, a watchman's round, a kind of walk called *ūkāval.* But a Dhobi taking such a walk inverts all expectations, for in all other contexts, kāval belongs to the Thevars of the village. Thevars, sanctioned by the Tamilnadu state that has created government positions that village Thevars have the right to fill, staunchly guard their right (urimai) to be the village watchmen (kāvalkāraṅkaḷ), and in the story I am about to relate, it was Vellalakantan's original attempts to perform kāval that led to his brutal murder at the hands of the enraged Thevars. As Vellalakantan walks his rounds, however, the Thevars also wait and so participate in constituting a version of the village that refutes their own version in which they figure as dominant and central as well as the rightful village guardians.

NARRATING VELLALAKANTAN

The walk Vellalakantan walks and the talk he talks as he stops along the way extend the space (*veḷi*) of the ūr and reverse some relations of high and low, center and periphery. The stories people told me about Vellalakantan's origins and about his surprising rights to perform kāval indicate along a different channel (narrative in an everyday context versus movement and transaction in a ritual one) the heterogeneity of peoples' assessments of social reality. Storytelling, in other words, is another venue for politics.

I recorded three versions, and heard a fourth, of the Vellalakantan story. The differences among the tellings show how a story's telling is potentially powerful action. Let me start with the longest story, the one told to me by Kantan, who claims to be a patrilineal descendent of the man-who-became-the-god Vellalakantan. I recorded this story on the outer stoop of Kantan's house. Kantan is a Dhobi, a Washerman, and he lives on the edge of the Big Ūr in a mud hut surrounded by clothes to be washed, clothes hung to dry, clothes folded, stacked, and bundled into old sheets.

The story of Vellalakkantan

In the beginning, this ūr belonged to the Ukkirankottai king—this place (*iṭam*) was his. When the Raja of Ukkirankottai ruled over this village, he would come on a trip once every six months to see how things were. One day when he came, the Dhobi Matavannan and his wife were in this house. They had just one daughter, Matippillai. She was very beautiful. When the Maharaja came into the village, all the people went and saw him. When the Maharaja came around on his horse, Matippillai too went and looked.

D: This very house, you mean?

Yes! When the Maharaja came passing by this very house, Matippillai became pregnant in his gaze (pārvai). She became pregnant, and when she was in her tenth month he came again to this very place (iṭam).

This time, the Raja sent a man to Matavannan and his wife to ask them to wash and return his veṣti. When the guard came and called to Matavannan, he angrily replied, "My daughter is pregnant. Her time has come. You tell your Maharaja that because of this I'm unable to come."

The Maharaja sent his man back again to bring the Dhobi, commenting, "If he doesn't come, cut off his head and bring it to me."

When the guard returned to the Dhobi, what did Matippillai say to him? She said, "I'll give you two heads instead of one. No need to go with only one head. Just wait a minute and I'll give you my child's head too." Seeing the situation, the guard gave up and left.

A boy was born and he grew steadily as a boy should. He grew up, and he didn't know the labor of washing clothes. He grew up into a big strong youth and he passionately studied all the labors like fencing and stick-fighting. He was a tough giant. Because he wasn't born in the way an ordinary person is [i.e., conceived by a "gaze"], they had decided to give him the name Vellalakantan.

One day the Pantimar (Thevars)[4] from here went off together for a hunt. When they went, he went too. He had two dogs—Kacci and Pocci—and he took them with him. That day he killed deer and he killed boar and he brought them down from Velli Malai.

He came back with the Pantimar (Thevars) to Pattamadai, where they placed their kills on the rock on the south side of the village at the place called Matarapatai and divided the shares. When they were dividing the shares, he said, "I want a double share."

"We can't give you a double share." they said.

"Don't tell me that! My dog killed the boar. For that I want an extra share," he requested.

It seems they wouldn't give a share for that.

"You're a cunt, born without even knowing your father. There's no double share for you," concluded a Thevar.

He said, "Oh really? OK, fine!" and concluding that he shouldn't go with them anymore, he returned home angrily.

Here at home his mother had heated water and was ready for the meat she thought would be coming. Her son entered the house angrily. As soon as he entered, he called his mother into the house and bolted the door.

He said, "The Thevars of this village called me a cunt who doesn't even know his father. Where is my father?"

She said, "Son, what can I tell you? I've never taken money from anyone. I've never even bought betel. I've never looked improperly at a man. How can you come at me with a sword! I've done nothing wrong, son."

All this was of no use to him. "Where is my father? I'll let you out only if you tell me. If you don't I'll stab and kill you and then I'll kill myself too."

She relented. "Son, in those days, the Ukkirankottai Maharaja would come on his horse to make rounds. When he came, all the people went and saw him. I also saw him from the roof of our house. And he saw me. That was my only fault (tōcam). In that fault, you were born."

Learning of this, he said "I'll go see and speak to the Maharaja, then I'll return," and he climbed on a horse and set off for Ukkirankottai.

There at the fort were four gateways. At all four stood guards. When they saw him stopping there, they thought that the king had come back from outside; he and the king were of exactly the same type—the same height, the same dress, everything the same. That's why they thought that the Maharaja had gone out another gate without their knowing and was now returning. So they opened the gate. He went straight in. When he went in, there the Raja and Rani were playing backgammon seated on their thrones. The Maharaja looked up and saw him.

"Hey there! Where are you from? You look just like me, so tell me, where are you from?" he asked.

Without listening to his questions, Vellalakantan asked "Have you ever been to the village Yanaimangalam?"

" . . . Yes . . . "

"When you came along the south side of my house, you had a look at my mother," he said.

The Raja admitted it.

"OK then. I want the right to do village watch (kāval)," he said.

The Raja said "Hey, wait. Don't ask for that! That will incite the enmity of the Thevars. You're my son, so I'll write over to you all the wealth of the village. Leave it at that."

He said, "No way, no how! I want the guard's staff."

The Raja said "Alright, son!" and told him to approach the throne. "If you're so determined, that watch (kāval) is yours." The Raja wrote him a title on a copper plate and handed him the guard staff, then sent him off on his horse with a warm goodbye.

When he came back here, the watch of the whole village was turned over to him. He would go on watch rounds. When he went around on watch, there was hardly room for him to circle the village because the fields were so packed with growing rice paddy: there wasn't even a path (vaḻi) for a dog to walk! He was sitting in this midst of such bounty. At harvest, the paddy would pile up in heap upon heap!

Now, they (the Thevars) went off to the six regions of their allies—that is, to Mangulam, Marakuricci, Tenni Malai, and so on—and gathered men. They gathered men and returned, saying "Look here! Can't we even kill a Dhobi boy? With this many men together, we should be able to kill him."

At that time there was a Leatherworker living within the precincts of Vellalakantan's watch who was hired to graze the cattle. That day, when he went to round up the village cattle, the Thevars caught him and tied him up. Then they stuck all the cattle inside a thorn fence and locked them up. Then, at six o'clock in the evening there were no cows here to milk, and all the calves, left at home, were moaning.

The villagers all noisily complained, "Hey Vellalakanta! Go check your pastures, why don't you! There isn't a cow to be seen. Who knows what terrible thing has happened!"

He said, "There's no need to talk to me like that! I'll go at once and bring back the cattle, wherever they are," and so he set off. He went there.

When he got there, the six sections of Thevars were there expecting him. He went and chopped down the thorn fence. He chopped it down and freed the cattle. A hideous battle ensued. He cut down a thousand men.

A crippled Thevar (*kallaṉ*)[5] had hidden. What did he do? He, in murderous rage, went and lay down expectantly behind a tree there. That Thevar then advanced, step by step, took his long spear and lunged with one great thrust. He stabbed Vellalakantan brutally, as if he desired his intestines. The Thevar stabbed and felled him.

Vellalakantan saw his intestines falling out and he bound them tightly with a cloth, then killed his attacker. Realizing that he wouldn't survive long, he grabbed hold of his dog, went to the irrigation ditch [Kantan gestures to the main irrigation sluice out in the fields beyond his house], and died.

When he lay down by the ditch, the ūr people there [i.e., in Middle Ūr, which is the ūr nearest the sluice] saw that he was very badly off. When they arrived there they saw that his life was finished and said, "We have to tell his mother."

But by this time, the dogs he had raised—Kacci and Pocci—had rolled in the blood and had already gone home. When they came to the house, Vellalakantan's mother saw that something bad had happened. Not knowing what had happened to her son, she followed the dogs. The dogs led her to the ditch, and there her son lay dead. She cried and wailed and really made her tears flow.

All the village people of Middle Ūr came out. They put him on a plank, lifted him, and brought him to the eastern side of Yanaimangalam, put him down near the irrigation channel [just behind the Dhobi's house, still in the fields but closer], burned his body, then scooped up his remains and put them into the channel.

As soon as they put his ashes in the channel, he became a god at that very place. There he would frighten and threaten passersby. He changed into a cruel god. His mind wasn't like a god's, but he was comparable (in power) to a god. We decided that we couldn't keep (*vaicciru,* to place and have) him here by the channel and took him near the big temple and put up a place (*nilaiyam*) for him there. We took him out to the big Cutalaimatan temple on the Tambraparni River, thinking that there should be a guardian deity in front of that temple. We decided that once a year when we give a festival to our god, Cutalaimatan, we would also give a festival for him. So to this day our twelve families come together to give a festival for Vellalakantan. . . . That's the end.

In a rather straightforward way, this story authorizes Vellalakantan's temple practices. It gives Vellalakantan and his descendants (who include the god-dancer, the storyteller, and those twelve families who worship at the shrine) the king-granted right—not to mention the biological-moral capacity as people descended from a king—to perform kāval in Yanaimangalam. The story connects Kantan's lineage, as well as the residents of Middle Ūr whose ancestors found the body, to the god and to the places from which his power emanates.

It is Kantan's *telling* of the story that makes the connection between the past event and his own family's current temple practices. Kantan told the story in some ways as a historical narrative, in the past tense as an event that happened to third persons ("hes," "shes," and "theys") no longer present. Yet at the same time, through his use of indexical (deictic) references to places and persons and relations—to the wider context in which the story was told—he pragmatically linked present realities to the past he narrated: he placed the story in Yanaimangalam and in his own family compound using phrases such as "in *this* same house," "*those* Thevars," "*that* field over *there,*" "*that* irrigation ditch" and by using gestures to indicate particular places. At the end of the story, Kantan lifted the past into the present when he suddenly shifted from "they" to "we": "we decided," "we took," and now "we give." First when that "we" breaks in and then when the tense switches to present, Kantan dramatically shifts the temporal frame from an objective "past" that involved objective others to a subjective "present" continuous with "our" actions here and now.

Kantan's creative use of indexicals not only connected him, his house, and his family to Vellalakantan's past and present (so that the story temporally overtook the telling, as Genette [1980, 221] might put it). His use of such indexicals was also what made the story into discourse: first, by telling the story in the here and now and, second, through the directed use of pragmatic indexical signs (pronouns, deictics, gestures) that tellers everywhere use to make their stories part of a discursive present.

As Benveniste pointed out, the kind of first-person "presence" that first-person pronouns such as "we" announce makes for *discourse,* makes for "inter-subjective communication" in the here and now (1971/1966, 219; see also Genette 1980, 28–30). Ramanujan too analogizes that the difference between a story and discourse is the same as the difference between a sentence (that says something) and a speech act (that, as Austin showed us, *does* something) (Ramanujan 1991, 25). The story tells us something, and the telling of it *does* something.

The story's *tellings* are, along with Vellalakantan's walk, then, part of a current discourse on spatial and social relations in the village. That is, while the Vellalakantan *story* is a kind of history of past events that authorize Vellalakantan's present agency, its *telling* is discourse about present circumstances, relations, persons, and events.

That residents of Yanaimangalam understand their tellings of past events to be potentially productive acts in the present is nowhere more evident than in the two tellings—or rather the difference between the two tellings—of the Vellalakantan story that Ariraman, the young leader of S. C. Middle Ūr, told me on the veranda of his house. In both tellings, he highlighted the role that members of his community, the Middle Ūr Pallars, played in retrieving Vellalakantan from his embattled fields and carrying him to the irrigation stream where he died. It was they who cremated him, who threw his ashes in the stream, and who thus brought him to the place where he became a god on the spot. They were the first to see him as a god. Ariraman's two tellings were set apart, however, by elements of context.

The first telling he launched into angrily and spontaneously after telling me of the incident I referred to in Part I as the "ash theft," in which a group of Thevars, including their headman and some local police, concocted false charges in order to expel Middle Hamlet residents from the goddess temple. As Ariraman told the Vellalakantan story, he named jātis—*those* Thevars, *the* Dhobis, *we* Pallars. He gestured toward the Thevar street with an angry wave of the arm when he mentioned them in the story, making a clear connection between living Thevars "over there" and ruthless actors in the story. He identified with Vellalakantan's fate at the hand of Thevars.

Ariraman's second telling, a few days later, was one I staged: I came to his house with a tape recorder and asked him if he would tell me the story again. He agreed, but he told it differently. He omitted all references to jāti, and when I urged him to provide jāti names, he claimed he did not know what he had so vehemently asserted only a few days previously. He narrated that the Dhobi boy was out hunting (and maybe guarding, he added, with some unscholarly prompting by me) and "many people" (*niṟaiyapēr*) came and attacked him and killed him. My assistant, a young master's degree student I had hired named Hari, who also self-identified as S. C. (though he asked me to hide this fact from the ūrmakkaḷ and Brahmans in the Big Ūr), pushed him a little, asking "*Who* is it who did that?" and Ariraman replied, "I couldn't say which jāti. The big bosses who *were* in charge of protection" (*enta cāti eṉṟu colla muṭiyātu. anta patukāppil* irunta *mutalāḷimāru*), using the past tense.

In the second telling, Ariraman did not use the name Vellalakantan even once, perhaps because he saw the enunciation of "the Dhobi boy's" name to be an act with pragmatic, discursive potential. Indeed, the name is a pun.[6] The core pun turns on the different double "l" and on the easy slip between short "a" and short "e" in the first syllable. "Vallāḷakaṇṭaṉ" appears in Tamil dictionaries and translates as the "powerful among the powerful" (Fabricius, 852), the "mightiest of the mighty" (*Tamil Lexicon* 1982, 3529). "Veḷḷāḷakaṇṭaṉ," on the other hand, means something like Lord of Peasant Farmers, or Lord of Urmakkal, Lord of Veḷḷāḷas (a name applied to peasant land-controlling jātis all over Tamilnadu, such as the Pillaimar in Tirunelveli District and the Kavuntar in Konkunatu [Beck 1972], and by connotative extension to any dominant landowners in a region, such as the Thevars were in Yanaimangalam). It is significant that to Raja Balasubramaniam, a native speaker and Tamil scholar who pointed out the pun to me in the first place, the term also suggested the meaning "Killer of Veḷḷāḷas." The word "kaṇṭaṉ" connotes forceful domination. Its dictionary glosses include warrior, hero, king, lord, and husband.

Kantan, the Dhobi teller, clearly calls the hero "Veḷḷāḷakaṇṭaṉ." The Dhobi boy is a lord of or even killer of dominant peasant jātis. In a version we will see below, Ramayya Thevar, a prosperous landowner, calls the hero "Vallāḷakaṇṭaṉ," the mightiest of the mighty.

Ariraman avoided the name altogether. He was well aware that his telling of the story was a creative and potentially consequential discourse about present social relations and not a mere recitation of an objective history of events. It was, remember, only a couple of weeks previously that the Thevars—upon whom many laborers among Middle Hamlet residents depend for their own economic well-being—had threatened Middle Hamlet with violence over the "ash theft." When Ariraman saw that I was trying to preserve his telling, that I could repeat it, that others could hear him tell it outside the context of his telling, he further "hid" (Scott 1990) the presence of the story he had voiced to me previously. Not only did he avoid mention of the hero's name (an elision that in its totality was far from silent)—sticking simply to "the Dhobi boy," and, post-apotheosis, the "*cāmi*," or god. He used the anonymous third person, he mentioned no jāti names except his own, and he kept the story stowed firmly in the past tense.

A fourth version, this one told by Ramayya Thevar, who we know as a relatively well-off landowning neighbor of mine, resembles Ariraman's second version and drives home the distinction I am making. Ramayya Thevar's version makes the incident of the story not only temporally but also spatially remote. The events take place "on the road" (versus in the ūr, as the others tell it—perhaps what is ūr to them is mere kāṭu to him). He uses jāti names but omits any particular identification (a Dhobi out on the road versus Kantan's personal naming of the characters and indications of the house they lived in) and refers to the Thevars as "they," not "we," using a common alternative jāti title, Pantimar. He sticks solely to the third person and the past tense. Ramayya Thevar's ending to the story differs somewhat from the others as well. While the others end with the erection of a shrine for the god, they usually talk of the shrine in the context of the whole village. They list different shrines, note the continuing importance of the shrines in rituals involving many jātis from the village and the movement of the god across the village. "Veḷḷāḷakaṇṭaṉ" in these versions is recognized as a powerful village resident in the here and now. In contrast, Ramayya Thevar makes "Vallāḷakaṇṭaṉ" into a distant god located on the village periphery (on the road) and says nothing of his continued activity: "Vallāḷakaṇṭaṉ" was killed, he told people there to construct a shrine for him and to bury his mother near him when she died; thus the place became a cremation area. The end.

Ramayya Thevar's story minimizes "Vallāḷakaṇṭaṉ" and makes him remote, something to see through a keyhole perhaps, small and distant but not relevant to experience in the here and now. Kantan the Dhobi's story is the opposite. It literally lifts the past into the present and conditions possible futures as well. His telling opens the door, to stick with that metaphor, and pulls the past right into the present.

Michel de Certeau (1989, 2–4) contrasts what he characterizes as two strategies of time in western discourse. One he defines psychoanalytically, invoking Freudian concepts of memory. The other kind of time is the one we use to write history. Memory in psychoanalysis, he points out, is treated as a kind of residue, hidden and problematic, of some past event. The past of memory, that is, is present in the person and conditions—usually in a negative, hindering way—present and future capacities for action. "Historiography, on the other hand," he continues, "is based on a clean break between the past and the present" (ibid., 4). In the first case of memory, then, the past is conjoined with the present and conditions present and possible future experiences. In the second case, the time of academic history, we certainly may posit a continuity in time, a causal link, between past and present, but, and this is important, the past is different from, disjunct from, the present. I find this distinction, between what I will call conjunctive and disjunctive temporalities, relevant to the material at hand.

Kantan and Ariraman (in his first version only) conjoined past and present, bringing the past to bear directly on the present. Unlike the problematic memory Freudian psychoanalysis works to unbury, the past of

Vellalakantan is something of an enabling past. The story's telling is a way for Kantan and Ariraman to remake themselves in the context of current social relations which in many other ways bury them in disadvantageous social positions (low, poor, workers outside the dominant village). Telling the story and making it present put the two of them into central agentive positions relative to others. Kantan shows his genetic connection to a village hero, and Ariraman explains how his own hamlet is also connected to the god's power: they in effect made the god and now they let the god make them, which he continues to do. It is important to remember that rituals for Vellalakantan are key events in the village, events in which many village residents, rich and poor, Brahman and ūrmakkaḷ and S. C., participate. While all the different jātis participate, it is the Dhobis and the S. C. Pallar who control Vellalakantan's movement, who speak Vellalakantan's words, who make Vellalakantan a present agent in the social reproduction of the village. Kantan and Ariraman and their kinsmen are the enablers of village reproduction once a year. Their way of narrating the story stresses the present powers they may access through their connection to the past making of the god.

The historiographical narratives of Ramayya Thevar and Ariraman (in his recorded version) are quite effective at maintaining another state of affairs entirely: that was then, this is now. Ariraman, with his use of the past tense, closed the door between past and present. With his avoidance of indexicals linking then to now he locked the door shut: his second telling made the event of Vellalakantan's death into something remote, past, and more or less unconnected to any current social realities. It becomes a bland causal explanation: how that god happens to be here in the village. Ramayya Thevar clearly peripheralized the story: outside of this time and even outside of the village, something that happened out on the road to some people who used to live around here a long time ago.

It may seem on the surface that Ramayya Thevar and Ariraman (in version two) are simply not bothering to make a connection between current social realities and this past event but are simply telling stories about an objective, possibly boring, and perhaps even mythological past. On the contrary, I would like to suggest that these latter two versions too are definite political statements about current social realities: while Kantan's version puts Kantan, his kinsmen, and the Pallar of Middle Hamlet into positions of some power in village affairs, Ramayya Thevar's telling placed Kantan, and Ariraman and all their kinsmen, outside the ūr and peripheralized them from participation in the social production of the village. If the action is all past, and all of it took place out on the road (outside the village), then it is certainly removed from any ongoing processes of village organization or political debate!

Kantan and Ariraman (in version one) use a different mode of narrative to construct a different kind of temporality, one in which past events take on real force in current social realities. They both pose ritually backed alternatives to the dominant version of the village. They centralize the powers and agency of those whom the analytical/historiographical versions peripheralize and make anonymous outsiders, give names and places to otherwise unnamed people out on the road. While de Certeau might conceive this as the past pulled into the present, here, invoking an existentialist mode of temporal reckoning,[7] it may be better said that Kantan, and even more so Ariraman, are both retrojecting a past based on a present anger which itself is defined against a hope for the future.

These narrative choices are political choices and, as Ariraman's second telling shows, matters of personal safety. His second version was clearly an attempt to hide the past (make it more like a memory in the Freudian sense, perhaps—repressed and best left so in order to avoid present pain, in this case the pain of Thevar threats and fists). He would not even mention Thevars in his second telling. Why? Because even his disjunctive narration of the event was possibly still a character statement about Thevars today. He could not mention the caste name without indexing those of that name living in the present, so he wisely omitted the name Thevar altogether—as well as the name of their Killer—and made his second story into a story not about the past or its relation to the present so much as a veiled story about his present fear of possible future injury at the hands of the Thevars who had so recently exhibited their will to dominate by force.

We have moved, temporarily, away from Vellalakantan's walk. To conclude, let us return to it briefly. The story and the walk, I have shown, are not unrelated: the story authorizes the walk. The walk Vellalakantan takes is, however, more like the *tellings* of the story than it is like the story itself. The walk, like the tellings, is about present relations and realities. In fact, Vellalakantan's actions at the festival do not follow the story line at all. He does not reenact the story or repeat its history. Rather, he makes a different story as he walks the story discursively into the present through movement and speech. Vellalakantan speaks for himself. He centers himself as a present first person, an interlocutor in dialogue with persons and in motion across the territory. Vellalakantan speaks for himself as he crosses the present terrains of the village on processions and talks to those he meets. This time the Thevars do not spill his guts. They wait along with everyone else.

Because Vellalakantan is a walking and talking double agent (an agent of the god and of his jāti and lineage), his actions, like those of any agent, effect real outcomes. Among them are the ontological expansion of the space called ūr to include those otherwise excluded. He also, as I indicated, reconfigures dominant social orderings of center and periphery. As Vellalakantan makes his guard round, he makes it possible for his community, his kinsmen, and for Middle Hamlet residents as well to refigure their relation to dominant village jātis, especially to the Thevars.

Vellalakantan's walk is heroic. Like the steps Visnu takes to open a field for others to act, to wage battle (de Certeau 1984, 124), so does Vellalakantan's lonely night walk open and create a space for the activities—including discourses—of others. And it also gives these others, not only Dhobis but in this case the Middle Hamlet S. C. too, a place *in* an ūr of his—and their—own making.

Residents of Yanaimangalam debate and contest their village through a politics of movement. The kind of refigurings that Vellalakantan's walks effect are not at all uncommon in and around the temples to fierce gods in Yanaimangalam. In several fierce-god temples in Yanaimangalam, the dominant social orderings instantiated in the goddess temple are redefined and often undermined. A thorough analysis of fierce-god temple rituals in Yanaimangalam complicates the common understanding of the social place of these fierce gods in south India. As I have noted earlier, in many South Indian studies on religion, fierce gods are considered to reflect and parallel the position of their allegedly low-caste worshippers. That is, fierce gods are often thought to belong to "low castes" and, like them, to rank low in a rather static village pantheon (see, for example, Fuller 1987; Dumont 1986/1957; Babb 1975, 237–246). But, as we have seen, these temples often include dominant high jātis among their temple-association members. Furthermore, what authorizes the social orderings in fierce-god temples is not political and economic dominance. Nor is it essential static jāti character or rank, but rather events inscribed in narratives such as the Vellalakantan story and made real in practices such as telling stories and taking walks. These practices constitute the village itself as a highly contested spatial unit.

FIERCE GODS AND ALTERNATIVE POWERS

It makes sense that fierce gods are a creative source of alternative discourses on village relations. To begin with, fierce gods in South India are well known for their disruptive and potentially transformative energy. Shulman lists common features of such gods, most of which fit Vellalakantan exactly, including mixed ancestry (King and Washerwoman), violent death of the hero (the Thevars overpower him and spill his guts), the god's place as village guardian (inscribed on a copper plate, no less), aided by low-caste helpers (the Pallars of Middle Hamlet who, at his death, carried him to the irrigation channel and cremated him and who yearly, in ritual, carry his coin-laden heavy body back to the temple). Shulman furthermore describes how such deities are characterized by "transformability and transformative power." This power is moreover an "antinomian" power, a power that potentially subverts extant orderings (1989, 47–48, 60–61).

The violent origin of fierce deities is not just violent. It is often a violence born specifically of a moral delict. We saw that persons may remove evils and other faults arising from past actions, whether they are their own or those of their ancestors, from the interior places of their lives (their bodies, their houses, their residential clusters) and dispose of them, often throwing them out into the kāṭu, the wild place "outside" (see also Raheja 1988, 172). By these disposing actions they at once reconstitute that outside's wildness (its "unmatching" incoherence, to borrow a term from Marriott) and render this outside place a present repository of the past. It's a dangerous and often painful place to go to—the kāṭu, the past. Ghosts linger there.

Fierce, disordering gods, the gods that the non-elite have best access to, are similarly outcomes of evil or sinful actions. And the kāṭu is the place for their many shrines. As the kāṭu is in general both repository and reminder of evil acts and dangers, the shrines that reside there, like scars on the body, also remind inhabitants of past violence. Consider the fierce-god stories recounted in this book so far. They follow a similar form: a human being—often but not always of some socially powerful jāti (see also Shulman 1989, 38–39)—commits a moral failing or injustice (making a false oath about bananas, lying about the theft of a plow, killing a valiant young Dhobi-Guardian, cutting down a tree inhabited by spirits), and from that negatively valued act—that evil (pāvam)—comes a negative result: a permanent aṭimai (slavery) between the family of the evildoer and the deity that their act brings into the ūr. Or, rather, into the kāṭu. The evildoer becomes, in effect, a slave to his or her own sinful action, the results of which become emplaced in shrines to fierce deities out in the kāṭu. Vestiges of violence, these shrines become places from which emanate real disordering and violent powers, which continue to shape the present. The past is emplaced in the kāṭu and to that extent the past remains, as David Carr writes, "an element of [the] experienced world" (1986, 4).

So while some embodied evils are "passed on" and "scattered," given away and digested, or thrown out into the distance (*tūram*), the kāṭu, and in this way become finished for the person, separated completely from the actor as from the ūr proper, the crimes and evils that bring fierce gods into a person's life do not finish so easily. They may be relocated—removed from the possessed body and sent out to permanent shrines in the kāṭu. However, the separation of the fierce god from the body is only partial. These fierce deities come to have permanent power over, through bodily connection to, those who committed the delict.

In many cases, this reversal of fortunes gives the non-elite some moral ground on which to stand and critique the dominant group. In short, the past economic, political, and moral misdeeds of the elite take on a life of their own, giving the victimized non-elite some semblance of power. Fierce gods in Yanaimangalam provide such powers to many non-elite and cannot therefore be reduced to mere mystifications of elite power. They serve rather as enabling powers for the non-elite, powers that give them not only a kind of moral authority but also a pragmatic power source (the god's power) that lends them an embodied political voice and a ritual means for political action. We have seen how the Dhobi reigns over Muppanars and how a Dhobi god enunciates an alternative reality of the ūr itself. We shall see this process repeated when the god Panaiyatiyan gives S. C. Pallars an edge over some ūr Thevars, and hence a wedge toward a reconceptualization of their place in the world.

NINE

Hindu Nationalism and Dalit Reform

TWO RESPONSES TO THEVAR DOMINATION

[P]eople need to have some say in the world into which they are thrown . . . they must in some measure choose their own lives and feel that they have a right to be here, to be free to make a difference, to be loved and affirmed, to be more than piano keys, ciphers, names, at the mercy of the gods, of oppressive laws, of impersonal injunctions, or mere fate.

—Jackson 1998, 195

The kinds of reconfigurations that Vellalakantan's practices effect are not at all uncommon in and around the temples to fierce gods. In fact, in several of the eleven fierce-god temples in Yanaimangalam, the social orderings instantiated in the goddess temple are in some ways refuted and reconfigured. At the same time, the language of rebellion in these temples does serve in some ways to reconfirm extant forms of domination even as it attempts to invert them. That is, inversions of rank and power that occur during a temple festival may reverse the specific relations of dominance and so exhibit an awareness of the dimensions of dominance, but they do not alter the overall form of dominance, the terms of its discourse. The idiom of competition favors precedence, mariyātai, inclusion, and exclusion, all of which are terms of the dominant discourse. It would be a mistake, however, to conclude that ritual in temples can never be more than rituals of rebellion, ultimately confirming the form of dominance. Not only do ritual inversions have the capacity to leak over and affect political discourse and everyday life, potentially feeding into real rebellion, as Natalie Davis (1975) and others (e.g., Sahlins 1994; Singer 1972, 231–232; Peacock 1968) have argued; temple festivals may also more radically alter the very terms of political discourse and pose real challenges to hegemonic forms of domination.

In two examples presented below, relatively disenfranchised residents of Yanaimangalam drew on regional and national movements as they contested the social and spatial contours of their local lives and their village in a ritual idiom. Their struggle in this politics was not only to contest and reshape their local social relations; to this observer it seemed they were also struggling for a "say" in life, for gaining a language of self-making and existence, for finding a way to matter in this world.

MIDDLE ŪR, THE GOD AT THE FOOT OF THE PALMYRA TREE, AND DALIT REFORM

On the side of the road leading to and from Yanaimangalam sits a set of earthen obelisks called *pīṭam.* Some are shin high, others chest high. For the first twenty months I lived in Yanaimangalam I did not notice these figures, even though I must have passed by them dozens of times on foot and by bus. Inconspicuous, they were the color of the red earth from which they were formed and they were hidden by the brambly thorn bushes that line the roadside here and there. One day I passed by on the bus, gazing out the window at the mountains that rose across the rice fields. Suddenly the shrine shouted out at me. The brambles were cleared, the obelisks refreshed and painted bright white.

This was the shrine to Panaiyatiyan Cāmi ("The God at the Foot of the Palmyra Tree"), and it belonged to the residents of S. C. Middle Ūr. For forty years, Middle Ūr had not performed a festival for Panaiyatiyan out of fear. During the festival forty years before, this fearsome god had lashed out and caused the deaths of several devotees and passersby, including a pregnant woman.[1] But as Ariraman, the young leader of Middle Ūr, told me, his generation—many of whom had not even been born at the time of the last koṭai—wished to distinguish itself by performing the festival again. In order to assure its success and to quell community fears, they planned a lavish festival that would without a doubt please the god immensely and turn all that rage into goodness and greatness for Middle Ūr. Consequently, the festival expenses far exceeded the means of many community members. Many went into debt in order to pay their share of the head tax, a whopping 350 rupees per adult male plus half that amount for each woman and child. This was a huge sum, considering that most Middle Ūr residents worked as agricultural laborers for a daily wage—collected sporadically over fluctuating agricultural cycles—of 15 to 20 rupees per day (in 1990), less for women laborers.

Among the victims of the god's rash anger forty years previously was a Thevar youth who was not even married yet. According to Ariraman, the youth was killed because as he walked past the shrine he had ridiculed the temple proceedings. The youth, I learned, was the granduncle (*tātā*) of a Thevar family in the village. In fact, he was the uncle of Ramayya Thevar. Now, about fifty yards up the road, just on the periphery of the main village and behind a small goddess temple and supposedly on the very spot where the youth died, stands a single obelisk in a small palmyra grove. This was the ancestor shrine to the fallen Thevar youth. The shrine attests to his continuing presence in the village at the very place where he is said to have dropped dead forty years before. Many village residents now conflate the slain Thevar with the god, calling them both "He at the base of the palmyra tree," as if the power (cakti) of the murderer (the god) is now the (potential) power of the murderee (the youth). As noted earlier, a moral delict such as a false oath or, here, ridiculing a god can lead the god to possess the transgressor in a maleficent or unmatched way. The fallen Thevar youth had come to partake of the god's powerful substance in this way, enslaving himself and his descendants to the fierce god's power emplaced at the site of his death.

Middle Ūr's koṭai festival must be understood against the backdrop of the ash incident, for the koṭai took place only a few weeks after the local police had barred Middle Ūr from the goddess temple. The Thevar headman's retaliation for what he chose to interpret as an incursion (and name as a theft) effectively put Middle Ūr in its place—outside the dominant ūr, out in Middle Ūr with their own ūr's goddess temple—and reestablished what for many ūrmakkaḷ, and certainly for the Thevar headman, were the desired and proper social and spatial relations of distinction (mariyātai) and other relations of dominance between themselves and the residents of Middle Ūr. As we saw in earlier chapters, and in keeping with the common South Asian formula in which temple, society, and cosmos are all homologues of one another (Beck 1976; Inden 1985), excluding a person from the central temple of a place is the same as excluding them from social centrality, power, and place. In this case, keeping Pallars out of the goddess temple was the same as keeping them out of the ūr and keeping them out in the kāṭu where their hamlet is located. Such exclusions, we know now, are powerful statements about social rankings in this society, where a person or group's spatial proximity to gods confers upon them relative high rank and status.

Middle Ūr residents proved to be reluctant subjects to Thevar domination. What started out as what Scott (1990) calls "hidden transcripts," statements made in the relative safety of home and hamlet about mythohistorical incidents of Thevar treachery (killing Vellalakantan) and of historically informed discourses on the originality of Untouchables (weren't they the Original Dravidians?) became public politics. Nowhere was this politics more evident than in the Panaiyatiyan koṭai, as Middle Ūr residents used their festival to assert an alternative future for themselves.[2] They drew not only on the familiar language of inversion but also on a hoped-for future informed by changing national discourses on Untouchability. Contemporaneous to the demographic shifts leading to Thevar dominance in Yanaimangalam, S. C. communities in the region had been subject to a range of programs promoting the uplift and equality of rural Untouchables. Over the years, these programs have included Tamilnadu's Self-Respect (cuya mariyātai) movement, Gandhian movements, Ambedkar-inspired conversions to Buddhism, and some nationally controversial conversions to Christianity and Islam (e.g., the famous case of Meenaksipuram[3], whose proponents held out promises of equality regardless of caste). In part through the implementation of these programs, many of the lower castes in Yanaimangalam had come to speak openly about egalitarianism (camattuvam) as a value or right (urimai).

In the wake of the ash incident, in a context of well-publicized and increasing clashes between S. C. and Thevars throughout the region, and armed with awareness of their own oppression as well as hopes for a different future, Middle Ūr residents used their own temple festival to assert different relations of power, different spatial prerogatives, and different definitions of inclusion. They put on what was one of the grandest and densest and most visible koṭai festivals of the year, a festival that also proved most disruptive to the movements of others.

This festival was, in short, an open inversion and subversion of ūrmakkaḷ domination in general and Thevar domination in particular. In public rituals, they inverted relative rank and centrality by making themselves higher, bigger, and more central. But they did not limit their moves to mere inversions or reversals that left the structure of inequality intact. They also subverted the dominant village by bringing the big villagers under the purview of their alternative vision of a different, egalitarian future. They accomplished these feats through several overlapping channels, four of which I will discuss here: they *cut across* the sociospatial contours of the dominant ūr in a bold procession through the ūr; they *centered* themselves through attractive displays of wealth and largesse; they *expanded* their influence and renown, their "bigness" (perumai), by taking over a road. But it was through the use of *national signs* of political belonging that they tied their future to an alternative formulation of the social order.

Cutting Across

Middle Hamlet worshipers and community members took an unanticipated route when they went on procession from their own hamlet to the temporary temple they had constructed over the god's image. Rather than plod the direct path across the clodded summer fields, they circled around and cut right through the Big Ūr. Starting from Middle Ūr (Figure 9.1), out in the uncivilized kāṭu, the Big Ūr's wasteland, they headed north to the big village, walked in procession up Muppanar Street, and then turned south again, heading down the road to the temple. This route en-

Figure 9.1. A procession starts out in Middle Ūr.

compassed specifically the Thevar neighborhood (Figure 9.2). The S. C. claimed that much territory as their god's and as their own.

Cutting this deliberate and boisterous path through the Big Ūr echoed that earlier transgression, just a few weeks before, when the S. C. man had walked into what was for him a restricted portion of the goddess temple to pinch some ash. Both transgressive walks lay claim to space and asserted inclusive rights in village places and processes. And both walks countermanded exclusions defined by Big Ūr processions and Thevar banishments. Both came as surprises to the Big Ūr people. And both were expansive acts, acts that effectively announced the existence of the S. C., as if to say, "Here we are, right here in our (*namma,* the inclusive first-person plural) ūr!" Where the two transgressions differed was in their power: unlike the lone man walking on his own into a goddess temple that the ūrmakkaḷ claimed as their own and that the Thevars protected as such, the S. C. community was enabled—literally empowered—by their exclusive and real links to their own powerful, protecting, and vengeful god. This time, the Big Ūr people consented to S. C. movement through ūrmakkaḷ, and even more so Thevar, space. Like the S. C., the Big Ūr people recognize the powerful, material link between gods and the members of their temple associations, their human servants, who become suffused with the qualities of the god with whom they have a "connection" (cērkkai).

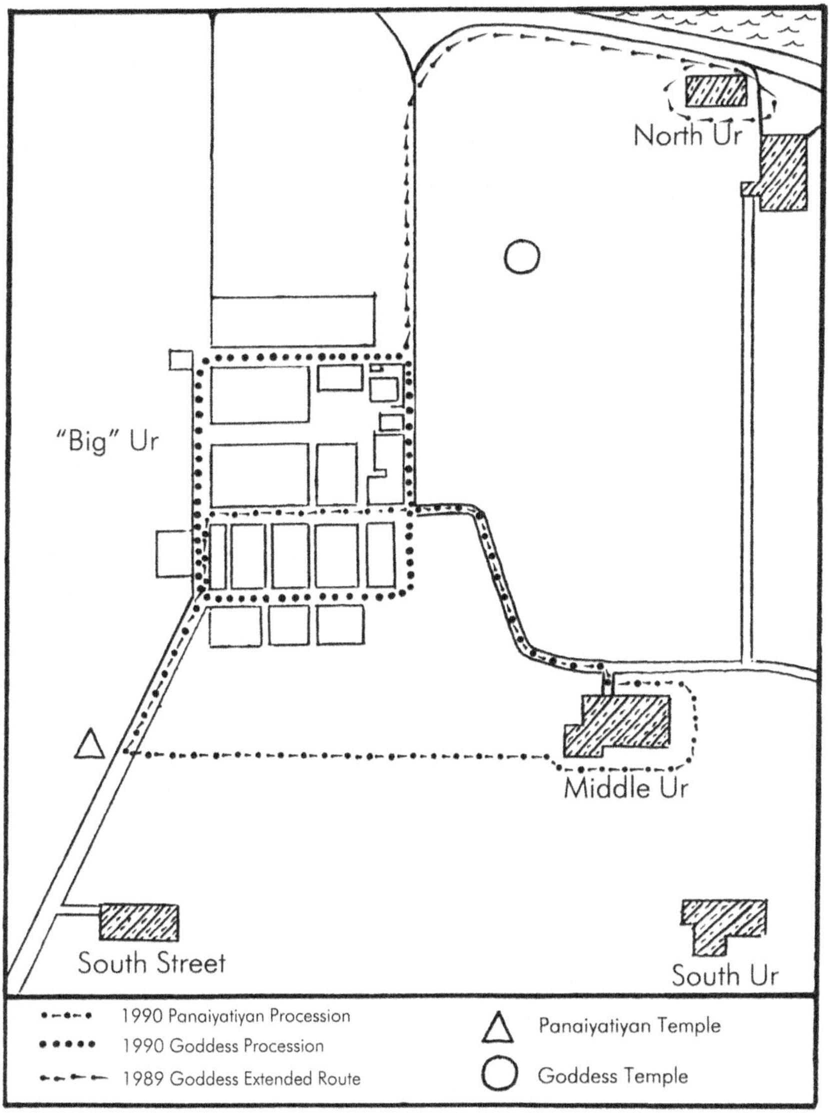

Figure 9.2. Diagram of Middle Ūr procession.

Though tolerated by the ūrmakkaḷ, this procession did prompt discussions of past transgressive processions. Parvathi, for example, recalled a procession of protest taken by a group she referred to as "Harijans." Several years previously (from her reports, as many as thirty years before our conversation in 1990), these "Harijans" had marched right up the Agraharam, from which they were at the time banned altogether. Parvathi and some of the other old-timer Brahmans on the Agraharam occasionally lamented the good old days when kuṭimakkaḷ (S. C. as well as Dhobis and Barbers) stayed off the Agraharam street in a show of deference (mariyātai) to its Brahman residents, a time when they approached houses from the back or stood just off the street on paths between houses, calling out from there to the householders to whom they needed to speak.[4] The Harijan protest march she described was meant to announce the rights of all to walk wherever they would. Protesting exclusions from the Agraharam, the procession also broke through that exclusion and transgressed expected mariyātai distinctions.

Parvathi could not recall who marched in the protest, and in all likelihood the participants came from outside Yanaimangalam, organized by Gandhian or other activists. Even at the time of this research, S. C. residents of the village were generally reluctant to cross boundaries of mariyātai. In 1990, the district collector's office (the collector at that time was a Tamil Brahman raised in Delhi), in an attempt to demonstrate intercaste harmony and equality at a time when in scattered sites in Tirunelveli District, as elsewhere in Tamilnadu and India, S. C. were still being harassed and beaten out of their homes, sponsored an "all-caste lunch" inside the Brahmanical Visnu (Perumal) temple at the riverbank (it might be obvious why he chose a Brahmanical temple instead of say, the goddess temple, given the former's relative unimportance in matters of local politics). The idea was that everyone—Brahmans to S. C.—would dine together in a sign of social equality. I asked Ariraman of Middle Ūr if he was planning to attend. He responded with a bewildered look that backed up his verbal reply—"No!" Neither he nor any other S. C. from Yanaimangalam would be going—"We have to live here, don't we?" he said—and then he added that the collector would bring in some S. C. from other places for the purpose. I was away when this event occurred and so could not attend. Later when I asked around, no one else—of any jāti—seemed to have gone either. This all-caste lunch, it seems, was not one of participation. It was merely for display.

On a different occasion, a big man among the Pillaimar jāti told me his thoughts on certain groups walking through the big village. He recalled a case involving the Illuttuppillai, Aruna's low-ranking jāti, a group whose members live peripheralized in the hamlet referred to as South Street. Several years previously the Illuttuppillai had made a temple procession along the edge of and then through the big village in order to get from the river to their southern hamlet during their ūr's Mariyamman goddess festival. Some important ūrmakkaḷ objected to this route and filed an apparently unsuccessful case in the district court to disallow it. As my informant stated the issue, the ūrmakkaḷ had the right to say who would walk where in *their own* ūr! I asked to see the court records which he claimed to have locked up in an ancient teak cabinet in his house, but he said "We don't give that to anyone." So this court case is a different kind of hidden transcript, proof perhaps of a losing decision that favored the subordinate group over the dominant. Regardless of the outcome of the court case, stronger arms prevailed and today the Illuttuppillai take a route that skirts but does not cut through the big village streets.

The nostalgic discourse of both Brahmans and ūrmakkaḷ tells a story of continual competition, but is not about stopping the S. C. from their present activities so much as it is about locating a time when a "proper," uncontested order still held. (It is the Kaliyuga, after all, the age of deterioration, the time when things fall apart, so disorderings such as S. C. processions through the Big Ūr are not completely unexpected.) Nevertheless, nowhere is it more obvious that restrictions on movement in or through certain spaces are still enforced by big people in Yanaimangalam than in the case of the ash theft.

Centering

As the S. C. moved in procession through the Big Ūr and lay claim to that much space, they also made themselves into central nodes in the distribution of desired substances, most particularly Panaiyatiyan's divinely transvalued ash. While some Big Ūr people hastily grabbed their own ash from the cups that S. C. deferentially proffered up to them, others reversed expectations and received (rather than took) their ash with public gestures of deference (mariyātai) of the kind that the S. C. are usually expected to show to them: they bent at the knees, covered their mouths, bowed their heads. These big village people made themselves relatively small, acknowledging in that act the power that the S. C. owned as the human conduits of Panaiyatiyan's power. These public displays of reverse deference are important, for as Levinson (1982) argues, and as residents of Yanaimangalam confirmed, mutual displays of deference connote relative equality (camam) between the transactors. Through this procession, then, the S. C. not only asserted the inclusion of their village but they effected at least a temporary public social symmetry.

As we have seen, god-dancers (cāmiyāṭikaḷ) are ritual experts who attract a following. During this koṭai, Middle Ūr men and women—the god-dancers in particular—are the central sources of divine power, called on not only by their own temple-association members but by other village people as well. For the time of the festival and for the time that talk about events at the festival will linger afterward, members of the Panaiyatiyan temple association must be seen as centers within the larger ūr of Yanaimangalam. Those who were on their periphery of the festival—those who gave vows, waited for ash, watched and in some cases followed the procession—included some of the big ūrmakkaḷ.

As noted earlier, during koṭai festivals devotees crowd around successful god-dancers, asking for oracular advice and promising vows in return for positive changes in their lives. Outside the festival, well-known god-dancers may also receive visitors and mail asking their advice all year long. Centered this way as foci of attention and vows, god-dancers—like the gods themselves—swell in size (garland after garland draped over their bodies) and in fame over the years as one piece of advice succeeds another. The number of bracelets, armbands, and necklaces that adorn their bodies is a measure of density over time, over generations even, as fathers give way to sons. At this particular koṭai for Panaiyatiyan, the vows were not dense nor were the god-dancers thickly adorned. A forty-year hiatus in the festival proceedings had offered little opportunity for devotees to transact with the god through the god-dancers, and consequently the god-dancers had very few vows to redeem. Despite the low density of the god-dancer's populace, a few vows did center attention upon the god-dancers, foregrounding the dancers' divinely delegated power, bolstering their centrality, and suggesting a future growth of fame and power.

One vow in particular stood out in this respect. During the festival, the oldest god-dancer at the temple received a heavy silver bangle, a *kaṭayam,* from an equally old Carpenter. Giver and receiver were both bent and wrinkled, but this bangle was a return on a powerful intervention that the god, via the god-dancer, had made when both men were young. Forty years previously, the Carpenter had been walking home along the road and passed by the Panaiyatiyan temple when the festival was under way. Unlike the taunting Thevar youth, the Carpenter had paused to offer a prayer, and as he did he vowed to the god-dancer that if only his wife would carry her current pregnancy to full term and bear a healthy child he would give the god-dancer a silver bangle in return. The couple was childless, and the wife had miscarried her first four pregnancies. This time she did carry the pregnancy to full term, and she did give birth to a child, a boy who was now, forty years later, a father himself. It was this very son's wife who told me the story. After that last koṭai and all the death and fear associated with it, Middle Ūr failed to hold a Panaiyatiyan temple festival until 1990. And so on the first day of the 1990 koṭai festival, the stooped and wrinkled Carpenter was finally able to fulfill his vow and present the bangle to the ancient god-dancer. This gift, inscribed with the donor's name, will endure beyond the lives of these men to be worn and displayed on the arms of the future descendants of the god-dancer as a sign of the god's continued delegation of his powers to the god-dancer's lineage. And over the years, perhaps, the density will increase.

After midnight the first night of the festival, I noticed the same god-dancer walking away from the temple, up the road toward the Big Ūr, with a few Thevars, including one of the grandnephews of the slain Thevar. I asked someone where he was going and was told that the god-dancer was going to dance in front of the Thevar shrine. The grandnephews of the slain Thevar were conducting a pūja of their own, funded from their own family funds, timing their activities at their granduncle's shrine to coincide with events at Middle Ūr's koṭai. The Thevar family hoped that one of them would become possessed by the granduncle (whose identity was conflated with that of the divine Panaiyatiyan) and would then give prophecy (kuṟi). It wasn't happening, so they had come to fetch the god-dancer, who was already channeling that power, to see if he could help. By making this request the Thevar family acknowledged their dependence on this man from Middle Ūr, another inversion of rank. Ariraman later emphasized the power inversion when he insisted that, of course, his community would never give—*koṭukka maṭṭōm*—that power away to the Thevars.

Though the scene around the god-dancers was not dense, the scene at the temple was very dense indeed. Middle Ūr built up fame or "bigness" for their community through largesse and dense display. The koṭai was visually and aurally packed. Energy was palpable, as many young men were for the first time seized in possession by the gods (Figure 1.5). One youth's parents kept him locked inside their house far from the temple for fear their boy would become possessed and possibly harmed. So much power to bear at such a tender age—not even a man (i.e., married) yet! The koṭai attracted the participation of many people, some from other villages. Middle Ūr spent collectively almost 20,000 rupees on the koṭai, money squeezed out of meager incomes, a sum Ariraman compared favorably to the 28,000 rupees raised by the more prosperous and numerous Big Ūr people for the goddess festival.[5] The 20,000 rupees raised by Middle Ūr went to purchase several things. They enlarged, renewed, and decorated the shrine elaborately; they rented a sound system to blare music across and beyond Yanaimangalam's fields to reach neighboring villages; and they hired an excellent and popular troupe of bow-song performers—they happened to be Thevar—who attracted an audience from all over the village as well as from other villages nearby (Figure 9.3).

Expanding

Through their koṭai activities, the small and excluded made themselves big and inclusive: they expanded themselves through spatial, verbal, and other gestures that produced bigness (perumai) for the temple association and its members, a perumai they could not easily produce without the koṭai. The activities discussed up to now are part of this expansion. Walk-

Figure 9.3. Bow-song performers play while god-dancers dance.

ing en masse through the village requires others to make way for their movement. Giving kuṟi, or oracular predictions and directions from the god, centers attention on the community and, with the spectacle of the koṭai itself, attracts onlookers and possible future vows which can convert into greater perumai in the future.

Middle Ūr further asserted their power through their use of space around the temple. In short, they expanded the space of their temple to cover the only road leading into and out of Yanaimangalam. In contrast to this temple's usual inconspicuous roadside existence as a set of small earthen mounds (each one a deity in Panaiyatiyan's retinue), the gods were large with bright painted faces and arms wielding weapons during the koṭai festival. They were, moreover, sheltered by an expansive pantal that the community had commissioned to cover not only the shrine but also the road in front of the shrine. This pantal transformed the road into a part of the temple's interior for the three central festival days. The pantal routed anyone traveling to or from the village right through the temple, effectively forcing all village residents and visitors, big and small, to pass through a space over which the S. C. had clear command and in which they were the indisputable power, the only legitimate agents of a fearsome god who demanded polite deference from all passersby, regardless of caste. Bicycle riders dismounted and walked their bicycles through the temple. Some passersby removed their shoes, as they would at any temple, before walking down the pantal-covered portion of the road. The pantal-makers had taken pains to make the roof of the pantal high enough to accommodate the bus that ran to the village five times a day (except on those days of unpredictable breakdown). The bus, along with other large vehicles, waited with relative patience for god-dancers to stop their heated dancing before honking on through the temple. In this way, the S. C. took command not only of space but also of time, as they required others to wait for them. Mutual waiting (and many S. C. often find themselves waiting—waiting for orders, waiting for the last shares from temple distributions, waiting for the remnants of wedding feasts, etc.) connotes, and in this case asserted, symmetry, sameness (camam), equality.

Earlier I wrote of the ancient god-dancer who accompanied some Thevar youths up to the shrine of that slain Thevar youth, their granduncle. The Thevar family had called on him to come to their own shrine and help them get possessed by their ancestor. This old god-dancer, a poor man I often saw waiting quietly for remnants on the peripheries of ūrmakkaḷ domestic and temple festivities, approached me at one point during the festival. He wanted to make certain that I noted in my notepad how he had made the Thevars wait for him. Eventually he did accompany them as they requested, but he took his own sweet time getting there. They waited.

While this first pantal took over the road, a second pantal converted an adjacent field (empty of crops at the time) of a high-ranking Pillaimar man into a rest area-cum-kitchen and café for those attending the koṭai. The Pillaimar man got wind of the fact that these "Pallars" were setting up shop on his field. He sent an irate message that they should pack up and move off. They ignored the message. Shortly after uttering his order, the Pillaimar man dropped dead. Ariraman insisted that the god Panaiyatiyan had killed him for trying to kick them off the land, suggesting that the theory of a heart attack put forward by the man's family mistook the result for the deeper cause.

A National Sign: Ambedkar

At all temple festivals in the region, sponsors crown their temples with the image of a protector and patron for the festival. Usually this protector is a popular deity, quite often the beneficent hero Murukan, son of Siva and Parvathi. But in this case, the S. C. (one of whom had dismissed Murukan as a *paṇakkāracāmi,* a "rich man's god") crowned their pantal with twin portraits of the Dalit leader named Ambedkar. Ambedkar (1892–1956) was a Columbia University–educated lawyer who was among the drafters of the Indian constitution in the 1940s. An advocate for the rights of Untouchables and an opponent of Gandhi's condescending policies concerning "Harijans," Ambedkar converted to Buddhism in 1956 and encouraged other Untouchables to do the same in order to promote a neo-Buddhist egalitarian ideology as an alternative to deleterious Hindu caste distinctions and exclusions.[6] Whether or not the S. C. of Yanaimangalam were ever encouraged to convert to Buddhism is unclear. But Ambedkar's portrait—widely available in affordable prints—hung in many S. C. houses in the village. As far as I know, this was the first time he had shown up for public display. Here, mounted on top of the pantal that covered the only road leading to and from the big village, were two portraits of Ambedkar. Like the Roman god Janus, the gatekeeper whose two faces look in opposite directions, here too Ambedkar's two faces looked in opposite directions: one faced in toward the big village, and the other faced away, down the road and out of the village. And like the Janus, here Ambedkar too may be said to symbolize change and transition "such as the progression of past to future, of one condition to another, of one vision to another, and of one universe to another" (en.wikipedia.org/wiki/Janus_ [mythology], accessed August 30, 2004).

The incorporation of Ambedkar into the temple festival was not merely symbolic. It was a powerful pragmatic use of a nationally recognized sign that indexed an explicitly egalitarian political ideology. Making flagrant processions, distributing ash to respectful big villagers, and making others wait for them—these also were creative and highly visible strategies of self-expansion through which the S. C. asserted alternative versions of an ūr where there was room for them to exist as powerful, self-asserting human beings. Yet these strategies were limited to the extent that they were created out of the very system of meaning—a language of caste differences (jāti vityācam) based on dominance and subordination, mariyātai distinctions, inclusions and exclusions—which the S. C. were seeking ultimately to move away from. They were, in other words, strategies that, like classic "rituals of rebellion," served to reproduce the very structures they were pushing against.

Bringing Ambedkar into the festival was something new. Here, one of their own, an S. C. (the term "Dalit" was not used in Yanaimangalam until very recently) who was a respected and bespectacled nationalist, a drafter of the nation's very constitution, sat Janus-faced atop their temple, dressed smartly in his signature "modern dress" of suit, tie, and horn-rimmed glasses, as if to announce both out to the world and into the village that the S. C. of Yanaimangalam identified their future in him. In phenomenological terms, the S. C. created a new horizon that shifted their self-making focus away from given forms of village ritual/politics and toward a future that belonged to them, specifically, *as* S. C. By giving Ambedkar the reigning position in the festival, they defined their space in part as a new kind of space for the constitution of alternative understandings of social and political relations in a village of their own making.

Ambedkar's position on the pantal also worked as a way for Middle Hamlet residents to force other village residents into a place ontologically imbued with the message of a social movement calling for equal rights regardless of caste. The bus, anyone on the bus, anyone riding their bike or walking to the next village (where one could find a makeshift cinema, lively coffee shops, and a road leading to larger towns)—all were routed under Ambedkar's gaze and brought into participation in S. C. ideology and purpose.

The use of Ambedkar connected them with a powerful national S. C. movement; it publicly defined the temple association's activities as nationally Dalit rather than locally Pallar and likewise defined the association's spatial frame of reference as not the limited Yanaimangalam, however defined, but as the nation itself. This particular national movement is perhaps the only one from which the big village people were themselves excluded *because of their jāti.* By defining themselves and their gods as agents of a national hero and a political movement, the Pallar reconstituted themselves as central actors in society and peripheralized those whose dominance is merely local.

KEEPING THE SMALL SMALL: CUTTING IN, DECENTERING, AND BELITTLING

If all of the actions described in this and the previous chapter indeed operate discursively—if, that is, they comment on and pose alternatives to dominant statements of social orderings such as that articulated at the goddess-temple festival—then we might expect some counterdiscourse or reaction from the point of view prevailing in that dominant discourse. Indeed, this seems to be the case. The reconfigurings effected by the activities at the Panaiyatiyan festival, and indeed at the Cutalaimatan temple too, are matters of concern to the ūrmakkaḷ, and at almost every turn in the three koṭai festivals described above, big people intervened. They attempted in both subtle and blatant ways to return the Dhobis and S. C. to their subordinate places, to peripheralize them, lower them, keep them small. In so doing, they reasserted their own dominance.

In the case of Middle Ūr's festival for Panaiyatiyan, the interventions were perhaps the most blatant and direct. During the course of this festival many big village men intervened disruptively in the temple proceedings. For example, they cut in the line of worshippers receiving ash at the temple. Several walked past rows of devotees in front of the god, moved straight to the front of the distribution rows, and took their own ash from the cup that was set next to the gods. They thus repeated exactly that act for which Middle Ūr as a whole was banned from the goddess temple only one month previously. While the latter act was treated as a theft and a blatant lack of mariyātai to the goddess as well as to previous social-spatial distinctions, this cutting into line had to be tolerated. Middle Ūr men here had to give way to their landlords and employers, and the mariyātai gained by receiving the ash ahead of others had to be allowed them.

In addition to snatching rank from the ash cup, several big village people competitively *decentered* Middle Ūr leaders by centering themselves but used subtler nonviolent procedures. They ostentatiously contributed large amounts of cash to the Panaiyatiyan temple, thus centering themselves as benefactors of the festival and of their kuṭimakkaḷ who put it on. In return for their large donations, these big men received special honors (a mariyātai called curuḷ) that placed them at the top of rankings established during festival distributions.

Other big village men *belittled* festival participants by ridiculing the participants. Big Ūr youths hung around on the edges of the festival area and belittled it with gazes and insults directed at koṭai participants, including those men and one woman who were dancing the god. While their fathers were perhaps playing into the validity of the event in order to garner mariyātai and centrality from it, their sons were denying the god's power by hurling insults and taking risks against the god's anger.

This ritual is politics. Nowhere is such a temple politics more clearly demonstrated than in the next example, where yet another set of Yanaimangalam's disenfranchised residents—Brahmans—brought Hindu nationalist rituals home to bear on their own self-making capacity in a village where Brahmans are reduced to whispers.

A BRICK TO AYODHYA

One morning in October 1989, I traveled on the early bus from Tirunelveli town to the village. I was surprised to see policemen leaning on their rifles at every crossroad and every bus station along the twenty-mile route and even more surprised to see two more policemen in Yanaimangalam! They were settled in chairs in front of the Krishna temple sipping coffee. I asked what the occasion was, and Parvathi answered, "We're sending a brick to Ayodhya."

Ayodhya is a pilgrimage town in North India. It is the mythical birthplace of the Hindu god Ram (an incarnation of Visnu) and is well known for both its mosques and its temples. Today it is better known for a communal dispute (here pitting "Hindus" against "Muslims") of national urgency. While the conflict at Ayodhya has been simmering for about 150 years, it was only in the 1980s that it became a pan-Indian issue. The dispute, in briefest outline, concerned a mosque built in 1528 under the auspices of the Mughal emperor Babur. In 1857, partly in response to another dispute at a nearby site—this one a Hindu temple that some Muslims claimed was built from the ruins of a mosque—some Hindu worshipers claimed the Babur mosque (Babri Masjid) to have been built from the ruins of a Hindu temple, perhaps on the very birthplace of the popular god Ram. Since that time, the site has been claimed by both Muslims and Hindus, with various compromises, conflicts, and closures occurring throughout this century.[7]

In 1984, a political-religious organization called the Vishwa Hindu Parishad (VHP)—an organization closely allied to a political party, then minor but now prominent, called the Bharata Janata Party (BJP)—launched a national campaign calling for the "liberation" of Ram from his "prison" inside the mosque (van der Veer 1987). The conflict surrounding the mosque was real, but it was also symbolic of the national goals of the BJP and its allies to garner support for their Hindu nationalist platform, one that constructed Muslims as enemies of the Indian nation from time immemorial and retrojected a pure Hindu kingdom which would return one day soon. One prominent goal of the VHP and BJP at the time was to oust the ruling, secular Congress Party government. Because the Congress Party publicly objected to the destruction of the mosque, they were denounced by some as Muslim sympathizers or at best as "pseudo-secularists" (Kakar 1995, 16). The VHP created national awareness of their version of the site's history, and thus Ram's plight, through several nationally ritualized and televised events, including a motorized pilgrimage to Ayodhya.

The conflict continued to intensify over the next several years, and then in 1989 the VHP organized a new kind of ritual pilgrimage to Ram in Ayodhya, one that they claimed would eventually end in the mosque's destruction (the destruction occurred only later, in December 1992). This was to be a pilgrimage by proxy. Instead of pilgrims journeying to Ayodhya, devotees from all parts of India and even the globe were encouraged to consecrate and then send bricks to Ayodhya. These bricks were intended to be used in constructing a grand temple at Ayodhya on the site of the mosque. Here was a unifying ritual that could occur in multiple sites simultaneously all over the world. It was in this context that residents of Yanaimangalam sent a brick to Ayodhya.

In 1989, the Brahman schoolmaster started things off with a small ritual in his house while others waited outside. Then, a small group of Brahmans together with several other higher-jāti residents—some of whom were relatively middle class, with white-collar jobs they commuted to in town—took a red brick in a short procession to the edge of the village. The brick was stamped in Tamil with the name of the village on one side and the name of the god Ram on the other. Along with the brick, they carried other offerings, including dozens of sheets of paper on which girls and women had written Ram's name an auspicious 1,008 times each. As the group walked through the village, they chanted, "Ram! Ram!" and the schoolmaster rang tiny cymbals. They stopped at the edge of the big ūr, where the road enters the fields, and handed the brick and other offerings over to the young priest Subramaniyam, at the time a teenager. He mounted his bicycle and, flanked by the two policemen, rode to the next village about two miles away. From there, the worshipers imagined, their brick would join other regional bricks on a train to Tirunelveli Junction, from there journey to Madras to join other Tamil bricks and then to Ayodhya via Delhi, where it would find its niche in the grand new temple—built from multilingual and even transnational bricks sent by Hindu supporters now residing overseas—a full-color photo mock-up of which had been published in the Sunday edition of local newspapers. They watched the young priest and the policemen and the brick disappear down the road, turned, and went home.

This brick pūja could be given a simple critical reading: Hindu nationalist ideology had brought Yanaimangalam into its network, turning an act of faith irrevocably into an act of ideology, as Nandy (1992, 70) has described such acts. Indeed, the state's presence in the form of coffee-sipping police spurred ideological "communalist" interpretations, such as that demonstrated by my Brahman neighbor Parvathi when I asked her why the police were necessary. She answered, "To protect the brick." "From whom?" I asked. "Muslims," she said. I asked, "Which Muslims?" then I pressed, "The Muslims in the next village wouldn't do anything!" "Muslims *from the North*!" she insisted. This was the first time I had heard any anti-Muslim sentiment in Yanaimangalam, but, sadly, not the last. When I returned in 2003, several village residents openly supported the BJP and participated in local political meetings. The Muslims in the next village were no longer spoken of in benign terms but were described as potential "terrorists" (*tīviravāti*), members of a group named al-Ummā. And in support of this view, I heard several times the story of a young BJP member who had been murdered the previous year at the hands of Muslims. It seems that the brick pūja had wrapped this small group of worshipers into someone else's nationalist script, one that they then brought home as their own.

One could stop the analysis there. But the brick ritual takes on meanings both more complex and more local if also read in the context of Brahman alienation from power and say in village affairs. For many of Yanaimangalam's Brahmans, sending the brick was less a cynical act driven by nationalist sentiment than it was an exertion to redefine and expand this community's sense of belonging in the world by also finding new ways to define their place in the village.

Several Brahman residents, some of whom were old, alone, and living in the corners of their ancestral homes, waxed nostalgic about the old days when, as they told it, the village operated as a self-sufficient unit,[20] when their street—their fully Brahman Agraharam—was filled with Brahman activity and teeming with Brahman youth eager to stage gratifying yearly performances of the epic Mahabharata, a popular story of dharma, when lower castes showed deference (mariyātai) by not entering their houses at all, and when "Untouchables" would not even enter the street but would, when required, call out from the bylanes running between houses or from the backyards abutting the fields. Some Brahmans told me of how they used to own most of the village land. They spoke of how they had been the leaders of the village, how their kinsmen were civil servants who ran the whole district, how the biggest festivals of the year were in the grand Siva temple, now sitting in disrepair at the end of the Brahman street where the large, intricately carved teak temple chariot leans on its broken axle, enduring both monsoon and drought. As far as the Brahmans were concerned, the village was degenerating. Its breakdown, one old man insisted, had started with the end of colonialism and with Gandhian movements that came to the village bringing in "Harijans" who marched for recognition up the heart of the Agraharam. The "breakdown" had continued with the more-recent influx of Thevars.

We have seen how Thevars spatially dominated the S. C. by excluding them from the goddess temple, effectively pushing them to the subordinate periphery of Thevar dominance. The Thevars' displacement of the Brahmans was more intimate, less an exclusion than an encroachment. Brahmans had been slowly moving from rural Tirunelveli District to towns and cities since the early part of the century. First lured to urban areas by more lucrative economic and political opportunities for a literate, educated elite under colonialism, Brahman migration only hastened under postcolonial land reforms that eroded the rights of noncultivating landowners with large holdings (e.g., Brahmans) in favor of the rights of cultivating tenants. Their migration opened up prime riverine agricultural areas for non-Brahman control and thus, as the Brahmans left, other peasant castes—Thevars prominent among them—moved in and bought up their land as well as their vacated houses. The Agraharam—the heart of the Brahman community—was slowly becoming the interior place of Thevar life too. At night, many Thevars slept out on the breezy street and sometimes on the outer verandas of their Brahman neighbors' houses. Some Brahmans (but by no means all) resented Thevar visits to their homes, and they whispered complaints about how Thevar neighbors barged right into their houses as if they were the ones who lived there, regardless of any sense of mariyātai! The Thevars explained their visits as neighborly gestures: it would be a lack of mariyātai not to come and visit on certain occasions. Rumors of improper sexual liaisons between Thevar men and Brahman women were encouraged by the fact that the Thevar headman had openly shacked up with a Brahman widow who lived near the Krishna temple on the west end of the street.

In this context, the brick pūja provided a way for Brahmans to circumvent what they saw as their inappropriate displacement from the heart of the village, and it had several outcomes. First, the pūja connected Yanaimangalam to a different political center, an important, newsworthy, and policeworthy center that the Brahmans found to be rhetorically akin to their own aims and goals, for this nationalist "Hindutva" movement is particularly associated with a high-caste, literary, Sanskritized, and universalizing Hinduism with which village Brahmans and other high-caste residents identified. Because Brahmans were the organizers of the pūja, they in particular were linked to this important political future centered in Ayodhya, thus bolstering their sense of belonging to the nation and of taking charge of their own political futures.

Second, the pūja and all the rhetoric associated with it held out the promise of a return to their own retrojected version of village history, as influenced as these memories seem to have been by what Inden (1990, 131–143) and Fuller (1989) have shown to be Orientalist and anthropological myths about glorious "traditional" self-sufficient village communities and their historical decline in "modern" times. Were the nation to be reconstituted and Hindu hegemony "regained," perhaps they too would recapture something of this desired past they constructed when they sat down on their verandas to speak to me of better times.

Third, the brick pūja was a way for them to regain some centrality in the village and region. They brought home a national movement that had the capacity (as the 1998 national electoral victory of the BJP attests) to subsume the entire nation—including local Thevars—under its governance. They could now define themselves as the local link to a Hindu national and transnational network. The brick—made from local soil in a nearby kiln, stamped in Tamil with the name of the village, and accompanied by handwritten devotions of women and girls—would, they imagined, become a material part, literally one brick among many, of a future temple in a future nation's capital of Ayodhya. That temple would be a tangible sign of a nation, a sign constructed of myriad acts of devotion, of myriad metonyms of places and language groups. The brick, then, was to be Yanaimangalam's Brahman-mediated link—its existent tether—to that would-be center. Brahmans in Yanaimangalam mediated this spatial relation to the nation and hence regained some sense of centrality in the world and, at least on that day, in the village too.

Village residents draw on a discourse of dominance as they also draw on regional and national movements, ideas, and signs to contest the social and spatial contours of their local lives and their village. Through both inversionary tactics within the discourse of dominance and through national signs—the rule of Ram, the idea of social equality, "self-respect," the leadership of Ambedkar—they at once refigured their imagined future place in the nation and asserted their present belonging in the village in different and sometimes new ways. In particular, it was by bringing regional and national signs and ideas home to bear on the practical reality of the village that villagers took hold of meanings and moved them from the realm of the "imagined" future (what we wish to become) to the realm of the pragmatically real present, where they became material for historical transformations that local actors made and continue to make for themselves.

Such imagined futures are an integral part of present makings of self and community. As we have seen, these futures are at the same time retrojected into the past as "histories," such that what will be is in line with what was. As May summarizes a phenomenological understanding of time, "What an individual seeks to *become* determines what he remembers of his *has been.* In this sense the future determines the past" (May 1993/1958, 69). Existentialist and phenomenological conceptualizations of time privilege the future (May 1993/1958, 68–69; Daniel 1996, 122–127), arguing that as humans move toward their intentional futures, they bring the present and the past into line with those futures, constructing coherent narratives (Carr 1986, 18–44) and experiences (Desjarlais 1996). Indeed, both the Dalits of Middle Ūr and the middle-class and upper-caste residents, including Brahmans, constructed their imagined futures as recoveries of lost pasts. The S. C. defined their struggle as a fight to regain lost rights in a village where they were the "Original Dravidians," the ones with truly inalienable rights to the goddess. They desired some kind of justice for past wrongs, which would come into being in an egalitarian world, a place where we would see, as one S. C. man put it, "everyone eating together without jāti differences." For Brahmans, the struggle to crown Ram king of the nation was defined in terms of a return to a more coherent moral order (dharma), a reversal of the inevitable dharmic deterioration of which the texts speak. The Brahmans were the previous owners and centers of a dharmic (a coherent moral) order to which they wished to return: the ideal self-sufficient village where each caste had a duty, where each need had a caste to fulfill it, and where those eager youths performed yearly the Mahabharata, a tale of dharma.

Kakar (1995, 148–9) writes that it is, in part, a sense of loss that propels people, individually or in groups, to identify with larger cultural and revivalist movements such as Hindu nationalism. And indeed, the Hindu nationalist movement promotes itself through exactly such a rhetoric, calling for Hindus to regain a glorious past now lost because of the invasion of others—"Muslims" (and the liberal "secularists" that nationalists construct as Muslim accomplices) in the case of Ayodhya. For southern Tamilnadu's Dalits, the invaders are most immediately the Thevars but are ultimately all the "caste Hindus" who came to usurp the rights of Original Dravidians. Such rhetoric holds out hope for a paradoxically conceived future return to a lost past, even though the content of that past is retrojectively shaped in accordance with nostalgia- or myth-driven hopes for the future. There never was an original Hindu nation, and there never was a pure Original Dravidian past—indeed, the very terms of this past, "Hindu" and "Dravidian," are constructs from the much more recent colonial period.

TEN

Conclusion

> Without places, regions would be vacuous and thus all too easily collapse into each other—ultimately into abstract space. As it is the essence of a place to be regional, so it is equally essential to a region to be anchored in particular places.
>
> —Edward Casey

A village is a place that is always open to the world (not bounded, closed, inward-looking). A village, through its inhabitants, reaches out into the world of which it is always-already a part and thereby constitutes itself over and again. Charles Peirce once said of the person: "he is not 'shut up in a box of flesh and blood'" (Peirce, cited in Colapietro 1989, 39). Colapietro explains that for Peirce, "the body is not principally something in which the self is located: rather it is [a] medium through which the self expresses" (ibid.). We can say the same of the relation between person and place: place is not a dead or limited container—a box of earth and stone—in which we are shut up or to which we are stuck like pins in a map. Like our bodies, our being-in-places is an inseparable part of our outreaching selves, our expressions, our perceptions, our makings. Our places, as much as our bodies, are a part of our engagement with the world at large. They are both literally and figuratively "where we're comin' from." Yanaimangalam is such a place. It is a place open to and formed in part through its inhabitants' engagement with one another, with their pasts and futures, as with the wider world. As village residents make and remake the village through their own outreaching actions, their makings are always already informed by the places they inhabit, places formed by previous lives.

This ethnography has been constructed against the background of my interest in existential anthropology, a perspective on life and the world most directly framed in the work of Michael Jackson but also consistent with a wide range of phenomenological, philosophical, psychological, and semeiotic perspectives on what it means to be human and on how human action works to make and remake the world. In Chapter 1, I stated that I see culture as what Daniel calls a "co-production" of the ethnographer and her informants or, perhaps better stated, her guides and interlocutors. By way of conclusion, I would like to offer a brief account of one such cultural co-production. It concerns Tamil concepts of action that I learned about through my conversations in Yanaimangalam, concepts which inform as they are also informed by my understanding of existential anthropology.

BEING-IN-YANAIMANGALAM

For existential anthropology, the relation of self and other and world is always co-productive. That is, the self is, again, not shut up in a box called the body, much less the mind. Rather, the self is created socially, between people who live in particular places that are themselves the product of previous lives, previous social activity. While the self is so created, so, at the same time, are others. So also are structures and ideologies and relations of power. Various writers have conceptualized this process in different terms. Michael Jackson (1998) speaks of the "intersubjectivity" of emergent lives. George Herbert Mead also spoke of the self as product and not the source of social interaction. Rollo May discussed the dynamism that binds what he sees as three aspects of our existence: our Eigenwelt (our own world, the self), our Mitwelt (the social world of our face-to-face relations with others), and our Umwelt (the environment most broadly conceived, what might also be called the given world, the contingencies that enter as if by chance into our capacities, which can include our place, our biology, our "caste" as an accident of birth, and our given social structures built up by the activity of previous lives). Peirce, for whom the human being too is a sign, wrote of semeiosis, the growth of signs through action, as a meaningful and active engagement with others in the world of signs. The point for all of these writers is that relations among self, other, and given world are all aspects of human action and are all co-productive of one another. This is a pragmatic approach to the world, one that eschews the distinction between "truth" and "appearance" and recognizes instead the real productivity of action-in-the-world or being-in-the-world. Action is what action does. This understanding of action, and of human "becoming," as May puts it, is consistent with what I understand of Tamil concepts of human action. That is, for Tamils, one's actions produce all at once self, other, and world, a world that is (precisely because of action) always changing (and not necessarily for the better).

Tamils live in an active and changeable material universe. In such a universe, it takes work for a person to change or remain stable in desired ways. As actors, Tamils have some control over their lives. They can make themselves and alter the world around them, just as the world and its actions may alter them (gods may attack, state policy may mandate certain actions, colonizers may change land-tenure arrangements or criminalize your entire caste). Regular actions—from daily sweepings and god-worshiping to sin-disposals and yearly processions—are required to keep oneself stable (dharmic) and capable of further life-making processes. Women sweep their houses and thresholds clear of dirt and debris once in the morning and then again in the late afternoon, after the life of day has brought in more disorder from outside. This housecleaning is not at all unlike the disposal actions described in Chapter 3, where those who are incapacitated by their own or ancestral actions may remove hindrances, their bad karma—whether through tiruṣṭi, evil, or fault—from their bodies through sweeping circular motions followed by disposals to outside places (the street, a field, a temple far from home) or persons, kuṭimakkaḷ or Brahmans, who take on the negatives, accepting them (not always willingly) into their own bodies and places, at least temporarily. Nor is housecleaning unlike the processions, described in Chapter 2, that ūrmakkaḷ make around the ūr during goddess koṭais. These actions also make and protect orderly interiors by sending negatives outside through sacrifices performed on boundaries and crossroads and through social exclusions that keep the lower and disordered bodies out of the temple, as out of the ūr. Whether they consist of the dirt of the day, an evil deed done by an ancestor, or any one of the plethora of faults (evils, tiruṣṭis, malign possessions by jealous gods) that may disorder a person or family or ūr, in all cases the negative materials are removed and disposed of from an inside (uḷḷē) and sent to or thrown away to an outside (veḷiyē). Once they pass on (kaḻi) to the outside, they may scatter or simply abide in other bodies in other places. Tamils in Yanaimangalam clear themselves for future action through such spatiotemporal disposal processes that keep them "coherent" or "dharmic" and capable then of further positive transformative actions that ensure well-being through further growth and productivity.

Self-making processes such as these disposals are always at the same time other-making processes. By making oneself stable and coherent, one makes another less stable and different (capable of handling evils you cannot, for example). Self-makings also create spatiotemporal distinctions. By sending things outside, actors create spatial distinctions between inside and outside, between ūr and kāṭu, for example. These spatial distinctions are at the same time temporal ones, for one's past, contained in material form as evils or faults or unwanted gods, comes to inhabit the outside, the kāṭu, where it remains, outside but like memory really still present, emplaced on the landscape. The kāṭu is such a dangerous place to go. Ghosts do linger there.

Some self-makings are also village-makings. As people relate to gods through temple associations, for example, they both promote and participate in the making of varied social and spatial orderings among residents of the village and so participate in making the multiple, overlapping, and contested communities that in fact compose the ūr.

In other words, like the existential and semeiotic concepts noted above, here too actions are understood to operate simultaneously in at least three modes or aspects: self, other, and social-spatial world. Culture itself is produced as human actions reproduce as well as amend the values and concepts and feelings through which people understand and operate in the given (and always given again) world.

SELF-MAKING IS OTHER-MAKING

Centers require peripheries. Insides presuppose and create outsides. Bigness invokes smallness. Ups depend on downs. Making oneself big and central requires making someone else peripheral and small. Making oneself high, say in a ranked line of mariyātai, requires making someone else low in that same ranking. Making oneself ordered and coherent requires another to be disordered and incoherent. In this way, self-makings are other-makings. These makings, it is important to note, are not singular, structurally reflective processes. As I have argued in this book, these makings are contested, reversed, and potentially changed. Each contest, reversal, and denial of one social prerogative sets up alternative makings of self and other, and the multi-accentual process continues heterologically. Social structure, that is to say, is not lurking "behind" our actions like an invisible hand. Structure is itself constantly under revision because it is made in action by humans interacting with one another in complex ways.

Take the Thevars' place in the social life of the village, for example. Although most of their own ancestors were likely farmers, still Yanaimangalam's Thevars link their present lives to historical actions that their ancestral caste-mates conducted as fighters and kings who protected a social realm even as they dominated it. These ancestral pasts, distorted through the cultural lens of British colonialism, set both past and present Thevars up for an "othering" as fearsome criminals. The entire colonial enterprise, a contingency thrown like a wrench into regional polities, fed into processes that have now culminated in the ethnicization of caste, including a transregional self-identification among Thevars that allow them to act as a political constituency and to compete for (and, as conceived by some, regain) power not just locally but in the state as well. So, while Thevars have made their lives and have had their lives made through social activities in a complex field of structure and politics, their lives as lived within that field have also contributed to the formation of new structures and new modes of political engagement, new perceptions of the past, new concepts of self, and new concepts of other.

Take, also, the fierce god rituals. The alternative assertions of power and ideology that temple associations make with the help of their gods make it clear that ritual is not "merely religion" and religion is not "merely expressive of" social structures. Temple rituals are complex sets of actions that pragmatically—that is to say, really—constitute social orders, as other South Asianists have shown (e.g., Tambiah 1985; Appadurai and Breckenridge 1976). Temple rituals are, moreover, metapragmatic actions. That is, through their rituals, residents of Yanaimangalam make relations and social configurations that are themselves statements about how life should be, statements about life's coherence, statements about the future that would be. The alternative orderings posited in fierce-god temples are thus in some ways political directives about how to understand everyday relations, about what to hope for in social life. And because residents of Yanaimangalam consider these rituals to be essential for their own growth and well-being, participation in these directives, in this politics, is inevitable for most. Ritual is dangerous, it is political, and for residents of Yanaimangalam it is a critical aspect of their struggle for dignity in this world.

SELF-AND OTHER-MAKING IS PLACE-MAKING

The outside (whether it be outside the house or outside the ūr) is a place of incoherence for Tamils. What makes that so is precisely the kinds of disposals discussed above. The chaotic aspects of self are sent out to the kāṭu, and the beings who inhabit the kāṭu (low castes, fierce gods, ghosts, wild animals, weeds, thorns, strangers) partake of the nature of that place, just as those who inhabit the interior are thought to be relatively orderly and stable by paḻakkam—that is, by the habit of their lives in those places.

The outside is in fact suffused with the quality of changeability and instability. As such, it makes sense that the outside fierce gods would be understood as agents for change, as unpredictable contingencies.

Fierce gods, like other outside forces that become emplaced in the village, are apt examples of the "thrown" world, the contingencies of the Umwelt (environment) over which actors appear to have no immediate control. As discussed in Chapter 6, fierce gods are emplaced in the village through events that result often, but not always, from villagers' actions, often accidental actions. Fierce gods may follow villagers home from other places, they may burst from the earth where a murder occurred, they may demand a shrine from a person who has benefited from a chance event—a banana shoot arriving from upriver—but who has failed to fulfill a vow. They may also just appear suddenly for reasons unknown. Fierce gods are not so different from—indeed, they are logically similar to and may be considered metaphors of—other powerful historical realities (the state, colonialism, Untouchable politics in the wake of nationalism, precolonial idioms of kingship) that emplace themselves in the village and become part of local life in powerful ways. Fierce gods force themselves into the daily life of villagers. Fierce gods come into the village from outside, either from other places or from the kāṭu itself, the chaotic and unpredictable site of disordering relations and beings. Fierce gods appear at first as uncontrollable forces that inhabit one's world and make demands that upset the previous balance of one's life. Once emplaced in the village they become irreversibly part of one's self-, other-, and world-making potential. Fierce gods, like other outside powers, ideas, and structures, are powerful agencies in villagers' lives. Unlike ancestral evils and faults that persons may dispose of, send "out" of themselves, these fierce powers stick around. They stay, they grab, they possess, they demand action.

RITUAL IS DANGEROUS

I visited Yanaimangalam for three months in the summer of 2003. I planned to arrive in time to attend another festival for Middle Ūr's Panaiyatiyan. I wanted to know how and if, in the thirteen years since I attended the festival described in Chapter 9, the festival had changed. Would it still command attention and assert alternative futures of justice and hope? But the festival did not take place that summer. When I asked why, some said it was due to lack of funds. Others said it was because of the trouble surrounding a recent murder and the fear that holding a festival would lead to violence between the Pallars and Thevars of Yanaimangalam.

Aruna filled me in on the murder, and this is what she told me. Two young men from Yanaimangalam, one Thevar and one Pallar, both attended the same college in a town about one hour away by bus. Both young men commuted daily to school. At college, their common origin in Yanaimangalam did not form the basis for any friendship. Reportedly, each hung with his own crowd: the Pallar youth with other S. C. students and the Thevar youth with other Thevar students. One day, some months prior to my visit to the village, the Thevar youth with some friends approached a table in the college canteen where the S. C. youth and some of his friends were eating lunch. The Thevar group loudly complained within hearing of the whole room that these Pallars should not be allowed to use the same plates and cups as the rest of the college, and wouldn't the canteen manager please provide them their own utensils too. This deflating insult collapses what for S. C. are years of work to overcome prejudice and hearkens back to the most painful signs of caste injustice, the "Untouchability" that disallowed S. C. to eat food or drink water from the same plate or cup as a higher-caste person or even touch something that a higher-caste person would subsequently touch. A fight broke out. At some point during the altercation a death threat was issued. The Thevar youth, Aruna reported, threatened to kill the S. C. youth. The murder, as it turns out, turned the tables on the threat, for it was the Thevar youth who was murdered allegedly by the S. C. youth and some of his running mates from Middle Ūr. The murder took place at night, out in the kāṭu, behind the shrine of an S. C.–controlled fierce god.

It was in the aftermath of this murder that my husband snapped several photographs of some Middle Ūr youth, including the one where they posed under their party flag. In several other photos, the young men posed in the hamlet and out in the surrounding fields. In all the photographs, one or more of them wield their machetes, sometimes at their sides and sometimes held high above their heads in a pose more prototypical of Thevar imagery or of the fierce gods themselves who, as guardians, resemble none so much as the guardian Thevars. Rick was about to present them with copies of the photographs to keep when Aruna, seeing the images, advised him not to give them out or even show them around to anyone else. Such evidence of what she described as the Pallar youths' arrogance (*timir*)—but was it not also defiance?—would, she was sure, only lead to further bloodshed. The temple festival I had come to see was cancelled because of high tensions in the village resulting from the murder. Middle Ūr's leaders feared the violence that could result.

Daniel writes that a "discordance" between two modes of being-in-the-world is a precondition for violence (1996, 50–51), and indeed such a discordance may be said to be operating between S. C. and Thevar modes of existence. Consider: while the S. C. are struggling for an egalitarian future where they are free to move through any village spaces, the Thevars in Yanaimangalam are also struggling for a future of domination, an aim that depends in part on the subordination of the S. C. These two modes of existence, of intersubjective becoming, are discordant not just because they are different but because they are incommensurable: each requires the recognition of the other to fulfill their own project. But for either group to recognize the other's future means giving up their own future: trading dominance for equality or equality for subordination. When two parties are engaged in struggles for such discordant futures, schismogenetic escalations of violence between the two parties may occur (cf. Bateson 1972, 61–72). And indeed both at the time of this research and in the intervening twelve years, violence between Thevar and S. C. communities has in fact escalated (Amnesty International 1997; Ananth 1998; Manikkam 1997; Rangaraj 1998). Often the violence has grown from attacks on statues and portraits of the leaders who embody each community's desires for the future—Ambedkar for the S. C. and Muthuramalinga Thevar for the Thevars —as the following report by D. Sivarajan illustrates:

> The first bout of the present clashes was triggered off on April 24 with the desecration of the statue of Muthuramalinga Thevar at Kandamanur. In retaliation, Thevars set fire to the huts of [S. C.] Dalits. The [S. C.] Dalits set fire to a few Thevar houses, unleashing a chain of attacks. (Sivarajan 1997)

Thevar/Pallar conflict is not the only conflict that has escalated in the years since my first research from 1988 to 1990. The Hindu nationalist movement that led some village residents to send a single brick to Ayodhya has redefined local social relations in potentially violent ways, and stories of murder circulate in this sphere, too.

So, what about that brick? The Ayodhya temple still is not built, but the political will behind it is as strong as ever. The violence associated with Hindu nationalism has been widely reported in the international media —hundreds dead here, a thousand there—though unlike the Pallar/Thevar conflict, violence in the cause of Hindu nationalism has until recently been quite rare in the "Dravidian"-dominated Tamilnadu, which still constructs itself as independent of North Indian Brahmanical hegemony. Yet here too local violence is escalating. Local Muslims from Pattamadai two miles away have become increasingly subject to a new fixed identity, propagated not only by Hindu nationalists but also by global media beamed into many village houses by satellite. Muslims in Pattamadai, if you recall Aruna's whispered warning to me one day in 2003, are now categorically vilified as "terrorists." In 2002, one local member of the BJP was murdered by a Muslim gang in Pattamadai, she told me.

Neither the brick, the imagined Hindu nation, nor the success—now quelled by the 2004 Congress Party victory in national elections—has translated into political power for Yanaimangalam's Brahmans. Brahmans here still only whisper any criticisms they have about village affairs. Their population continues to fall. Their houses continue to be occupied by other jātis who gained from postcolonial land reform measures. So while the pūja created a local tie to a growing national political movement and has held out some hope to the community, it expressed at the same time further alienation. It expressed Brahman alienation from the village as a valued place of belonging. It also expressed an alienation of the Agraharam from the state as well as the nation, for the brick ritual succeeded only in making the Agraharam small, one small and almost anonymous node in a national network, a place linked by a simple brick to a large hope embodied in a future temple they would likely never see. The only signs of change for Brahmans' local lives is the surface renovation of the Visnu and Siva temples by a rich donor from Chennai. These renovations are something local Brahmans are proud of, but they do not enhance their voice in village life. Those temples are still largely treated as antiquities by most village residents. And the chickens and goats still scratch and multiply in the dirt outside Parvathi's door.

The power of place is a power of persons to extend themselves (our selves), a power to express ourselves and our memories, a place from which to move out into the world, to move through space and to assert temporal extensions. Pasts and futures extend back and forward from place, they extend from a here and now forward toward a projected future (Hindu nations and caste equalities) and they extend back to a retrojected past (the Brahman's self-sufficiency, the Thevars' kingship, the S. C.'s primacy). There are as many extensions, as many spaces and times, as there are actors in place (see May 1994, 59). The more divergent the futures of different sets of village inhabitants (caste "equality" for the S. C., domination in the manner of little kings for the Thevars and national belonging for the Brahmans), the more divergent their versions of the past and the more contestable and changeable their present. This is the village.

The village conveys regional and national disputes. It is in places, whether they be bus stands, statues, temples, streets, city neighborhoods, or villages, that these "national" movements take place. This book has attempted to show that whether or not villagers are conscious of historical precedent, the ins and outs of nationalism, the colonial construction of Thevar criminality, the radical alteration in land tenure, and so forth, the truth is that they are self-aware actors who work to make lives that matter. They struggle for a world in which one's life has meaning, whether through change or stability.

Aruna was both right and wrong when she lamented from the rooftop that nothing in this village ever changes. Things have changed. The village is not as it once was. Violence itself is an expression of the struggle that comes with change, in this case the expression of the difficulty that S. C. and Thevars, Muslims and BJP members experience as they exert themselves to alter or maintain their prospects in the world. But she is also right, for the struggle of the powerless and disfranchised against oppressive forces that inhibit their freedom, however they perceive freedom, probably has not changed. And this may be what she meant.

I end with a question, borrowed from Michael Jackson (1998, 54). It is a question worth posing here, in the context of violent conflict between two modes of being-in-the-world, and it is a question worth posing to all of us who, through our actions, inevitably make others as we work to make ourselves. "How [will] the claims of any individual . . . be adjusted to the claims that others make on him or that he makes on himself on their behalf, such that everyone finds validation and dignity in the many?"

GLOSSARY

abhisekam: ablutions in which priests pour various fluid substances such as water, honey, and milk over a deity's image.

acuttam: unclean, impure.

akam: interior; also a genre of Tamil Sangam poetry.

aṉpaḷippu: "gift of affection"; a descriptive term dominant landowners sometimes use to describe the prestations that they offer their kuṭimakkaḷ.

anyāyam: injustice.

ārati: A practice in which substances are waved around in a circle in front of a deity or ritual subject. Often the substance waved in front of a ritual subject is intended to remove and transfer unwanted negatives from the person. In temple worship, ārati usually consists of the priest waving a camphor flame in front of the deity, making possible the mode of visual worship called darśan.

aruḷvākku: "voice of grace"; the oracular prophecies uttered by the men and women who become possessed by deities.

aṭimai: slavery; in this context, the term refers to the devotees of a goddess as those enslaved to her.

camam: equivalent, equal to.

camattuvam: egalitarianism or equality as a social fact or ideological principle.

cāmiyāṭi: "god-dancer"; men, and less often women, who hold a hereditary right to become possessed by, or "joined with," a particular deity.

cāmiyāṭṭam: "god-dance"; the possession of a man or women by a deity. It is described as a dance because the possession involves much bodily movement. These movements may be agitated but usually resolve into a rhythmic dance to drums and musical instruments.

cāpattīṭu: the deleterious affects a curse has on a person.

ceri: to digest; in this case, the term is used to describe the digestion of a person's "evils" once they are consumed in the form of food by an appropriate recipient.

cērkkai: a joining, combination, or association; in this context, a word used by god-dancers to express their relation to the gods who possess them.

cīr: auspiciousness, orderliness; a type of gift or prestation given on the auspicious occasions of weddings and puberty rituals; a kind of dowry.

contam: one's own people; relatives in the broadest sense of the term.

curuḷ: a small token gift usually consisting of rolled betel leaf and areca nut. This gift often accompanies wedding invitations and is given out to guests at weddings and puberty rituals.

cutantiram: a polyvalent term meaning in some contexts independence, freedom, and right; here most often used to refer to prestations given by landowners to *kuṭimakkaḷ* who have the "right" to receive these prestations in return for services.

cuttam: cleanliness, purity.

dān: Hindi term for *tāṉam.*

darśan: visual contact with a deity or other auspicious being, person, or place. Vision is thought to transfer positive qualities between seer and seen.

iṣṭatēvaṅkaḷ: favorite or desired deities, the deities that people favor and feel a personal connection to regardless of any obligation or association.

jajmān: literally "sacrificer"; the term most often refers to the landowning patrons in Indian villages who are responsible for upholding the order or dharma of the place through right conduct.

jāti: often translated as "caste," the term more exactly means type or genus. Humans, animals, plants, indeed all things in the universe are classified into ranked types that vary according to their proportional constituent qualities.

kaḻi: to pass or pass on; this term can be used in the context of time (passing the time), finances (currency passes the bank or passes in the market), or bodily wastes (to pass urine). Here the term is used in the context of evils and other biological-moral negative substances that can pass out of the body like other wastes.

kaṭṭāyam: required, obligatory, compulsory; certainly.

kāṭu: wilderness or uncivilized place; here the areas of the village which lie outside the boundaries of the ūr. These are the places thought to be disorderly and unpredictable and inhabited and frequented by fierce gods and lower castes.

kāval: guard or watch duty.

kīḻ: low, in reference to objects in space as well as to rankings of living beings including castes. The term also means "east," which, in Tamilnadu, is the lower-elevation part of the state.

koṭai: literally "gift"; in Tirunelveli District, the name for the temple festivals that take place in the summer months.

kōṭṭai: a measure of grain approximately 70 kilograms, an amount that fills two large burlap bags.

kōyil: temple.

kulatēvam (pl. kulatēvaṅkaḷ): the particular deity or deities associated with one's lineage, often over generations. Particular rituals are due to these gods, often on a yearly basis and/or on special occasions such as weddings.

kuli: cash wage.

kuṇam: quality; colloquially used to describe people as having a good or bad moral/personal quality, but the term also has relevance in textual explications of the qualities that make up the universe and that differentiate one jāti from another.

kuṭimai: personal attachment (as of a person to a house or family or landlord) and dependent subordination (as in servitude, tenancy, subject). Many ūrmakkaḷ use this term to describe the subordination of their laborers and tenants.

kuṭimakkaḷ: the people in the village who are involved in the service end of kuṭimai relations.

māṉam: honor or dignity.

mariyātai: social distinction (often translated as honor). Higher-ranking persons are accorded more mariyātai than lower-ranking persons.

māṭaṉ: fierce god.

mēlam: a kind of drum played during rituals such as weddings and temple festivals. During the latter these drums accompany the god-dancers during possession and play to celebrate the deities as they undergo abhisekams.

metuvāka (adj. metuvāṉa): softly, quietly, gently.

mōcam: bad, ugly, unpleasant. This term can refer to places, persons, moralities.

muṟai: right and proper life-sustaining order, moral rules, dharma.

ocanta: high ranking.

oḻuṅku: orderliness, discipline, moral conduct; see also muṟai.

paḻakkam: habit, practice.

palaṉ: result, outcome, fruit (as of a ritual or vow).

paṅku: share or portion; here, rightful shares in the leftover substances from temple rituals.

paṇṇaiyāḷ: bonded laborer.

pantal: a temporary awning-type structure fashioned of woven coconut-frond walls and roof, all supported by bamboo poles.

pārvai: view, sight.

paṭi: a small measure of grain, about a day's ration for one person.

pāvam: evil, sin. The term refers both to the act and to the results of the act. Evils can "stick" to the body/soul, affecting the afterlife; they can also pass down to children or grandchildren. They can sometimes be removed from the body/soul through ritual procedures.

payaṅkaramāṉatu: that which is fearsome.

periya ūr: the big village; here the main residential area of the higher and more-powerful landowning castes.

piracātam: leftovers from the gods; these are substances first used in worshiping a deity and then passed out to human devotees who eagerly consume them. Devotees consider these divine leftovers to be positively transvalued by contact with the deity and to be therefore potentially transformative of their own nature (at least temporarily).

piṭiccatu: a past-tense verbal form meaning literally "grabbed," but used here to describe a kind of malign or harmful possession of a person by a god.

piṭimaṇ: "a handful of earth." Many Tamils think that divine and human substances alike reside in the soil. Taking a handful of soil from one place and moving it to another can transfer qualities from one place to another, including, for example, the transfer of divine power. This is one way to establish new temples to gods who already reside elsewhere.

poṅkal: a boiled (poṅku) rice dish prepared in a special way on open fires, often cooked on thresholds. This dish is cooked on special occasions including temple festivals and the yearly Tamilnadu state holiday named for the rice dish, Poṅkal or Tai Poṅkal. This holiday is associated with agricultural productivity, kinship connections, and celebration of the Tamil New Year.

poṟuppu: responsibility, duty.

potu/potuvāka: common/commonly; public/publicly.

potumakkaḷ: the common people, here referring particularly and ironically to the ūrmakkaḷ as a collective agent.

prasad: common Anglicized spelling of piracātam.

puṟam: exterior; often used as complement to akam; also a genre of Tamil Sangam poetry.

talaimai: literally "headness"; leadership, command.

talaiyāris: a village servant whose duty it is to oversee protection of fields from animals and to accompany the local government officials and revenue collectors on their rounds of the village. In Yanaimangalam, this position is reserved for a member of the Thevar jāti.

taḻnta: low, often in reference to caste rank.

tāṉam: a kind of prestation that can transfer negative substances from one person to another. The term is also used in a more neutral sense to mean simply donation.

tappu: mistake, error, ethical blunder or blunder in etiquette.

tīmai: evil.

timir: arrogance.

tiruṣṭi: the negative effects of emotion-laden gazes, often translated as "the evil eye."

tīṭṭu: impurity; the kind caused by contact with substances conceived of as polluted (human and animal waste, blood, dead bodies, animal carcasses) or contact with persons considered polluted (often those who work with polluted substances.)

tōcam: fault, blemish. These can be physical faults or moral faults, sometimes caused astrologically.

ukkiramāṉa: fierce.

uḷ: in, inside.

ūr: residential place, native place, village.

ūr pūrāvum: the whole village, the whole population of an occupied place.

*ūrammaṉ: the village goddess, the deity in rural areas most closely associated with agricultural and human reproductive capacities.

ūrmakkaḷ: the village people, a term which in fact refers only to the dominant castes of the village.

vaḷḷaṉmai: largesse, liberal generosity.

varikkāraṇkaḷ: taxpayers; a term used to describe the members of a temple association, such as those who must pay a head tax to fund a temple's festival.

veḷi: out, outside, exterior.

vesṭi: the white wraparound cloth men commonly wear. Tied at the waist, the cloth extends to floor length and can also be hiked up to knee or thigh length for convenience of movement.

viḷaiccal: harvest, yield, productivity in general.

vipūti: ash, usually made of cow dung. This finely textured ash is used in temples and given as prasad to smear on foreheads or other parts of the body. It has significant symbolic associations with the god Siva.

vivacāyi: cultivator, a term of self-reference used by farmers when they describe their occupation.

NOTES

1. INTRODUCTION

1. *Annual Report on Epigraphy,* 1916: Nos. 565, 569, 588, 591, etc.); Araṅkācāri n.d.; see Ludden 1985, 35–41.

2. This proposal was inspired in part by the multi-aspectual model of social organization that Raheja (1988) identified in an Uttar Pradesh village dominated by a non-Brahman caste of cultivators.

3. The *Settlement Register of Tinnevelly District* for 1879, a document compiled by the British government to detail and define landholdings, shows that at this time, Brahmans in Yanaimangalam were assigned ownership to a vast majority of the land. Colonial land-tenure practices assured Brahmans "ownership" of the land. Legislation shortly after Independence put the land more readily into the hands of tenants.

4. By "pragmatic," I intend to invoke the philosophical pragmatism of American philosophers Peirce, Dewey, and Rorty.

5. This point of view characterizes a great deal of both past and present ethnographic and historical research among South Asianists who have written on how Indian localities, be they villages or towns or cities, have been affected by their relations with the wider world, whether through precolonial political and economic relations (Fuller 1989; Ludden 1985; Stein 1980), colonialism (e.g., Cohn 1987, 1996; Appadurai 1981; Dirks 1987; Mani 1992), democratic practices (Bate 2000; Fox 1969; Wadley 1994, 223–224), modernity (Hancock 1999; Singer 1972), state practices (Arnold 1986; Gupta 1995; Springer 2000), and land reforms (Mukherjee and Frykenberg 1969; Gough 1989; Kapadia 1995; 181–253), to name but a few examples.

2. WHO IS THE ŪR?

1. Appadurai and Breckenridge 1976; Appadurai 1981; Beck 1972; Dirks 1987 and 1991; Ludden 1985; Mines 1994; Price 1979; Nilakanta Sastri 1955; Srinivas 1952; Stein 1980.

2. For a more detailed account of why only certain temples convene for koṭai festivals, see Mines 1995. For a study on how the very decision to convene a festival may be already fraught with conflict and potential subversion, see Dirks 1991.

3. Maloney (1976, 123–125) notes that this type of ārati in part protects the god from harmful eye-flows—the so-called evil eye—of devotees. Babb (1981, 394) adds, following Marriott, that ārati may also be a way of "tying" or "binding" the god's qualities to the worshiper.

4. While Naidu, Saiva Pillai, and Brahman jātis are considered "high" castes, due to their low population they cannot be said to command the political and economic power of these other three jātis who, indeed, own most of the land and in the village.

5. This is the term commonly used to refer to temple "trustees," government-appointed temple administrators. In this case, the "appointment" was not governmental but

local. The village people appointed a Brahman headman because, according to some, he was neutral among the three other temple-community jātis and, according to others, because it was a sign of respect (mariyātai) that they chose to accord to the Brahmans of the village. The Brahmans of the village do not pay tax to the goddess temple or to any other temple (they collect donations for things they wish to fund), but they nonetheless consider her their goddess as well.

6. A long and loud reed instrument resembling in shape and tonality something like a giant oboe.

7. When I described this ritual and others like it to students in a Hinduism course I was teaching in St. Louis, one of my Indian-American students suddenly sat up straight and volunteered, "Oh! Is that why my parents did that thing with my car?!" She explained that when her parents brought home a car for her to take to college, they performed a circling ritual in their suburban driveway before they allowed her to drive it. They circled a lime "bloodied" with red vermilion powder around the car and threw it out into the street. Only then would they let her drive it. In this case, the shiny new car could have attracted dangerous gazes cast over suburban lawns.

8. See for example Bhattacharya 1991, 130–131; Kakar 1995, 44–47; Kumar 1989; Sax 1991; van der Veer 1994, 124–125; Inden 1990, 229–230, 244–262; Inglis 1985; Mines 1994, 65–83. Not only in South Asia but in many places throughout the world processions instigate conflict, as is most evident today in Northern Ireland and has been reported historically as part of carnivalesque rebellions in Europe (Davis 1975, 152–180). In the United States, clashes have also taken the form of disputes within the community over who should be included and who excluded from the social unity the processions proclaim. Both Irish-American and South Asian–American groups in New York City, for example, have tried to ban gay and lesbian groups from participating in yearly celebratory parades, effectively banning them from the community.

9. The territorial and political ramifications of processions and even individual movement through space have both mythical and historical precedence in South Asia. The earliest Hindu text extant (ca. 1200 B.C.), the Rg Veda, praises Visnu's great heroic strides: three footsteps that create the spaces of earth, heaven, and the distinction between the two (e.g., 1.154). A later myth dramatizes these footsteps. Visnu, in his dwarf incarnation, reclaims the earth as a territory for human occupation by tricking the demon Bali. The dwarf asks the demon to grant him just that bit of space he can stride in three steps. The demon is amused and so grants the dwarf his three steps, upon which the dwarf reveals himself as Visnu, grows immense, and takes three strides that cover earth and heaven.

As Visnu claims mythical overlordship of heaven and earth with footsteps, so too have historical kings effected and pronounced their overlordship of earthly regions in royal processions. The *dig-vijaya,* for example, "the conquest of the quarter," was a procession meant to "display the performer of it as the overlord of the four directional regions" (Inden 1990, 229). In the *asvamedha,* the famous "Horse Sacrifice," a king established his control over a territory by releasing a horse to wander as far as it wished during the course of the year, followed by (and perhaps coaxed along by) a band of warriors ready to defend the horse against those whose territory it crossed. If they won their battles or continued unchallenged, the territory was considered to belong to their king.

10. The only exception was the fourth procession, the Capparam, one reason being that the chariot could not practically be carried over the fields to and through North Ūr and another reason being that the Brahmans did not want this hot, transformative, meat-eating, rice beer–drinking goddess on their street.

11. The term "Thevar" is a title meaning in Tamil something like "heavenly immortal" (*Cre-A's Dictionary of Contemporary Tamil*). The Thevars are also collectively known as

"Mukkulathors" (those of the three lineages) and include three jātis, namely Kallar, Maravar, and Agamudaiyar. Yanaimangalam's Thevars are Maravar. For more on the Thevar designation, see Chapter 5.

12. I should note that it was Arunacalam Pillai's style to repeat himself in order to make people listen, and it was Parvathi's habit to repeat things to me because it often took a while for me to catch on to the meaning of things.

13. The mills are specifically government-licensed ones. The government regulates the flow of paddy across the territory in order to control prices and distribution. I was told that to evade regulations, rice is sometimes loaded up for transport in the middle of the night, oxcarts rumbling wooden wheels over the stone and dirt roads of the village and fording the river in order to transport the paddy to other markets where the harvest is not yet in full swing (irrigation leads to a staggered harvest in season that takes place later as one moves downriver). The price fetched on this black market exceeds what the government pays at the mills.

14. There is a similar contractual arrangement among the Thevars called *kāval kuttakai.* Several Thevar men pay a small fee for the contract to guard the fields during planting and harvest. The money they pay for this contract goes into the village's general fund. Such kuttakai contracts are not common to all villages. There may be several ways to collect public funds. In one hamlet in a village where associates of mine had affines, for example, the jāti headman (it is a single-jāti hamlet) collects a small fee (7 rupees in 1990) from each household when they perform an auspicious life-cycle ritual—puberty and weddings particularly. This money is set aside and used to finance the goddess of that hamlet.

15. The governmental subdivision of panchayat, or village council, oversees funds earmarked for such purposes as these—that is, for maintaining and constructing drinking-water systems, sanitation, roads, public electricity, health care facilities, and irrigation channels. Yanaimangalam belongs to a panchayat that includes more than one village and is centered in a village other than Yanaimangalam (the same village that has the rice mills), to which Yanaimangalam sends three elected representatives (including the legally required one S. C. member and, as of 2001, one woman). During my research from 1988 to 1990, this panchayat did not necessarily fulfill all its functions (at least not in a timely manner), so the "village people" keep a fund for emergency repairs.

3. THE ASH THEFT

1. "Darśan" refers to the visual exchange that occurs between devotees and gods, where devotees meet with their own gaze the return gaze of the deity who is present in the image. Diana Eck has suggested that in Hindu devotion, "seeing is a kind of touching," a physical channel through which a transforming auspiciousness moves from deity to devotee (1981, 3–9; see also Fuller 1992, 59–62).

2. Pfaffenberger elaborates that Pallars, the caste name belonging to residents of North and Middle Ūrs, were in older schemes considered to be related to landlords not by kuṭimai but rather by *aṭimai,* a term that British colonizers translated as "slavery." This distinction depicts a difference between jātis who have a specialized, ritual occupational function (toḻil) and those who "merely" labor. That is, other S. C. such as Cakkiliyar (Leatherworkers) and Palaiyar (Drummers) may participate in kuṭimai relations, while Pallar have no occupational toḻil other than labor. In Sri Lanka, and likely the process was similar in Tamilnadu, the kuṭimai-aṭimai distinction (which corresponded in part to a Right-Left caste distinction) collapsed under British rule and law, such that now Pallars are included in a kuṭimai idiom along with the others (1982, 33–50; see also Dirks 2001, 76–78). However, the distinction still echoes. It may be relevant, for example, to Gough's observation in 1973

that Pallars more than other S. C. jātis showed "an almost fanatical passion for equality within their caste group" (cited in Moffatt 1979, 18), and today too, it is mostly Pallars who clash with Thevars in Tirunelveli district, much more so than other S. C. jātis.

3. Sarah Lamb (2000, 57–67) shows how the forms and meanings of caste also apply within families.

4. This list probably originates from directives of kingly rule in South India. Pfaffenberger (1982, 35) cites a similar list used by Tamil kings of Jaffna, Sri Lanka (see also Hocart 1950).

5. This contention is supported by land ownership recorded in the *Settlement Register of Tirunelvelly District* (1879), which clearly lists Brahmans as the predominant landowners.

6. Raheja (1988, 1990) shows us that indeed either relation may be foregrounded, depending on context.

7. During the heyday of village studies, many if not most authors concentrated a great deal of effort on detailing changes that state political and economic transformations made in village organization (e.g., Bailey 1957, 1963; Beals 1955; Beteille 1965b; Epstein 1962, 1973; Gough 1989; Marriott 1955, to name but a few). Very few anthropologists of this era treated the village as an isolate.

8. See for example, Beteille 1965b, 99–101; Beck 1972, 15–17, 44–49; Gough 1989, 128, 294; and Ludden 1985, 87–94; Srinivas 1976, 164–167; Pfaffenberger 1982; Dumont 1986/1957, 44–47.

9. See, for example, Gough 1989, 128, 137; Epstein 1973, 123–125; Beteille 1965b, 100. But see also Mencher (1970, 208–210), who saw no significant changes such as those marked by Beteille and Epstein for the same period.

10. "Bad karma" is, indeed, what it is. While rural Tamils do not tend to use the term "karma" in this way (see also Daniel 1983), they do indeed understand these negatives to be the material effect of previous immoral acts committed either by themselves or by their ascendant ancestors (see Mines 1997b). Karma, literally, means "action" as well as the effects of action on the actor (see also Potter n.d.). In Yanaimangalam, the term "pāvam" similarly refers to morally negative acts as well as the outcomes of those acts that remain tied to (and incapacitate) the souls of persons.

11. It is important to mention that "tiruṣṭi" is not impurity. Nor is "evil" (pāvam) or "fault" (tōcam) the same thing as impurity. Like Kapadia (1995, 120–121), I found that Tamil distinctions between impurity (tīṭṭu) and these other kinds of negative substances that Raheja's North Indian informants call "inauspiciousness" (as opposed to "impurity") (1988, 46) are not always clearly marked. Some of my informants, as did Kapadia's (and see also Parry 1991, 268–269, cited in Kapadia 1995, 121), did state that Barbers and Washermen took away the impurity (tīṭṭu) from certain life transitions, such as death and birth and puberty. Inglis also reports that South Indian Potters are capable of removing impurities (Inglis 1985, 99). But my informants were adamant about the fact that weddings generate no impurity (tīṭṭu) (see also Mines 1990). Barbers, Washermen, Carpenters, Brahmans, and others—and gods too—do receive prestations that are said to remove other negatives that resemble more what Raheja's informants call inauspiciousness, namely faults (tōcam), evil eye (tiruṣṭi), and evils (pāvam).

12. Much of the following passage appeared first, in somewhat altered versions, in Mines 1997b.

13. This could be the father's actual sister or the mother's brother's wife, for example. The point is that the woman is defined as an affine. (All fathers' sisters—attai—are potential mothers-in-law—attai—given the pattern of cross-cousin marriage.)

14. See also Kapadia (1995), who refers to the whole set of acts involved in a circling ritual (107–110) and Good (1991, 100).

4. MAKING SOCIAL DISTINCTIONS

1. While it is true that mariyātai does not inhere in any thing by itself (for mariyātai is always relationally defined), some items are used so habitually to constitute mariyātai in exchange that the transaction and the thing are reified as one category, mariyātai. Sometimes people will speak of a distributed item as "a mariyātai," but they would agree, if asked, that the item is only mariyātai because of the context in which it was given.

2. Epstein (1973) and Gough (1989) discuss at length how economic class has been gradually gaining precedence as a means of social rank in rural Tamilnadu.

3. Marriott (1990) suggests that "non-transitivity" would be a more appropriately inferred axiom, since it allows for imperfect transitivity that often actually eventuates from the acts of multiple agents.

4. Mēlam is a large drum that musicians beat with sticks, altering rhythms according to event and action. Two mēlam usually accompany one nataswāram, a loud reed instrument that plays tunes.

5. In network terms, the "reach" has a distance of one. That is, the center (giver) creates a set of included allies by transacting with each one directly, thus distinguishing them. This network measure called "reach" is, also in network terms, a measure of a network's centrality (Hage and Harary 1983, 69). It would be more accurate, perhaps, to name these inclusion sets parity sets, for parity defines relations not of equality but rather as sameness in relation to a center. (So all devotees of the goddess have parity to the extent that they can each receive prasad from her, and all receivers of curuḷ or other door-to-door prestations have parity in relation to the giver, regardless of how they might otherwise rank along a dimension of high to low.) Parity in relation to a god is the dominant structural idiom of bhakti, for example, because in bhakti all devotees (no matter how they are ranked among themselves) are equal in the sight of the god or goddess they worship.

5. HABIT, HISTORY, AND THEVAR DOMINANCE

1. "Aṭimai" means both slavery and ardent devotion.

2. As Karl Potter (n.d.) writes, outlining a philosophical theory of karma drawing on textual sources, karma (action) is not merely a "doing" but is in fact a "making" of future capacities and qualities of experience. Actions thus are never mere functions; they are embodied, emplaced, and have a real effect on ourselves, our relations, and our world.

3. See for example, Stein 1980; Breckenridge 1977; Price 1996a; Appadurai 1981; Dirks 1987.

6. GODS OF YANAIMANGALAM

The first portions of this chapter originally appeared in "The Hindu Gods in a South Indian Village," in Mines and Lamb 2002.

1. The use of Brahman priests at temples to fierce gods is not universal, nor (for the Brahmans) is it very prestigious. However, communities with sufficient funds to hire a Brahman priest (many of whom are poor enough to take what work they can get) may do so in order to increase the prestige of their temple.

2. Portions of the following section originally appeared in the *Irish Journal of Anthropology* (Mines 1997a).

7. MAKING GOOD AT KOṬAI FESTIVALS

1. In Madurai district and northward, this term is not used.

2. Viḷaiccal is a noun formed from the verb *viḷai,* which means in general to cause or produce; that is, to make. Another context in which I heard this term used, mentioned in Chapter 3, is in relation to menstrual clothing. If a woman washes her own, the viḷaiccal (productivity) of the house is said to be endangered. She should send these cloths out with the Dhobi.

3. Auvayar was a Tamil poet from the Sangam period (approximately 300 B.C. to 200 A.D.).

4. Many aspects of koṭai festivals tie in to agricultural processes, which may be generalized as reproductive processes. For example, every koṭai, and every wedding as well, commences with an event called "planting the post" (*kālnāṟṟutal*). Sometimes performed more perfunctorily than at other times, planting the post in either context minimally involves taking a wooden branch (the *kāl*) cut freshly (usually from a peepol tree), cleaning the branch by stripping the bark, dunking it in water, and painting it with red and white stripes. Then the post is literally planted (*nāṟṟu*) in a hole near the ritual site (by the side of the temple wall or by the side of the house or pantal area for weddings). The post is watered with milk by important people in a sequence that produces mariyātai. Much of the preparation of the post (its cutting and stripping) is performed by an Acari, a Carpenter whose duty and right it is to perform this work, especially at the temple. At the Cutalaimatan koṭai, I watched the kālnāṟṟutal. There, paddy too was thrown into the hole. It was then that Ramayya Thevar told me that the post had to be forked on top to represent the growth (*vaḷarcci*) of the branches of the family (as in English, in Tamil too a family is said to have "branches," *kilai*).

5. Marriott (1990) has emphasized quantity ("bigness," "dominance") and "maximizing" as one effect of what he identifies as the "mixing" variable, a product of heat.

6. The district collector is the head posting of the Indian central government in the district. He administers and oversees the local functioning of government agencies and programs.

8. WAITING FOR VELLALAKANTAN

This chapter appears in an altered version in the forthcoming *Tamil Geographies,* ed. Martha Selby and Indira Peterson (Albany: State University of New York Press).

1. In one short story by the well-known Tamil author from the district, Putumaippittan (a nom de plume meaning "He who is mad for modernity") a young man who is a devout "rationalist" (atheist) goes to the Cutalaimatan temple one night on a dare to show that he does not believe in either ghosts or fierce gods. He is startled by ghostly sounds, though, and in fear he scrambles up a tree from which he finds he has gained a view of the temple's interior. There he sees the source of his oracular fright: the priest and a woman making love.

2. Even those Thevars who are originally from North Ūr and who are lineally related to those in North Ūr pay tax both to East Cutalaimatan temple and to the main goddess temple by virtue of the fact of their place of residence. The fact that they live in the main ūr makes it necessary for them to pay tax to the gods worshipped by Thevars living in the main ūr.

3. A position normally assumed only by those capable of channeling the god's power, and too dangerous to all others.

4. "Pantimar" is a now somewhat archaic term for Maravar and its use here in this telling may be simply stylistic (the story is about "the old days") or it may be more pragmatic (the teller does not wish to implicate today's Thevars).

5. Meaning "thief"; also the name of one of the subjātis of Thevars (Kallar) designated "criminal" by the British colonial state.

6. I only noticed the discrepancy in pronunciation after returning from the field and working from tape transcriptions hurriedly made as I was leaving the field. Raja Balasubramaniam, a Ph.D. candidate at the University of Chicago who is a native Tamil speaker, first pointed the pun of the name out to me. He took me by surprise as he caught the pun with a burst of laughter upon first hearing me utter the name "Vellalakantan."

7. Existentialist and phenomenological conceptualizations of human temporality privilege the future (May 1994/1958, 68–69; Daniel 1996, 122–127). As humans move toward their intentional futures, they bring the present and the past into line with those futures, constructing coherent narratives (Carr 1986, 18–44) and experiences (Desjarlais 1996).

9. HINDU NATIONALISM AND DALIT REFORM

Portions of this chapter also appeared in Mines 2002b.

1. Alf Hiltebeitel notes that the violent deaths of pregnant women are also a specialization of Cutalaimatan (1989, 357).

2. Contrast this analysis of refutation and redefinition of relations through festivals with Moffatt (1979, 219–289) who argues that Harijan exclusion from village goddess festivals results in a replication of the goddess festival in the more limited confines of Harijan hamlets. While similar replications do take place in Yanaimangalam's S. C. goddess temples, the fierce-god temples allow a more direct and forceful response.

3. In 1981, several hundred S. C. in a village called Meenaksipuram in southern Tirunelveli District converted en masse to what was considered to be a more egalitarian Islam in order, they reported, to escape from domination by higher castes in what was understood to be a Hindu idiom. Subsequently, what are euphemistically referred to as "communal tensions" led to violent clashes between primarily Thevars and S. C. in this area. Several reports show that the S. C. who converted were not the poorest of the area but were more highly educated citizens who saw their move as an overt political protest.

4. It is not just the higher jātis who talk of the days when mariyātai distinctions were maintained. Perhaps even more common is talk from today's peripheries, talk by the S. C. and other little jātis (Illuttuppillai in particular) about how they have been and still are treated unfairly in Yanaimangalam, how only recently their children could attend the village primary school, how many people (the Thevars, for example) still exclude them from temples.

5. Good (1991) reports that in another part of the district, landowners actually fund the festivals of their kuṭimakkaḷ, making their patronage of them total. Here it is through independent financing of their koṭai that residents of Middle Hamlet can make something of and for themselves.

6. For a detailed discussion of the contentious discourse on Untouchability that brought Gandhi and Ambedkar into conflict, see Dirks 2001, 255–274.

7. For more detailed histories on the dispute see, for example, Gopal 1991; McKean 1996; van der Veer 1987, 1994.

REFERENCES CITED

Ambedkar, B. R. 1990. *Annihilation of Caste: An Undelivered Speech.* Ed. Mulk Raj Anand. New Delhi: Arnold Publishers.

Amnesty International. 1997. "India: Submission to the Human Rights Committee concerning the Application of the International Covenant on Civil and Political Rights." Available online: http://web.amnesty.org/library/Index/engASA200271997.

Ananth, V. Krishna 1998. "The Canker of Caste . . . and Conflagration." *The Hindu,* October 11, 1998.

Annual Report on Epigraphy. 1916. Archaeological Department. Madras: Government Press.

Appadurai, Arjun. 1981. *Worship and Conflict under Colonial Rule: A South Indian Case.* Cambridge: Cambridge University Press.

———. 1996. *Modernity at Large.* Minneapolis: University of Minnesota Press.

Appadurai, Arjun, and Carol Breckenridge. 1976. "The South Indian Temple: Authority, Honor, and Redistribution." *Contributions to Indian Sociology* n.s. 10 (2): 187–211.

Araṅkācāri, A. V. n.d. "Kariculntamankalam tirukoyilkal." Xeroxed publication. Pattamadai: [Publisher unknown.]

Arnold, David. 1986. *Police Power and Colonial Rule: Madras 1859–1947.* Delhi: Oxford University Press.

Austin, J. L. 1962. *How to Do Things with Words.* Cambridge, Mass.: Harvard University Press.

Babb, Lawrence A. 1973. "Heat and Control in Chhattisgarhi Ritual." *The Eastern Anthropologist* 26 (1): 11–28.

———. 1975. *The Divine Hierarchy: Popular Hinduism in Central India.* New York: Columbia University Press.

———. 1981. "Glancing: Visual Interaction in Hinduism." *Journal of Anthropological Research* 37 (4): 387–401.

Bailey, F. G. 1957. *Caste and the Economic Frontier: A Village in Highland Orissa.* Manchester: Manchester University Press.

———. 1963. *Politics and Social Change: Orissa in 1959.* Berkeley: University of California Press.

Bakhtin, M. M. 1981. *The Dialogic Imagination: Four Essays.* Trans. Caryl Emerson and Michael Holquist, ed. Michael Holquist. Austin: University of Texas Press.

Bate, John Bernard. 2000. "*Metaittamil*: Oratory and Democratic Practice in Tamilnadu." Ph.D. diss., Department of Anthropology, University of Chicago.

———. 2002. "Political Praise in Tamil Newspapers: The Poetry and Iconography of Democratic Power." In *Everyday Life in South Asia,* ed. Diane Mines and Sarah Lamb. Bloomington: Indiana University Press.

Bateson, Gregory. 1972. *Steps to an Ecology of Mind.* New York: Ballantine Books.

———. 1979. *Mind and Nature: A Necessary Unity.* New York: Bantam Books.

Beals, Alan. 1955. "Interplay among Factors of Change in a Mysore Village." In *Village India,* ed. McKim Marriott. Chicago: University of Chicago Press.

Beck, Brenda. 1969. "Colour and Heat in South Indian Ritual." *Man* 4 (4): 553–572.

———. 1972. *Peasant Society in Konku: A Study of Right and Left Subcastes in South India.* Vancouver: University of British Columbia Press.

———. 1976. "The Symbolic Merger of Body, Space, and Cosmos in Hindu Tamil Nadu." *Contributions to Indian Sociology* n.s. 10 (2): 213–243.

Beidelman, Thomas O. 1959. *A Comparative Analysis of the Jajmani System.* New York: J. J. Augustin.

Benveniste, Emile. 1971/1966. *Problems in General Linguistics.* Coral Gables: University of Miami Press.

Beteille, Andre. 1965a. "Social Organization of Temples in a Tanjore Village." *History of Religions* 5 (1): 74–92.

———. 1965b. *Caste, Class, and Power: Changing Patterns of Stratification in a Tanjore Village.* Berkeley: University of California Press.

Bhattacharya, Neeladri. 1991. "Myth, History and the Politics of Ramjanmabhumi." In *Anatomy of a Confrontation,* ed. Sarvepalli Gopal. London: Zed Books.

Blackburn, Stuart. 1988. *Singing of Birth and Death: Texts in Performance.* Philadelphia: University of Pennsylvania Press.

Breckenridge, Carol. 1977. "From Protector to Litigant: Changing Relations between Hindu Temples and the Raja of Ramnad." *The Indian Economic and Social History Review* 14 (1): 75–106.

Bronger, Dirk. 1975. "Jajmani System in Southern India." *Journal of the Indian Anthropological Society* 10: 1–38.

Brubaker, Richard L. 1979. "Barbers, Washermen, and Other Priests: Servants of the South Indian Village and Its Goddess." *History of Religions* 19 (2): 128–152

Carr, David. 1986. *Time, Narrative, and History.* Bloomington: Indiana University Press.

Casey, Edward S. 1996. "How to Get from Space to Place in a Fairly Short Stretch of Time: Phenomenological Prolegomena." In *Senses of Place,* ed. Steven Feld and Keith H. Basso. Santa Fe: School of American Research Press.

Chakrabarty, Dipesh. 1997. "The Time of History and the Times of Gods." In *The Politics of Culture in the Shadow of Capital,* ed. Lisa Lowe and David Lloyd. Durham, N.C.: Duke University Press.

Chatterjee, Partha. 1993. *The Nation and Its Fragments: Colonial and Postcolonial Histories.* Princeton, N.J.: Princeton University Press.

Cohn, Bernard S. 1987. "The Census, Social Structure, and Objectification." In *An Anthropologist among the Historians and Other Essays.* New Delhi: Oxford University Press.

———. 1996. *Colonialism and Its Forms of Knowledge: The British in India.* Princeton, N.J.: Princeton University Press.

Cohn, Bernard S., and McKim Marriott. 1958. "Networks and Centres in the Integration of Indian Civilization." *Journal of Social Research* 1: 1–9.

Colapietro, Vincent. 1989. *Peirce's Approach to the Self: A Semiotic Perspective on Human Subjectivity.* Albany: State University of New York Press.

Comaroff, Jean, and John Comaroff. 1986. "Christianity and Colonialism." *American Ethnologist* 13 (1): 1–22.

Corrington, Robert S. 1993. *An Introduction to C. S. Peirce.* Lanham, Md.: Rowman and Littlefield.

Cre-A's Dictionary of Contemporary Tamil. 1992. Chennai: Cre-A.

Daniel, E. Valentine. 1984. *Fluid Signs: Being a Person the Tamil Way.* Berkeley: University of California Press.

———. 1993. "Tea Talk: Violent Measures in the Discursive Practices of Sri Lanka s Estate Tamils." *Comparative Studies in Society and History* 15 (3): 568–600.

———. 1996. *Charred Lullabies: Towards an Anthropography of Violence.* Princeton, N.J.: Princeton University Press.

Daniel, Sheryl B. 1983. "The Tool Box Approach of the Tamil to the Issues of Moral Responsibility and Human Destiny." In *Karma: An Anthropological Inquiry,* ed. Charles F. Keyes and E. Valentine Daniel. Berkeley: University of California Press.

Davis, Natalie Zemon. 1975. *Society and Culture in Early Modern France.* Palo Alto, Calif.: Stanford University Press.

de Certeau, Michel. 1984. *The Practice of Everyday Life.* Berkeley: University of California Press.

———. 1989. *The Writing of History.* New York: Columbia University Press.

Desjarlais, Robert. 1996. "Struggling Along." In *Things as They Are: New Directions in Phenomenological Anthropology,* ed. Michael Jackson. Bloomington: Indiana University Press.

Dickey, Sara. 2000. "Permeable Homes: Domestic Service, Household Space, and the Vulnerability of Class Boundaries in Urban India." *American Ethnologist* 27 (2): 462–489.

Dirks, Nicholas. 1987. *The Hollow Crown: Ethnohistory of an Indian Kingdom.* Cambridge: Cambridge University Press.

———. 1991. "Ritual and Resistance: Subversion as Social Fact." In *Contesting Power: Resistance and Everyday Social Relations in South Asia,* ed. Douglas Haynes and Gyan Prakash. Berkeley: University of California Press.

———. 2001. *Castes of Mind: Colonialism and the Making of Modern India.* Princeton, N.J.: Princeton University Press.

Doniger, Wendy O'Flaherty, trans. 1975. *Hindu Myths.* New York: Penguin.

———. 1980. *Women, Androgynes, and Other Mythical Beasts.* Chicago: University of Chicago Press.

Dube, S. C. 1955. *Indian Village.* London: Routledge and Kegan Paul.

Dube, Saurabh. 1998. *Untouchable Pasts: Religion, Identity, and Power among a Central Indian Community, 1780–1950.* Albany: State University of New York Press.

Dumont, Louis. 1970. *Homo hierarchicus: The Caste System and Its Implications.* Chicago: University of Chicago Press.

———. 1986/1957. *A South Indian Subcaste: Social Organization and Religion of the Pramalai Kallar.* Delhi: Oxford University Press.

Durkheim, Emile. 1965/1915. *Elementary Forms of the Religious Life.* Trans. Joseph W. Swain. New York: The Free Press.

Eck, Diana. 1981. *Darsan: Seeing the Divine Image in India.* Chambersburg, Pa.: Anima Press.

Epstein, Scarlett. 1962. *Economic Development and Social Change in South India.* Manchester: Manchester University Press.

———. 1973. *South India: Yesterday, Today, and Tomorrow.* New York: Holmes and Meier.

Fabricius, J. P. 1972. *Tamil and English Dictionary.* Tranquebar: Evangelical Lutheran Mission Publishing House.

Fox, Richard. 1969. *From Zamindar to Ballot Box: Community Change in a North Indian Market Town.* Ithaca, N.Y.: Cornell University Press.

Fromm, Erich. 1973. *The Crisis in Psychoanalysis.* Harmondsworth: Penguin.

Fuller, C. J. 1987. "The Hindu Pantheon and the Legitimation of Hierarchy." *Man* n.s. 23 (1): 19–39.

———. 1989. "Misconceiving the Grain Heap: A Critique of the Concept of the Indian Jajmani System." In *Money and the Morality of Exchange,* ed. Jonathon Parry and Maurice Bloch. Cambridge: Cambridge University Press.

———. 1992. *The Camphor Flame: Popular Hinduism and Society in India.* Princeton, N.J.: Princeton University Press.

Genette, Gerard. 1980. *Narrative Discourse: An Essay in Method.* Trans. Jane E. Lewin. Ithaca, N.Y.: Cornell University Press.

Gold, Ann Grodzins, and Bhoju Ram Gujar. 2002. *In the Time of Trees and Sorrow: Nature, Power, and Memory in Rajasthan.* Durham, N.C.: Duke University Press.

Good, Anthony. 1982. "The Annual Goddess Festival in a South Indian Village." *South Asian Social Scientist* 1 (2): 119–167.

———. 1983. "A Symbolic Type and Its Transformations: The Case of South Indian Pongal." *Contributions to Indian Sociology* n.s. 17 (2): 223–244.

———. 1985. "The Annual Goddess Festival in a South Indian Village." *South Asian Social Scientist* 1 (2): 119–167.

———. 1991. *The Female Bridegroom: A Comparative Study of Life-Crisis Rituals in South India and Sri Lanka.* Oxford: The Clarendon Press.

Gopal, Savarapalli, ed. 1991. *Anatomy of a Confrontation: Ayodhya and the Rise of Communal Politics in India.* London: Zed Books.

Gore, M. S. 1993. *The Social Context of an Ideology: Ambedkar's Political and Social Thought.* New Delhi: Sage Publications.

Gough, Kathleen. 1989. *Rural Change in Southeast India: 1950s to 1980s.* Delhi: Oxford University Press.

Gould, Harold. 1958. "The Hindu Jajmani System: A Case of Economic Particularism." *Southwestern Journal of Anthropology* 16 (Winter): 434.

Guha, Ranajit. 1999/1983. *Elementary Aspects of Peasant Insurgency in Colonial India.* Durham, N.C.: Duke University Press.

Gupta, Akhil. 1995. "Blurred Boundaries: The Discourse of Corruption, the Culture of Politics, and the Imagined State." *American Ethnologist* 22 (2): 375–402.

Gupta, Akhil, and James Ferguson, eds. 1997. *Culture, Power, Place: Explorations in Critical Anthropology.* Durham, N.C.: Duke University Press.

Hage, Per, and Frank Harary. 1983. *Structural Models in Anthropology.* Cambridge: Cambridge University Press.

Hanchett, Suzanne. 1988. *Coloured Rice: Symbolic Structure in Hindu Family Festivals.* Delhi: Hindustan Publishing Corporation.

Hancock, Mary Elizabeth. 1999. *Womanhood in the Making: Domestic Ritual and Public Culture in Urban South India.* Boulder: Westview Press.

Harper, Edward B. 1959a. "Two Systems of Economic Exchange in Village India." *American Anthropologist* 61 (4): 760–778.

———. 1959b. "A Hindu Village Pantheon." *Southwestern Journal of Anthropology* 15: 227–234.

Hart, George. 2000. "The Seasons in Tamil: A Broken Template." Paper presented at the 29th Annual Conference on South Asia of the Center for South Asia, University of Wisconsin, October 14, Madison, Wisconsin.

Harvey, David. 1989. *The Condition of Post-Modernity: An Inquiry into the Origins of Social Change.* Cambridge: Blackwell.

Haynes, Douglas, and Gyan Prakash, eds. 1991. *Contesting Power: Resistance and Everyday Social Relations in South Asia.* Berkeley: University of California Press.

Hebdige, Dick. 1979. *Subculture: The Meaning of Style.* London: Methuen.

Hiltebeitel, Alf. 1989. *Criminal Gods and Demon Devotees: Essays on the Guardians of Popular Hinduism.* Albany: State University of New York Press.

Hocart, A. M. 1950. *Caste: A Comparative Study.* London: Methuen.

Holland, Dorothy, William Lachicotte, Debra Skinner, and Carole Cain. 1998. *Identity and Agency in Cultural Worlds.* Cambridge, Mass.: Harvard University Press.

Inden, Ronald. 1985. "The Temple and the Hindu Chain of Being (Kashmir)." *Purusartha* 8: 53–73.

———. 1990. *Imagining India.* London: Blackwell Press.

Inden, Ronald, and Ralph Nicholas. 1977. *Kinship in Bengali Culture.* Chicago: University of Chicago Press.

Inglis, Stephen. 1985. "Possession and Poverty: Serving the Divine in a South Indian Community." In *Gods of Flesh, Gods of Stone: The Embodiment of Divinity in India,* ed. Joanne Punso Waghorne and Norman Cutler with Sasudha Narayanan. Chambersburg, Pa.: Anima Press.

Irschick, Eugene. 1986. *Tamil Revivalism in the 1930s.* Madras: Cre-A.

Jackson, Michael. 1996. "Introduction: Phenomenology, Radical Empiricism, and Anthropological Critique." In *Things as They Are: New Directions in Phenomenological Anthropology,* ed. Michael Jackson. Bloomington: Indiana University Press.

———. 1998. *Minima ethnographica: Intersubjectivity and the Anthropological Project.* Chicago: University of Chicago Press.

Kakar, Sudhir. 1982. *Shamans, Mystics, and Doctors: A Psychological Inquiry into India and Its Healing Traditions.* New York: Knopf.

———. 1995. *The Colors of Violence: Cultural Identities, Religion, and Conflict.* Chicago: University of Chicago Press.

Kapadia, Karin. 1995. *Siva and Her Sisters: Gender, Caste, and Class in Rural South India.* Boulder: Westview Press.

———. 2000. "Pierced by Love: Tamil Possession, Gender, and Caste." In *Invented Identities: The Interplay of Gender, Religion, and Politics in India,* ed. Julia Leslie and Mary McGee. New Delhi: Oxford University Press.

Kapferer, Bruce. 1997. *The Feast of the Sorcerer: Practices of Consciousness and Power.* Chicago: University of Chicago Press.

Kearney, M. 1995. "The Local and the Global: The Anthropology of Globalization and Transnationalism." *Annual Review of Anthropology* 24: 547–565.

Khare, R. S. 1984. *The Untouchable as Himself: Ideology, Identity, and Pragmatism among the Lucknow Chamars.* Cambridge: Cambridge University Press.

Kinsley, David. 1986. *Hindu Goddesses.* Berkeley: University of California Press.

Knipe, David M. 1989. "Night of the Growing Dead: A Viirabhadra Cult in Coastal Andhra." In *Criminal Gods and Demon Devotees: Essays on the Guardians of Popular Hinduism,* ed. Alf Hiltebeitel. Albany: SUNY Press.

Kolenda, Pauline. 1963. "Toward a Model of the Hindu Jajmani System." *Human Organization* 22 (1): 11–31.

Kumar, Nita. 1989. "Work and Leisure in the Formation of Identity: Muslim Weavers in a Hindu City." In *Culture and Power in Benares: Community, Performance, and Environment 1800–1980,* ed. Sandria B. Freitag. Delhi: Oxford University Press.

Lamb, Sarah. 2000. *White Saris and Sweet Mangoes: Aging, Gender, and Body in North India.* Berkeley: University of California Press.

Larson, Gerald, and Ram Shankar Bhattacharya. 1987. "Samkhya: A Dualist Tradition in Indian Philosophy." In *Encyclopedia of Indian Philosophies,* ed. Karl Potter. Princeton, N.J.: Princeton University Press.

Levinson, Stephen. 1982. "Caste Rank and Verbal Interaction in Western Tamilnadu." In *Caste Ideology and Interaction,* ed. Dennis B. McGilvary. Cambridge: Cambridge University Press.

Levi-Strauss, Claude. 1963. *Totemism.* Trans. Rodney Needham. Boston: Beacon Press.

Ludden, David. 1985. *Peasant History in South India.* Princeton, N.J.: Princeton University Press.

Madras Institute of Development Studies. 1988. *Tamilnadu Economy: Performance and Issues.* New Delhi: Oxford University Press.

Maloney, Clarence. 1976. "Don't Say 'Pretty Baby' Lest You Zap It with Your Eye: The Evil Eye in South Asia." In *The Evil Eye,* ed. Clarence Maloney. New York: Columbia University Press.

Mani, Lata. 1992. "Cultural Theory, Colonial Texts: Reading Eyewitness Accounts of Widow Burning." In *Cultural Studies,* ed. Lawrence Grossberg, Cary Nelson, and Paula Treichler. New York: Routledge.

Manikam, K. A. 1997. "Caste Clashes in South Tamil Nadu." *Economic and Political Weekly* 32 (36): 2242–2243.

Marriott, McKim. 1955. "Little Communities in an Indigenous Civilization." In *Village India,* ed. McKim Marriott. Chicago: University of Chicago Press.

———. 1972. "The Feast of Love." In *Krishna: Myths, Rites, and Attitudes,* ed. Milton Singer. Chicago: University of Chicago Press.

———. 1976. "Hindu Transactions: Diversity without Dualism." In *Transaction and Meaning: Directions in the Anthropology of Exchange and Symbolic Behavior,* ed. Bruce Kapferer. Philadelphia: Institute for the Study of Human Issues.

———. 1990. "Constructing an Indian Ethnosociology." In *India through Hindu Categories,* ed. McKim Marriott. New Delhi: Sage Publications.

———. 1998. "The Female Family Core Explored Ethnosociologically." *Contributions to Indian Sociology* 32 (2): 279–304.

Marriott, McKim, and Ronald B. Inden. 1977. "Toward an Ethnosociology of South Asian Caste Systems." In *The New Wind,* ed. Kenneth David. The Hague: Mouton.

May, Rollo. 1994/1958. "Contributions of Existential Psychology." In *Existence,* ed. Rollo May, Ernest Angel, and Henri F. Ellenberger. Northvale, New Jersey: Jason Aronson Inc.

———. 1958. *Existence: A New Dimension in Psychiatry and Psychology.* New York: Basic Books.

McKean, Lise. 1996. *Divine Enterprise: Gurus and the Hindu Nationalist Movement.* Chicago: University of Chicago Press.

Mencher, Joan P. 1970. "A Tamil Village: Changing Socio-Economic Structure in Madras State." In *Aspects of Continuity and Change in India,* ed. K. Iswaran. New York: Columbia University Press.

Mines, Diane P. 1990. "Hindu Periods of Death 'Impurity.'" In *India through Hindu Categories,* ed. McKim Marriott. New Delhi: Sage Publications.

———. 1995. "Making and Remaking the Village: The Pragmatics of Social Life in Rural Tamilnadu." Ph.D. diss., Department of Anthropology, University of Chicago.

———. 1997a. "From Homo hierarchicus to Homo faber: Breaking Convention through Semeiosis." *The Irish Journal of Anthropology* 2: 33–44.

———. 1997b. "Making the Past Past: Objects and the Spatialization of Time in Tamilnadu." *Anthropology Quarterly* 70 (4): 173–186.

———. 2002a. "The Hindu Gods in a South Indian Village." In *Everyday Life in South Asia,* ed. Diane Mines and Sarah Lamb. Bloomington: Indiana University Press.

———. 2002b. "Hindu Nationalism, Untouchable Reform, and the Ritual Production of a South Indian Village." *American Ethnologist* 29 (1): 158–185.

———. In press. "Waiting for Vellalakantan." In *Tamil Geographies: Cultural Constructions of Space and Place in South India,* ed. Martha Selby and Indira Peterson. Albany: State University of New York Press.

Mines, Diane, and Sarah Lamb, ed. 2002. *Everyday Life in South Asia.* Bloomington: Indiana University Press.

Mines, Mattison. 1994. *Public Faces, Private Voices: Community and Individuality in South India.* Berkeley: University of California Press.

Mines, Mattison, and Vijayalakshmi Gourishankar. 1990. "Leadership and Individuality in South Asia: The Case of the South Indian Big-Man." *The Journal of Asian Studies* 49 (4): 761–786.

Moffatt, Michael. 1979. *An Untouchable Community in South India: Structure and Consensus.* Princeton, N.J.: Princeton University Press.

Moreno, Manuel. 1985. "God's Forceful Call: Possession as a Divine Strategy." In *Gods of Flesh, Gods of Stone: The Embodiment of Divinity in India,* ed. Joanne Waghorne and Norman Cutler with Sasudha Narayanan. Chambersburg, Pa.: Anima Press.

Mukherjee, Nilmani, and Robert E. Frykenberg. 1969. "The Ryotwari System and Social Organization in the Madras Presidency." In *Land Control and Social Structure in Indian History,* ed. Robert E. Frykenberg. Delhi: Manohar.

Munn, Nancy. 1986. *The Fame of Gawa: A Symbolic Study of Value Transformation in a Massim (Papua New Guinea) Society.* Cambridge: Cambridge University Press.

Nabokov, Isabelle. 2000. *Religion Against the Self.* New York: Oxford University Press.

Nandy, Ashish. 1983. *The Intimate Enemy: Loss and Recovery of Self under Colonialism.* Delhi: Oxford University Press.

———. 1992. "The Politics of Secularism and the recovery of Religious Tolerance." In *Mirrors of Violence,* ed. Veena Das. Delhi: Oxford University Press.

———. 2001. *An Ambiguous Journey to the City: The Village and Other Odd Ruins of the Self in the Indian Imagination.* Delhi: Oxford University Press.

Nilakanta Sastri, K. A. 1955. *A History of South India from Prehistoric Times to the Fall of Vijayanagar.* Madras: Oxford University Press.

Omvedt, Gail. 1993. *Dalits and the Democratic Revolution: Dr. Ambedkar and the Dalit Movement in Colonial India.* New Delhi: Sage Publications.

Parish, Steven. 1996. *Hierarchy and Its Discontents: Culture and the Politics of Consciousness in Caste Society.* Philadelphia: University of Pennsylvania Press.

Parry, Jonathan. 1980. "Ghosts, Greed, and Sin: The Occupational Identity of the Benares Funeral Priests." *Man* 15 (1): 88–111.

———. 1986. "The Gift, the Indian Gift and the 'Indian Gift.'" *Man* 21 (3): 453–473.

———. 1989. "On the Moral Perils of Exchange." In *Money and the Morality of Exchange,* ed. Jonathon Parry and Maurice Bloch. Cambridge: Cambridge University Press.

———. 1991. "The Hindu Lexicographer? A Note on Auspiciousness and Purity." *Contributions to Indian Sociology* 25, no. 2: 267–285.

———. 1994. *Death in Banaras.* Cambridge: Cambridge University Press.

Pate, H. R. 1917. *Tinnevelly.* Madras District Gazetteers. Vol. 1. Madras: Government Press.

Peacock, James L. 1968. *Rites of Modernization: Symbolic and Social Aspects of Indonesian Proletarian Drama.* Chicago: University of Chicago Press.

Peirce, Charles S. 1955. *Philosophical Writings of Peirce.* Ed. Justus Buchler. New York: Dover Publications.

———. 1931–1958. *Collected Papers of Charles Sanders Peirce.* Ed. Charles Hartshorne, Paul Weiss, and Arthur W. Burks. 8 vols. Cambridge, Mass.: Harvard University Press.

———. 1992. *The Essential Peirce.* Ed. Nathan Houser and Christian Kloesel. 2 vols. Bloomington: Indiana University Press.

Pfaffenberger, Bryan. 1982. *Caste in Tamil Culture: The Religious Foundations of Sudra Domination in Tamil Sri Lanka.* Foreign and Comparative Studies/South Asian Series no. 7. Syracuse, N.Y.: Maxwell School of Citizenship and Public Affairs, Syracuse University.

Pigg, Stacy. 1992. "Inventing Social Categories through Place: Social Representations and Development in Nepal." *Comparative Study of Society and History* 34 (3): 491–513.

Pocock, David F. 1962. "Notes on Jajmani Relationships." *Contributions to Indian Sociology* 6 (1): 78–95.

Potter, Karl. n.d. "Karma: The Metaphor of Making." Unpublished typescript, 15 pp.

Presler, Franklin A. 1987. *Religion under Bureaucracy: Policy and Administration for Hindu Temples in South India.* Cambridge: Cambridge University Press.

Price, Pamela. 1979. "Raja-Dharma in 19th Century South India: Land, Litigation, and Largess in Ramnad Zamindari." *Contributions to Indian Sociology* 13 (2): 205–239.

———. 1993. "Democracy and Ethnic Conflict in India: Precolonial Legacies in Tamil Nadu." *Asian Survey* 33 (5): 493–506.

———. 1996a. "Revolution and Rank in Tamil Nationalism." *The Journal of Asian Studies* 55 (2): 359–383.

———. 1996b. *Kingship and Political Practice in Colonial India.* Cambridge: Cambridge University Press.

Rabinow, Paul. 1977. *Reflections on Fieldwork in Morocco.* Berkeley: University of California Press.

Radcliffe-Brown, A. R. 1929/1952. *Structure and Function in Primitive Society.* New York: The Free Press.

Raheja, Gloria Goodwin. 1988. *The Poison in the Gift: Ritual, Prestation, and the Dominant Caste in a North Indian Village.* Chicago: University of Chicago Press.

———. 1990. "Centrality, Mutuality and Hierarchy: Shifting Aspects of Inter-caste Relationships in North India." In *India through Hindu Categories,* ed. McKim Marriott. New Delhi: Sage Publications.

———. 1996. "Caste, Colonialism, and the Speech of the Colonized: Entextualization and Disciplinary Control in India." *American Ethnologist* 23 (3): 494–513.

Ramanujan, A. K. 1967. *The Interior Landscape: Love Poems from a Classical Tamil Anthology.* Bloomington: Indiana University Press.

———. 1973. *Speaking of Siva.* Harmondsworth: Penguin.

———. 1985. *Poems of Love and War.* New York: Columbia University Press.

———. 1986. "Two Realms of Kannada Folklore." In *Another Harmony,* ed. Stuart Blackburn and A. K. Ramanujan. Berkeley: University of California Press.

———. 1990. "Is There an Indian Way of Thinking?" In *India through Hindu Categories,* ed. McKim Marriott. New Delhi: Sage Publications.

———. 1991. "Three Hundred Ramayanas." In *Many Ramayanas: The Diversity of a Narrative Tradition,* ed. Paula Richman. Berkeley: University of California Press.

Rangaraj, R. 1998. "In the Midst of a Churning." *Indian Express.* November 12, 1998.

Reiniche, Marie-Louise. 1979. *Les dieux et les hommes: Etude des cultes d'un village du Tirunelveli Inde du sud.* Paris: Mouton.

Reynolds, Holly Baker. 1980. "The Auspicious Married Woman." In *The Powers of*

Tamil Women, ed. Susan Wadley. Syracuse, N.Y.: Maxwell School of Citizenship and Public Affairs, Syracuse University.

Rg Veda. 1981. Trans. and ed. Wendy Doniger. Penguin Books.

Richman, Paula, ed. 1991. *Many Ramayanas: The Diversity of a Narrative Tradition.* Berkeley: University of California Press.

Roy, Beth. 1994. *Some Trouble with Cows.* Berkeley: University of California Press.

Sahlins, Peter. 1994. *Forest Rites: The War of the Demoiselles in Nineteenth-Century France.* Cambridge, Mass.: Harvard University Press.

Sapir, Edward. 1921. *Language: An Introduction to the Study of Speech.* New York: Harcourt, Brace.

Sax, William. 1991. *Mountain Goddess: Gender and Politics in a Himalayan Pilgrimage.* New York: Oxford University Press.

Scott, David. 1994. *Formations of Ritual: Colonial and Anthropological Discourses on the Sinhala Yaktovil.* Minneapolis: University of Minnesota Press.

Scott, James. 1990. *Domination and the Arts of Resistance: Hidden Transcripts.* New Haven, Conn.: Yale University Press.

Seizer, Susan. 2000. "Roadwork: Offstage with Special Drama Actresses in Tamil Nadu, South India." *Cultural Anthropology* 15 (2): 217–259.

Selby, Martha. 2000. "The Seasons, Sexuality, and Aesthetic Representation in Early Indian Poetry." Paper presented at the 29th Annual Conference on South Asia, Center for South Asia, University of Wisconsin, October 14, Madison, Wisconsin.

Selby, Martha, and Indira Peterson, ed. Forthcoming. *Tamil Geographies.* Albany: State University of New York Press.

Settlement Register of Tinnevelly District, Ambasamudram Taluk. 1879. Madras Government Archives.

Shourie, Arun, Harsh Narain, Jay Dubashi, Ram Swarup, and Sita Ram Goel. 1990. *Hindu Temples: What Happened to Them (a Preliminary Survey).* New Delhi: Voice of India.

Shulman, David D. 1981. *Tamil Temple Myths.* Princeton, N.J.: Princeton University Press.

———. 1985. "Kingship and Prestation in South Indian Myth and Epic." *Asian and African Studies* 19: 93–117.

———. 1989. "Outcaste, Guardian, and Trickster: Notes on the Myth of Kattavarayan." In *Criminal Gods and Demon Devotees: Essays on the Guardians of Popular Hinduism,* ed. Alf Hiltebeitel. Albany: State University of New York Press.

Singer, Milton. 1972. *When a Great Tradition Modernizes: An Anthropological Approach to Indian Civilization.* Chicago: University of Chicago Press.

Sivarajan, D. 1997. "Politicians Add Fuel to Caste Fire in TN." *Indian Express,* June 18, 1997. Available online at http://www.expressindia.com/ie/daily/19970618/16950183.html. Accessed September 4, 2004.

Springer, Jenny. 2000. "State Power and Agricultural Transformation in Tamil Nadu." In *Agrarian Environments: Resources, Representation, and Rule in India,* ed. Arun Agrawal and K. Sivaramakrishnan. Durham, N.C.: Duke University Press.

Srinivas, M. N. 1952. *Religion and Society among the Coorgs of South India.* Oxford: The Clarendon Press.

———. 1955. *India's Villages.* New Delhi: Oxford.

———. 1976. *The Remembered Village.* Berkeley: University of California Press.

Steedley, Mary. 1994. *Hanging without a Rope.* Princeton, N.J.: Princeton University Press.

Stein, Burton. 1980. *Peasant State and Society in Medieval South India.* Delhi: Oxford University Press.

Tambiah, Stanley. 1985. "A Performative Approach to Ritual." In *Culture, Thought, and Social Action,* ed. Stanley Tambiah. Cambridge, Mass.: Harvard University Press.

Tamil Lexicon. 1982. Chennai: The University of Madras.

Thomas, Nicholas. 1991. *Entangled Objects: Exchange, Material Culture, and Colonialism in the Pacific.* Cambridge, Mass.: Harvard University Press.

Tolen, Rachel. 1991. "Colonizing and Transforming the Criminal Tribesman: The Salvation Army in British India." *American Ethnologist* 18 (1): 106–125.

Trawick, Margaret. 1990. *Notes on Love in a Tamil Family.* Berkeley: University of California Press.

———. 1991. "Wandering Lost: A Landless Laborer's Sense of Place and Self." In *Gender, Genre, and Power in South Asian Expressive Traditions,* ed. Arjun Appadurai, Frank Korom, and Margaret Mills. Philadelphia: University of Pennsylvania Press.

van der Veer, Peter. 1987. "God Must Be Liberated: A Hindu Liberation Movement in Ayodhya." *Modern Asian Studies* 21 (2): 283–303.

———. 1994. *Religious Nationalism: Hindus and Muslims in India.* Berkeley: University of California Press.

Vincentnathan, S. George. 1996. "Caste Politics, Violence, and the Panchayat in a South Indian Community." *Comparative Studies in Society and History* 38 (3): 484–509.

Viramma, Jean-Luc Racine, and Josiane Racine. 1997. *Viramma: Life of an Untouchable.* London: Verso Books.

Volosinov, V. N. 1986. *Marxism and the Philosophy of Language.* Cambridge, Mass.: Harvard University Press.

Wadley, Susan S. 1994. *Struggling with Destiny in Karimpur, 1925–1984.* Berkeley: University of California Press.

Wadley, Susan S., and Bruce W. Derr. 1989. "Eating Sins in Karimpur." *Contributions to Indian Sociology* 23 (1): 131–148.

Wiser, William H. 1936. *The Hindu Jajmani System: A Socio-Economic System Interrelating Members of a Hindu Village Community in Services.* Lucknow: Lucknow Publishing House.

Zelliot, Eleanor. 1992. *From Untouchable to Dalit: Essays on the Ambedkar Movement.* New Delhi: Manohar.

Zimmermann, Francis. 1980. "Rtu-Satmya: The Seasonal Cycle and the Principle of Appropriateness." *Social Science and Medicine* 14B: 99–106.

———. 1987. *The Jungle and the Aroma of Meats: An Ecological Theme in Hindu Medicine.* Berkeley: University of California Press.

INDEX

Numbers in *italics* refer to illustrations.

Amnesty International, 215

Diane P. Mines is Assistant Professor of Anthropology at Appalachian State University. She is co-editor (with Sarah Lamb) of *Everyday Life in South Asia* (Indiana University Press, 2002).

CPSIA information can be obtained
at www.ICGtesting.com
Printed in the USA
LVOW04s1758250717
542589LV00020B/180/P

9 780253 217653